THE MIGRANT PASSAGE

THE MIGRANT PASSAGE

*Clandestine Journeys from
Central America*

NOELLE KATERI BRIGDEN

CORNELL UNIVERSITY PRESS
ITHACA AND LONDON

First published 2018 by Cornell University Press

Printed in the United States of America

Library of Congress Cataloging-in-Publication Data

Names: Brigden, Noelle, author.
Title: The migrant passage : clandestine journeys from Central America /
    Noelle Brigden.
Description: Ithaca [New York] : Cornell University Press, 2018. |
    Includes bibliographical references and index.
Identifiers: LCCN 2018012024 (print) | LCCN 2018017704 (ebook) |
    ISBN 9781501730566 (pdf) | ISBN 9781501730573 (epub/mobi) |
    ISBN 9781501730542 | ISBN 9781501730542 (cloth ; alk. paper) |
    ISBN 9781501730559 (pbk. ; alk. paper)
Subjects: LCSH: Central America—Emigration and immigration—
    Social aspects. | Central Americans—Mexico—Social conditions. |
    Central Americans—Violence against—Mexico. | Human
    smuggling—Mexico. | Illegal aliens—Mexico—Social conditions. |
    Illegal aliens—Violence against—Mexico. | Mexico—Emigration and
    immigration—Social aspects. | United States—Emigration and
    immigration—Social aspects.
Classification: LCC JV7412 (ebook) | LCC JV7412 .B75 2018 (print) |
    DDC 304.809728—dc23
LC record available at https://lccn.loc.gov/2018012024

For John

Contents

THE MIGRANT PASSAGE

ACT 1

Exposition

Chapter 1

The Opening Scene

A Journey Begins

Karla, who worked in a tourist café owned by *gringos*, prepared gourmet coffees for the international backpackers and surfers who flock to the coast of El Salvador.[1] She made friends with some of them on Facebook and so caught glimpses of their relatively glamorous lives and travels abroad. She had long imagined that someday she would join these friends and her older siblings in the United States. Karla was twenty years old, and life in rural El Salvador made her restless. She longed to leave her small town behind. One brother had been in the United States for a long time. A second brother had recently left and was followed by a sister the month before I met Karla in 2009. Her brothers had warned her that the journey was very difficult, but the second brother had a better *coyote* [human smuggler] than the first one, and they thought it was now safe enough for their sisters to follow. By March 2010, Karla had already begun to plan her journey, and she talked to me about it. When I asked her to imagine the route that would she would take north and to draw me a map of this route, she agreed without much hesitation (see Figure 1.1).

Figure 1.1. Karla's Map
The risks and the uncertainties of the journey, as understood by Karla before she left home.

Nevertheless, imagining the journey proved to be a daunting task for her. Karla delivered the map to me nearly a month later with an explanation that she had changed her mind; it was too dangerous to travel clandestinely. In her map, dangerous animals lined the trail, symbolizing the travel risks. A mountain looms ominously in the distance, obscuring the path forward. The journey is uncertain because the adventure cannot be foretold. Despite (or because of) her worldliness and the experiences of her family, Karla knew it would be preposterous to predict the route she would need to travel. Thus, the mountains in her map symbolized her uncertainty about the path she would take. Yet within a year of drawing the map, a frightened Karla braved the journey anyway; she suddenly left for reasons that she never explained to me. Perhaps the lure of adventure overcame the monotony of a rural woman's life. Perhaps one of her siblings offered her a once-in-a-lifetime opportunity to travel with an expensive coyote, and she seized the moment. Since such smuggling services could, at the time, cost $7,500 for a regular passage, it is easy to imagine that sponsorship for such pricey travel opportunities might be difficult to refuse.[2] I did not have the opportunity to ask Karla about the motives for her sudden flight. Instead, through the images Karla posted on Facebook, I have followed her from a distance for years, watching her create a new home in the United States and raise her daughter, who was born after her arrival and thus is a U.S. citizen. With a bit of luck, Karla will avoid deportation and will not have to travel the migrant passage through Mexico again.

The survival plays necessitated by the migrant passage can make heroes, victims, and villains out of Central Americans, such as Karla, who must brave it. These survival plays are the performances that structure encounters among strangers under violent conditions, and they become a source of cultural and territorial mobility within the migration corridor. Nevertheless, the State sets the stage by imposing borders and generating risk and uncertainty for migrants crossing Mexico. These everyday scenes of migration unfold within a larger political theater, in which the intensification of migration policing and migrant suffering play to a U.S. audience.[3] Taken together, survival plays and policing scenes depict a tragedy rather than an epic, often closing with senseless sacrifice instead of happy endings. For this reason, I hope that Karla's part in this spectacle is over.

To return to the image for a moment, the mountain motif in Karla's map is not just background setting serving an aesthetic purpose. The image is critical for understanding the plot structure of a clandestine journey from Central America to the United States.[4] In her map, the mountains obscure the way forward, because each journey is unique. She cannot know what may lurk beyond. The past offers little guide to the future. While Karla trusted her siblings, she had doubted her ability to learn from their experiences in the borderlands. The route north through Mexico changes dramatically from one journey to the next, limiting the capacity to predict whether migrants arrive successfully in the United States or not.

Using a theatrical metaphor, this book tells the story of how people like Karla navigate in shadow and cope with a double-edged micropolitics of information; it is this double-edged informational politics that animates the plot and creates unexpected twists, moving people in new trajectories as they grapple with unknowns. Karla is rational, but to imagine a journey to the United States, she must navigate an almost impossibly difficult problem of uncertainty. While risk is the probability of a danger and its potential harm, uncertainty characterizes a dangerous situation without a known probability.[5] A dynamic strategic setting and the accompanying clandestinity—a necessity during the journey due to policing and criminal predation—exacerbate uncertainty. In this setting, information is both a resource and a curse; migrants must learn past practices and protocols for negotiating the journey, but the very availability of this information renders it suspect. The spread of information about how and where to go may lead migrants north, but it may also lead police and criminal predators to migrants. As police and criminals attempt to intercept them, migrants cannot rely on information about past practices without reservation, even if reliable sources like trusted loved ones relayed that information to them. In fact, with the intensification of Mexican policing and criminal violence occurring since the mid-2000s, even experienced migrants and guides express bewilderment about recent changes along the route through Mexico.

Thus, in the shadow of Karla's mountains, as I contemplated their meaning, I studied two interrelated questions about migrant journeys:

1. If the most experienced migrants and guides feel daunted by this uncertainty and violence, how do people attempt to move along the route with the barest of social or financial resources at their disposal?

2. How do these wanderers, many of whom never arrive at their intended destinations, interact with people and places along the way, and what are the consequences for the societies through which they travel?

I argue in my answer that people *improvise* encounters with strangers and with the terrain to survive a dangerous and uncertain passage. Migration studies, focused primarily on the role of social capital as a mobility resource, have missed the importance of encounters among strangers as a survival resource.[6] These studies have also generally overlooked the physical encounter with terrain as a source of migration information. Much of this scholarship treats the journey from the homeland to a destination country as a black box.[7] Scholars emphasize the preparations, resources, adaptations, politics, and the socioeconomic impact of migration before or after migrants take their trips. Academic work that does unpack the journey tends to focus myopically on the border rather than the long-distance corridors that most migrants must traverse.[8] Nevertheless, during the journey, improvised performances of social scripts and improvised material practices become a resource for mobility. As we will see, migrants' loose reenactments of these scripts and practices also potentially reinforce or destabilize identity and place markers. These reenactments generate social ambiguity. As a result, migrants' encounters with people and places along the way restructure the route for the people that follow in their footsteps.

Importantly, this process unfolds whether migrants reach their intended destinations or not. Scholarship focused primarily on migrant destinations generally misses the story of the people who never reach them. A U.S.-only view of the migration process obscures the stories of people who never leave home, people who make failed journeys, and people who die or disappear en route. A view from the transit corridor, however, reveals the long-reaching shadow of the border for people who may never step foot in the United States.

Therefore, I analyze the journey and migrants' improvised interaction with the transit corridor through which they pass. In this context, improvisation refers to an irreverent resourcefulness—a leveraging of conventions and codes for unanticipated purposes.[9] As such, it is cultural mobility in action, and a theatrical metaphor spotlights this dimension of mobility.[10] By tracing these improvisations along the transit corridor from Central America through Mexico and into the United States, I show how fluid migration practices reshape the social landscape. Thus, I argue that migrants' responses to their uncertain passage transform the possibilities of the nation-state and the world around us, albeit with as yet undetermined outcomes for borders and humanity. This book, along with Karla's map, is a portrait of underground globalization in action.

An Ethnographic Journey

Drawing on the accounts of people like Karla, I take the reader on an ethnographic journey, introducing the people, places, and practices that compose the borderlands *within* nation-states. You will meet the priests and hustlers, cops and criminals, smugglers and good Samaritans, and adventurers and refugees who inhabit the transnational space that connects Central America, Mexico, and the United States. You will meet migrants who never arrive at their destinations; some of these migrants will wander indefinitely and others disappear, presumably into hidden graves. You will meet people who leave home, and you will meet the people they leave behind. Following in their footsteps, we will discover how people survive a human security crisis with imagination and improvisation—not just planning. These everyday improvisations generate an emergent transnational space where material and social practices become unmoored.

Until now, however, much of the literature exploring the immigrant experience has largely ignored improvised journeys in favor of migration-specific resources and social ties accumulated in migrant home communities and destinations. A focus on established social networks misses the resources that emerge from anonymous, fleeting encounters with strangers and terrain. As a result, this focus also misses a dynamic process of engagement between migrants and the transit corridor through which they pass. Indeed, migration theories rooted in ideas of social capital and networks have a difficult time explaining how migrants cope with uncertainty.[11] As explained by Ćetta Mainwaring, "network theories often present migration systems as fully formed without investigating the agency required to initiate, transform, or weaken such systems."[12] In other words, it misses the way migrants shape societies through which they pass and the reordering of geopolitics that occurs within and around these transnational spaces. These migrants reorder global politics simply by attempting to cross borders. Their attempted passage is reshaping the Americas, Eurasia, and the Mediterranean basin.

By exploring migration through the lens of the journey, this book responds to a recent call for international relations (IR) scholars to examine how ordinary people, sometimes unwittingly, impede the projects of nation-states and thus shape the world political economy.[13] Even if they never reach their destination, people embark on journeys that effect personal, social, economic, and political transformations along the route they traverse. Scholars of international politics have overlooked the flesh and blood travails of migrants who undergo dangerous long-distance odysseys. Much of this scholarship therefore supplies an incomplete view of globalization—one that focuses almost exclusively on top-down, collective challenges to the nation-state. However, ethnographic methods, a lens that focuses on the level of practice, reveal a more complex transnational social process. Through an anthropological lens we can see how the paths blazed by migrants complicate the cultural markers that the State requires to distinguish between migrants and citizens. We also see how they reshape the physical and socioeconomic terrain of the nation-state, leveraging aboveground economies and social relations for underground activities.

While the State may impede individual journeys and enforce a territorial boundary, neither collective action nor novel technologies are necessary to *complicate* borders. To be clear, I do not argue that territorial borders or the State are disappearing. The interplay between migrants and the State creates unintended consequences that we can best understand at the analytical and methodological borders of IR and anthropology. Viewing globalization "from below" allows us to trace how migrants and citizens adapt to existing roles, protocols, and rituals for the purpose of their survival. They also improvise on the material resources at their disposal. A more humble, speculative position emerges from analytical engagement with everyday people such as Karla. On the one hand, IR scholarship benefits from this humility because we explore politics that matter to the survival of marginalized actors on the world stage. On the other hand, ethnographic accounts of everyday practice benefit from the grand theories of world politics that allow us to transgress the particulars of local experience. This broad historical and global vantage point provides a countervailing narrative to heroic stories that underemphasize the larger political structures shaping individual action. By bringing together both perspectives, we arrive at a richer understanding of the uncertain future of the nation-state.

Through the Borderlands Within

To provide some context for the argument that migrants' improvisations reshape the possibilities of the global political order, it is important to remember that states regard their frontiers, and the people who come to embody those frontiers, with suspicion. Borders are contact zones where material and social boundaries must be continually renegotiated, often under conditions of threat, whether perceived or real. Mark Salter conceptualizes borders as a space where citizens, foreigners, and migration agents *perform* citizenship, thereby giving meaning to sovereignty.[14] Such state performances produce artificial boundaries between both territories and peoples, and these boundaries unwittingly generate the borderlands: social spaces inhabited by novel forms of cultural hybridity and contestation.[15]

States, however, have "thickened" and "transnationalized" their borders by outsourcing immigration policing to neighboring transit countries and further emphasizing immigrant apprehensions within their own territory, such as at worksites.[16] The policing of transnational flows in the states' interior extends and deepens the clandestine contestation that normally occurs at these frontiers. Policing extends contestation by moving clandestine activity into the heartland of the state, as it is no longer localized at its geographic periphery. It also deepens the contestation by incorporating more citizens into a clandestine social field. Thus, the routes become embedded in the nation-states through which they pass, incorporating both mobile and immobile people alike into their flows. In this manner, nation-states of both transit and destination develop borderlands *within* their borders. The dynamic between state and people internalizes the borderlands, within territories and the population within them.

Gilberto Rosas argues that these contemporary borderlands are uneasily situated along the rough edges of sovereignty, between war and peace, militarization and policing.[17] Such hybrid control tactics both function through and regenerate racialized illegalities:[18]

Nightmares of insecurity are effects of necessarily incomplete exercises of sovereignty at the new frontier. They underwrite the low-intensity warfare at the new frontier. Indeed, this kind of warfare is designed far more to regulate bodies than to conquer populations. Media spectacles of undocumented border crossings and processes of illegality more generally have been widely equated with the U.S. nation-state's loss of control at its borders. Nightmares of drug traffickers, terrorists, and illegal immigrants weigh down on the new frontier; these dark fantasies legitimate the continuing and ongoing amplification of militarized regimes of social control and a perverse birthing of criminal types in its necessary fissures.[19]

Indeed, these internal contact zones often become places of greater danger and deception when the State attempts to control them; such interventions boost insecurity for citizens and migrants, both directly through state violence and indirectly, by calling forth a variety of delinquent refusals of the state order.[20] For this reason, Karla's map emphasized her fears of the long trek *across* nation-states, not just the danger she associated with crossing the borders *between* them.

In fact, Karla and other Central Americans have good reason to be afraid of the journey to the United States. A consensus of scholars, journalists, and migrants suggests that the migration corridor from Central America through Mexico to the United States has become much more dangerous in the last two decades (see Figure 1.2).[21] Both risk and uncertainty are on the rise along the route. Bandits, corrupt officials, and unscrupulous smugglers have robbed and raped migrants ever since people began to travel through Mexican territory en route to the United States.[22] But in the last decade, even additional dangers, such as organized mass kidnappings in which the victims are systematically tortured in order to extort money from U.S.-based relatives, have emerged.[23] At the time of my fieldwork, Mexico's National Human Rights Commission estimated that more than twenty thousand migrants are kidnapped each year.[24]

Compounding the growing fear, Central American media began reporting, with greater frequency, crimes along the Mexican routes following the end of the Central American civil war period in the 1990s. And the increasing systematic organization and severity of this violence came to international attention in August 2010 with the shocking discovery of seventy-two corpses of Central and South American migrants in a mass grave in Tamaulipas, Mexico.[25] Mass murder is a tragic by-product of increased territorial competition among

Figure 1.2. Map of the Route
Primary migration land routes from Central America through Mexico. Credit: Rodolfo Casillas.

drug gangs as they attempt to control passage and to charge tribute from human smugglers, as well as to exploit the opportunities for kidnapping and extortion. Ask nearly any migrant and they will tell you that the journey is far more dangerous today than ever before.

Even though it might be tempting to describe this anarchy as a Hobbesian state of nature, it is, in fact, a by-product of the State. Borderlands are not a primordial place that predates the State.[26] The Mexican and U.S. governments have partnered to increase the risks to migrants traveling unauthorized routes, thereby deterring would-be border crossers.[27] Under a policy described as "prevention through deterrence," U.S. migration authorities have deliberately channeled the migrant stream toward the most dangerous places (such as desolate, and therefore deadly, desert zones) on the U.S-Mexico border.[28] Since 2001, Mexican migration policing has also funneled migrants to the most dangerous places within Mexico, such as the drug-running corridors where kidnappers and corrupt authorities prey on migrants with impunity.[29] At that time, under the first iteration of *Plan Sur*, Mexico established a series of internal control belts to intercept Central American migrants far north of the Guatemalan border, and in 2008 began to receive substantial support for these security measures from the United States through the auspices of the Mérida Initiative.[30] Most recently, in the aftermath of a wave of Central American children arriving at the U.S. border in 2014, the Mexican government implemented a reinvigorated program of policing in its southern corridor, principally targeting the train routes that the poorest and most vulnerable migrants ride north like international hobos and largely shutting down that transportation method.

The Mexican government announced the newest program, also known as *Programa Frontera Sur* or simply *Plan Sur*, as an attempt to protect migrants from the deadly train route. However, a consensus among human rights activists indicates that Plan Sur has increased migrants' exposure to crime by necessitating long, unprotected walks through the wilderness. States exacerbate the risks of the journey.[31]

Mexico and the United States have not only exacerbated the *risks* of the journey; under the banner of the drug war, the Mexican and U.S. governments have also allied to increase *uncertainty* by intentionally dislocating the routines and relationships that underpin the political economy of transit. To do so, police "decapitated" the drug cartels. They hunted down local terrain bosses in order to incite violent competition within and among gangs with the intention of disrupting illicit trafficking in drugs and people.[32] In doing so, states make illicit business, like the smuggling enterprises on which migrants are dependent, less predictable (as well as more dangerous).

For this reason, the Mexican government attempted to claim that the high death toll of criminal violence is a measure of success in the drug war.[33] In response to the August 2010 mass murder of migrants in Tamaulipas, Alejandro Poiré, a Mexican security official, offered the following analysis: "This act confirms that criminal organizations are looking to kidnapping and extortion because they are going through a difficult time obtaining resources and recruiting people willingly."[34] This massacre may be viewed as a "success" in a second way; as migration policing pushes migrants into the path of drug cartels, criminal violence against migrants strengthens state enforcement of its borders. In this sense, the heightened danger of criminality to migrants indirectly serves state purposes by deterring some Central American migration. State policy makers, if they are aware of their role in exacerbating this danger, are complicit accessories in these crime against migrants.

Put another way, migration and drug control efforts induced the growth of what Guillermo O'Donnell calls a *brown area* where informal and formal rules must be continuously renegotiated, and as a consequence, uncertainty is endemic.[35] In Mexico, few migrants avail themselves of official protection because they are vulnerable to violence committed by authorities and fear deportation. Thus, formal law only intermittently protects migrants. Since the drug war's intensification, the informal rules of the illicit economy have been subject to continuous renegotiation by criminal actors. Uncertainty along the route has risen because the routines and social networks that underlie clandestine migration have undergone profound change since intensified migration policing and the Mexican drug war (in 2006). As a result, past practice offers very imperfect guidance for migrants as they move through Mexico.

In sum, brown areas and borderlands, such as the migration route, are not beyond the reach of sovereign authority. They are constituted by governance and resistance to that governance. Incomplete sovereignty at borders calls forth a spectacle of violence to project state power and, through militarized policing practice, reproduction of the migrants' racialized illegality.[36] The combined effect of migration policing and the drug war is largely responsible for the dramatic increase in both risk and uncertainty. Indeed, Wendy Vogt traces both the contemporary migration policing and the drug war offensive to a neoliberal agenda pursued by the United States, and she argues that this militarized, free-market agenda continues the processes of colonial and Cold War social fragmentation in Latin America. In other words, the violent and unstable conditions that plague the migration route are state creations; they are not intrinsic to human movement, but an outcome of policy decisions.[37] The internalization of border policing introduced uncertainty and anarchy of a kind normally associated with the international realm into the domestic affairs of the Mexican state. The resultant humanitarian catastrophe, which spans from home through transit communities and destinations and then back again, is common knowledge across Central America.

Following Uncertain Trajectories; Improvising Survival

Ironically, however, a wealth of common knowledge concerning the route's dangers does not provide migrants much useful information about how they might cope with the challenges which face them once the decision to leave has been made. Thus, hundreds of thousands of Central Americans leave home each year and confront an ominous unknown.[38] Given the dramatic uncertainty they confront en route, migrants traveling the entire length of Mexico (which is roughly 1,200 miles from southern Mexico to the Texas border) must presume that each journey will be unique. Migrants face information constraints, but they are not naïve. They know that they do not realize what the future holds.

Strategic interaction between migrants, police, and criminals renders the iteration of successful tactics dangerous, because predators rapidly identify and respond to migrant practices.[39] For that reason, a ploy that had previously abetted safe passage may enhance risk a second time around. Criminals, ranging from drug cartels that control territory and collect passage fees from illegal traffic to local opportunists who commit rapes and robberies, stalk the migrant trail. Faith in a previously competent coyote could be misplaced in a world where even reputable smugglers sometimes make mistakes and die alongside their clients. Smugglers have been killed crossing territory that has suddenly changed hands among competing criminal organizations, turning cooperative gangs into implacable enemies. Migrants insist that "every trip is different," because the shifting strategic context of the route ensures that no two journeys are ever alike; specific information from a previous trip quickly becomes obsolete. Fully aware of this fact, migrants adopt uncertainty as their worldview.

Traveling the route changes people, and the continual presence of transient people changes society. It is perhaps cliché to remind readers that every journey across the globe has its parallel journey into the self.[40] Just as new experiences transform people, so does violence. However, this is not only a personal process. Violence and migration reconstitute not only personal motives, but also social roles and norms.[41] Thus, violence and migration produce a fundamental ambiguity and uncertainty along the route. At various places, the roles of the "migrant," "smuggler," "gang member," "state official," and "kidnapper" overlap or become fluid.[42] Migrants or smugglers may be forced to collaborate with kidnappers or police to survive, and police may be forced to collaborate with smugglers or kidnappers. Many social markers that might normally signal trustworthiness or solidarity, such as nationality, religion, gender or class, come to betray those who would rely on them. Treachery is rampant as loyalties shift under the strain because people are forced to make decisions in violent situations.[43]

The illegality of human smuggling and migration further exacerbates this uncertainty by reinforcing the need for secrecy and deception. Of course, if such practices were perfectly concealed, smugglers would soon run out of clients. So, there are also incentives for publicity. Unauthorized migrants share their travel stories, and they even make claims on the State for protection and services during their journey. As they do so, the location and protocols of unauthorized routes become common knowledge in the communities through which they pass. Nonetheless, illegal activities are undocumented, in the sense that there is no objective general record through which we can study migrant vulnerability along the route. For this reason, Susan Bibler Coutin defines clandestine terrain as territory that is simultaneously "hidden yet known."[44] While the veil of secrecy is far from opaque, diffusion renders information dangerous for migrants. By the time a rumor of a safe path or an effective ploy reaches migrants, they may also have attracted the attention of migration police or criminal predators.

Karla clearly understood the limits of information under conditions of uncertainty; she knew that the ever-changing strategic conditions of the route meant that the well-trod path of her brothers and sister could not be trusted. To follow an established trail through the wilderness is tempting, because it can lead you north. When migrants follow in the footsteps of previous generations of migrants, they learn to rely on the material artifacts their compatriots leave behind; to observe and mimic tactics of travel companions; to receive humanitarian support from Catholic shelters; and to access a political economy of transit when they hire smugglers and purchase supplies. In this way, the route provides a physical and social infrastructure for the acquisition of information. However, to uncritically follow an established trail is dangerous, because it may have also been identified by patrols or bandits. Consequently, institutionalized practice becomes both a source of vulnerability and a resource for survival. In this context, the accumulation of social capital and lessons learned over time cannot resolve the information dilemma confronted by migrants.[45] Migrants have no reassurance that past experience will provide a reliable guide for future journeys.

Confronted by this informational paradox, how do people make their way? Rather than solely rely on the past for reliable information, people must largely depend on imagination and improvisation. In other words, migrants and smugglers leverage established routines, roles, and resources to their advantage. When they do that, migrants reshape a transnational place, known colloquially as "el Camino" (translated to English as "the migrant trail," or directly as "the way" or "the road").

By promoting these improvisations, uncertainty destabilizes social and material practice along the route. Central American migrants must make decisions amid great danger and dynamic uncertainty. Despite their ingenuity, they often find themselves at the mercy of criminal gangs and police, who continually manipulate the rules of the game. The interplay of violence and evasion structures the migratory route by making improvisatory demands on migrants. Thus, without intending to, migrants and their smugglers transform the migration corridor into a space that no state securely controls. Faced with violent and uncertain journeys, everyday people like Karla complicate, but do not eviscerate, the social and territorial boundaries of the nation-state.

While migrants and smugglers are the vanguard, they are not alone. Migrants intermingle with a wide variety of people who live along the route. The relationships and roles of these people are also transformed by the passage of migrants. Both citizens and migrants creatively interact and thus complicate the governance of the unauthorized routes that have become a ubiquitous feature of globalization. Ultimately, this ongoing process blurs boundaries between foreigners and citizens, migrants and settlers.[46]

Globalization and the Nation-State at Disciplinary Borders

Since the 1970s, scholars have heralded the impending reordering of the nation-state under conditions of complex interdependence and overlapping sovereignties.[47] The inexorable forces of cultural and economic globalization shake, but do not dislodge, both the territorial and ideational moorings of the State.[48] Transnational media complicates the relationship between territory and cultural identity.[49] State efforts to impede unauthorized flows of people and contraband generate perverse results.[50] When IR theorists attempt to account for these complications, they often look to social networks and novel communication technologies as vectors for the diffusion and increasing resilience of transnational practice.[51] Indeed, a variety of organized actors, including diaspora activists, leverage these resources to challenge state sovereignty.[52] And while political scientists also use the lens of migration and trafficking to explore the discursive construction of national identity and sovereignty,[53] they make fewer attempts to understand the embodied deconstruction of the nation-state at the level of everyday practice.[54]

By emphasizing lived experience, anthropology points to how everyday material practice shapes place, identity, and common-sense understandings of the world around us. The experience of the journey is clandestine transnationalism that is called into existence by the very effort of the State to stop it. As the anthropology of criminalization reveals, clandestine activities are never autonomous from the state, but instead are constituted by their illegality.[55] As they return from deportations or failed border crossings, migrants continue to make multiple journeys not despite of the State but because of it. Both state and nonstate violence structure these practices, rendering trust and community ephemeral along the route. Thus, it should be no surprise that clandestine transnationalism is an incidental, not purposive, challenge to sovereignty.

Of course, we must not forget the human tragedy that necessitates migrant survival strategies, and we should refrain from celebrating these improvisations as intentional resistance to the State. Migrants also become unwilling props in the political theater of borders.[56] Here, anthropology can learn from the discipline of international relations and its broader understanding of the political and institutional structures that shape the global stage—thereby limiting the agency of actors. While migration practice troubles the links between nationality and territory, border policing painfully impacts the lives of migrants and citizens alike. The unending transience that emerges in the wake of mass deportation and border policing erodes the coherence of social and territorial boundaries, but it does not establish a transcendent regime for the protection of human life and dignity. An ethnographic focus on undirected mass movement, coupled with an awareness of ways in which the global border regime potentially perverts this movement, brings this reality into stark relief. Such an interdisciplinary approach adds nuance to triumphant accounts of transnationalism and globalization.[57]

The Path Forward

Like a tragedy with a three-act structure, this book is divided into three parts. The first is the *exposition*. It sketches concepts and describes the routes as uncertain and violent terrain. This part of the book discusses the transformative process unfolding along the route, and it justifies my methodological approach. In chapter 2, I describe my fieldwork methods and the concept of improvisation in greater depth. In chapter 3, I introduce the players who inhabit the route and how their relationships have changed over time. These fluid relationships generate social ambiguity and acute uncertainty for migrants.

The second part of the book is what playwrights might call a *rising action* with a character arc that develops the situations in which migrants find themselves. It demonstrates how migrants' responses to those situations transform social roles. To do so, I describe migration practice, fleshing out the concepts and methodology introduced in the first part and exploring the social and material dimensions of the journey in turn. Each chapter makes both an empirical point and further develops the argument in favor of ethnographic methods for understanding globalization and borders. In chapter 4, I examine how narratives and actions become *survival plays*. This chapter traces the performances of social roles and identity that become tactics in transit and how they become a source of cultural and territorial mobility. By exploring these encounters, I demonstrate the importance of *performing* ethnography. In other words, I show that reading interview narratives themselves as survival plays can reveal otherwise overlooked dimensions of the journey. In chapter 5, I analyze how migrants come to understand and employ material resources in unexpected ways during the journey, shaping the stage for future survival plays. To do so, I merge a critical cartography with ethnography in a series of mapmaking workshops that probe the origins of a transnational imaginary of the route. Maps orient us to how the narrative, characters, and stage setting interact, guiding us through the lived experiences of survival plays. This merging of mapping with ethnography follows Tom Conley's observation that the narrative structure of cinematic performances is also a map, insofar as, "like topographic projections, [maps] can be understood as an image that locates and patterns the imaginations of spectators."[58] Survival plays rearticulate the space of the transit corridor, and when asked to participate in a cartography of the route, migrants deployed maps within their performances of the interview about that corridor. Taken together, the second part of the book documents cultural mobility as migrants improvise on imperfect information. This second part also more fully develops a fluid methodology that mirrors migration practice, leveraging social encounters between strangers and the terrain itself to understand that mobility.

The final part, or *climax*, concludes by speculating about the implications of this analysis for the State and globalization, and it briefly explores these dynamics in other regions around the globe. Clandestine migration transforms territorial and symbolic sovereignty of the State but with indeterminate consequences for human dignity. The State cannot prevent the emergence of a transnational space, but it does have the power to pervert this social reality, thereby inflicting tremendous suffering on both citizens and migrants alike. I conclude with a melancholy reflection on the transnational homelessness that accompanies contemporary migration policing in the Americas. For migrants, destinations have become as ephemeral as the social interactions in which they engage en route; journeys along *el Camino* have increasingly become experiences with indefinite beginnings and ends.[59] The only definite end to the journey is death, and even then, the disappearance of corpses into unmarked graves renders that certainty ambiguous for the loved ones left behind.[60] The bodies of deceased migrants become unwilling props in an ongoing political theater of borders.[61] Whether they eventually arrive in the United States or disappear into the desert, migrants in transit participate in a contested, collective imagining of *el Camino*.

In the conclusion, I point to an analogous process unfolding across the Atlantic in the wake of the recent refugee crisis. At the periphery of Europe, sea and land routes persist in the face of escalating risk and uncertainty for migrants. Whether their lives are lost to watery graves in the Mediterranean or to the open graves left by Mexican narco-traffickers, whether they step foot in their intended destinations in Europe or the United States, migrants reorder these corridors around the world. Everyday people like Karla change the possibilities of the State and complicate borders. Sometimes they pay a tragic price for playing this pivotal role in the politics of place. Ultimately, it remains unclear where these transnational corridors lead us, as individuals or as a global society.

Chapter 2

The Plot

Migration Stories Take Shape

Their story begins on ground level, with footsteps. They are myriad, but
do not compose a series. They cannot be counted because each unit
has a qualitative character: a style of tactile apprehension and
kinesthetic appropriation. Their swarming mass is an innumerable
collection of singularities. Their intertwined paths give their shape to spaces.
They weave places together.

—Michel de Certeau, *The Practice of Everyday Life*

Roberto lived in a crumbling one-room adobe home at the end of a muddy
path in rural El Salvador. When we talked, we were never entirely alone.
An old, haggard-looking woman worked in the hot sun in the garden behind
the house. She occasionally scolded an equally haggard-looking dog. When
I explained my purpose and the rules of consent, Roberto agreed to be interviewed, and we talked about the journey he had made to the United States
in 2005.[1] I returned a few days later, and we discussed my life at great length.[2]
He asked about my sisters, their lives, and their husbands. He asked whether
there are decent jobs where they live, and he opined that my childless
half-sister works too much. Family must come first. While he confidently
offered advice for my sister, he was not so certain about his own plans for
the future. His elderly mother occasionally joined the conversation, but I
could not understand her slurred speech, probably a consequence of her
missing teeth.

I asked him to draw me a map of his journey to the United States, and
Roberto carefully tore off a smaller piece of paper to use from the large sheet.

He did not want to waste. He began by sketching the borders in orange crayon: El Salvador, Guatemala, Mexico. It took him awhile to figure out the correct spelling of Mexico, as he was writing and then rewriting the word. He did not write Estados Unidos (United States), but he pointed to where it would be at the top of the page. When I asked him how he knew where to go, he told me that I must understand that no one is traveling alone. He spread his arms wide to illustrate the mass of people that travel along the train route, and then he pulled his arms inward to show them moving forward in the same direction: "That is how you know where to go." He started north with his brother and an uncle, but a Honduran man who they had met along the way soon joined them. All nationalities traveled together on top of the freight train. Even though Mexican men pretending to be smugglers for hire had cheated him twice, Roberto maintained that the Mexican people were good to him, too: "The poorest people give the most." The people who lived near the tracks gave him shoes, food, and water:

> You do not travel alone. Your little group is not alone. You are with thousands of others. You meet people, and little groups form. You help one another. If you do not help people, you will not reach your goal. If you go in bad faith, you cannot get there. If you are hurting people, God will not reward you.

Roberto repeated this philosophy many times during my conversations with him. Through a repeated performance of reciprocity and humility, he navigated the route, finding his way to Catholic migrant shelters and into the United States.[3] He also followed a material infrastructure of migration through Mexico: well-trod paths, train tracks, and a string of humanitarian aid outposts that serve as signposts for people en route to the United States. In so doing, he, along with so many others, changed the social landscape of the route, giving rise to a fleeting transient community. In U.S. communities that receive migrants, Susan Bibler Coutin observes that Salvadoran youth confronted with social rupture—produced by their precarious position between law and illegality; between belonging and exclusion; and among different national cultures—improvise upon their context, changing it.[4] Thus, migrants do not just live in "gaps" between nation-states, but actively reinvent those spaces.[5] Indeed, this creative process begins before they arrive in the United States, as migrants reimagine and re-create the transient place between home and intended destination.

With Roberto's experience of the journey in mind, this chapter adopts a novel approach to understanding how migrants respond to uncertainty and violence. The chapter focuses on the micropractice of long-distance migration journeys, responding to Emanuel Adler and Vincent Pouliot's call to bring "scholarly debates down to the ground of world politics in order to empirically scrutinize the processes whereby certain competent performances produce effects of a world political nature."[6] This chapter thus constructs a methodological and conceptual framework that brings us down to ground level where migration practice produces larger political effects. While much of the international relations (IR) literature focuses on purposeful, collective challenges to the nation-state in a globalized world, the unchoreographed, individual survival strategies employed by migrants generate a dynamic transnational social space that complicates the governance of borders.

Such strategies are unchoreographed insofar that, outside of some of the advocacy in shelters, migration tactics generally do not represent a premeditated political challenge to the legitimacy of the State. Furthermore, despite the role of organized crime and smugglers, no monolithic, criminal conspiracy directs the flow of all clandestine traffic. Indeed, as we will see in the chapter that follows, different criminal actors play crosscutting roles in human mobility by sometimes working at odds with one another. Migrants sometimes move in unison and may sometimes collaborate with travel companions or political advocates, but without a single overarching coordination of their movement. In the aggregate, social practice, mimicry, and individual responses to incentives produce the synchronicity of their tactics, not collective strategizing. In this sense, we can understand the route as what Reece Jones characterizes as a *space of refusal*, as opposed to resistance: "a zone of contact where sovereign state practices interact with alternative ways of seeing, knowing, and being" that rejects binary territorial and identity categories.[7]

Along the route, migrants convert information into practice with imagination and improvisation, generating alternative ways of seeing, knowing, and being. While much of the migration literature focuses on social processes in home communities and U.S. destinations, the transit corridor through Mexico is also place where this conversion occurs. Over time, that practice becomes entrenched as a cultural form. However, unauthorized migration through Mexico also requires immense tactical innovation in response to intensified policing and criminal violence. Under these uncertain and dangerous conditions, conventional routines and tradition cannot be relied on as guides. As a result, entrenched cultural forms become unmoored, and the route becomes a paradoxical site of cultural continuity and continuous change.

The chapter opens with an explanation of how I arrived at this understanding of migration practice, outlining an ethnographic method for exploring a clandestine social reality. This method crosses the disciplinary boundaries between international relations and anthropology and its flexible engagement with strangers and terrain mirrors migration practice.[8] I discuss the conceptual framework that explores how migrants navigate the corridor and how the corridor evolves with sustained migration In particular, I analyze how migrants adapt both social and material artifacts to new ends, thereby destabilizing social identities and reshaping terrain. I describe both the physical and cultural mobility that emerges where people practice clandestine migration. In this chapter and throughout the book, I will revisit the stories of migrants like Roberto to elaborate key points in the analysis.

Importantly, this chapter does not portend to provide a causal theory of migration, but instead describes the process through which human mobility occurs and the impact it has on the possibilities for the nation-state. This chapter also leaves empirical evidence to be developed in subsequent chapters. However, it introduces a methodological and conceptual approach through which this process and its impact along the route become visible.

A Methodology

Yanira, a middle-aged woman, lived on the other side of town from Roberto. One day, she was working the coffee fields when she saw a strange, gaunt man lurking behind the trees. He wandered around, staring at her and her children. He had a shaggy beard and mustache and unkempt hair in dirty curls. Mosquito bites made his shoeless feet look like meat, and they were bandaged with rags tied with a belt. Terrified, Yanira picked up her children and ran home. But then he came and stared through her window. She was panic-stricken. He tried the door. She shouted at him to go away, and he shouted back that she was crazy. It was her husband. Like Penelope confronted with her long-lost Odysseus, Yanira did not believe him at first, but recognition slowly dawned on her. When he finally entered the house, he slept for two days and ate nothing. His almost lifeless body was both thin and swollen, telling her what she needed to know about his journey. It was the first of four attempts her husband made before successfully arriving in the United States.

I interviewed members of this Salvadoran family eight times in their home community over the course of a year, listening as those who had traveled and those who had stayed behind collectively reimagined the dangerous route. At first, Yanira only talked about her husband's experience; later, on my third visit to her family, she opened up and told me about the day her youngest son Wilian left town.[9] He did not come home one night. In the morning, she went to look for him, asking in the streets, but no one knew where he was. When she returned home, the smaller children were crying. They had found a note that Wilian had written in a notebook. He had left home carrying only twenty U.S. dollars. She cried when he left, and she cried again remembering that morning.

In the back room, I heard another cry above Yanira's sobs. Her three-month-old niece had awoken. The baby looked like a newborn, with her oversized head on a tiny body and bulging eyes already deformed by chronic hunger. Yanira explained apologetically that she knows her niece is hungry, but she can barely afford to feed her own children, let alone her sister's neglected brood. She washed the baby, and she dressed her in a fresh outfit with little booties, donated by some benefactor, but she mumbled that nobody ever gave her anything for her own babies. Her sister gave the baby unboiled water; it is amazing the baby survived. This baby is tough. She patted the baby and bounced her on her knee, but the baby continued to wail with hunger. My own chest grew heavy with the desire to feed the baby, but I dared not reach for the dying thing. Some vague trepidation held me back from embracing the infant. Finally, she gave the screaming baby to her youngest daughter, who ran off with her little cousin like she was holding a ragdoll.[10]

After this interruption, our conversation veered abruptly to the news. Yanira had heard about the earthquakes in Haiti and Chile, and she believes *something* is coming for El Salvador. A man passed through town a few weeks ago warning of an impending disaster. He travels the countryside telling people about his visions. She only believed him after seeing those distant events on the television. But she stayed in El Salvador, "waiting for God's will."

In moments like these, interviews instruct not only through words, but experience; ethnographers decipher a tangle of eyewitness observations, emotions and nonverbal communication that leads to new insights.[11] Through long meandering conversations with Yanira and others, I came to understand migration decisions in a larger context of precarity and ambiguity; the borderlands cast a long shadow, and the imaginings and improvisations moving with travelers across several nations fall on the ears and eyes of those who remain behind, waiting for God's will. The route becomes a reality even before anyone leaves home. These insights would be overlooked if researchers *only* focused on answers to survey questions.[12]

Migrants and Researchers on Parallel Journeys

In the course of my research, I developed a method that mirrored migration practice. I leveraged social networks for introductions and information. I engaged strangers, earnestly combining the professional role of researcher and the easy informality of Church volunteer, as well as the more personal roles of woman, foreigner, friend, mother, wife, customer, and tenant, in the communities where I lived. I used my intuition, based in part on stereotypes and my own cultural frames, about the reliability of people and their position vis-à-vis the wider community, and how to interpret my interactions with them. I observed the knowledge-based artifacts produced by the flow of people over terrain and time, as well as how people employed them in their own activities. In short, I developed, to the best of my ability, a sense of place.

Ethnographers, like migrants, rely heavily on serendipity.[13] Despite the role of subjectivity and chance in ethnography, neither ethnographic research nor migrants' knowledge of the route is purely impressionistic; both require preparation, thoughtful execution, and flexible planning.[14] Strictly followed plans stifle creativity, while randomly collected data cannot yield convincing results. New ethnographic insights, like innovative travel tactics, emerge in that mental space between accident and expectation. For this reason, Charles Tilly convincingly argues that ethnography is neither art nor science.[15] It requires a systematic method of observation and description that pure artists may forgo, and it can only be judged from a clear set of intersubjective disciplinary standards.[16] Thus, the work of ethnography is best described as craftsmanship.[17] By creating opportunities for inductive improvisation when unexpected insights arise, and thus partially liberating researchers from a deductive framework, ethnography is particularly well suited for tracing causal and conceptual mechanisms in a volatile and uncertain social situation.

Of course, parallel journeys made by participating observers very imperfectly retrace the path of migrants. Given my position of privilege as a researcher and U.S. citizen, I will never share the precarious experience of Central American migrants, and I did not attempt to follow migrants along the entirety of the route.[18] However, I did take seriously George Marcus's exhortation to "follow the people," not just to the places that they are going but also to the places they happen to go to along the way.[19] Thus, the entire route became my research site.[20]

Immersion along the route required more than two years of fieldwork, which began in September 2009. I divided my time primarily between Salvadoran hometowns and the Mexican transit corridor. However, I also made targeted follow-up visits with migrants in the transit corridor and destinations in the United States. I conducted 281 semistructured and unstructured interviews with migrants, human rights activists, community members, government officials, family members, clergy, and others.[21] In addition to formal interviews and mapmaking workshops,[22] I listened to countless real-time tactical discussions among migrants. In Mexico, to facilitate access and to gain inductive insights, I engaged in approximately five hundred hours of participant observation as a volunteer at a Catholic migrant shelter along the route's approximate midpoint. I visited transit communities with shelters along the train route across Mexico, including Tapachula, Arriaga, Ixtepec, Tenosique, Oaxaca City, Lecheria, Coatzacoalcos, San Luis Potosi, Saltillo, Monterrey, and Reynosa. I also accompanied unauthorized migrants on a sixteen-hour segment of their journey atop a freight train. I returned to Mexico for two weeks in December 2014/January 2015, and again in May 2015 and June 2016.[23] I revisited former fieldwork sites at the border between Guatemala and Mexico and along the migration route through Chiapas, Oaxaca, and Veracruz. I also visited three additional sites in Chiapas, Tabasco, and Oaxaca during three targeted trips.

Wilian's Story

I began by volunteering with the Catholic Church and walking door to door along the cobblestone and mud streets of two villages in El Salvador, which is how I had met Yanira and her family. Before I met Wilian, Yanira had explained that she is particularly protective of him. Perhaps this was why she did not tell me about him at first—why I did not know of his journey until my third visit. Her older boy, Carlos, was "pure campesino": tough, rugged, and aggressive, and capable of working the fields and defending himself in a fight. She did not fear for him when he took to the road like his father. Carlos returned home after working for a time in the tourist zone in Acapulco. He was always in trouble and always challenging her authority. Maybe she did not beat him hard enough, but Lord knows she tried. She beat Carlos until she ran out of strength, even leaving permanent marks on his flesh, but it did not teach him. This younger boy was not like that. When I saw Wilian, I understood. His eyebrows had been carefully groomed into thin arches, his build was slight, and his hands were delicate. He spoke softly, and I too could hear the gentleness his mother sought to protect.

Before I left the Salvadoran town on my way to Mexico to see the storied route firsthand, Wilian drew me a map of his own failed attempt to arrive in the United States. It was a map of a memory. With these contributions, this family was one of many that transformed my interviews into an ethnographic journey. Wilian prepared the map with a help of an artistic friend.[24] They made the journey together, leaving in secret, and they made the map together with the same carefully guarded privacy. In the picture, there are stylistically drawn adobe houses, stop signs, a bus, and some Guatemalan artifacts, connected by a meandering black line. His friend worked in the school library and read books in English and Spanish, an eccentric pastime in this small town. The map took a while to complete, because sometimes his friend was moody and unhelpful. I graciously accepted the map, late or not, and Wilian told me his story again.

He did not tell anyone about his decision to go—not even his mother. If he had told his mother, she would have stopped him. Wilian told her that he was going to his volunteer shift at the Red Cross, and he spent the night at his friend's house. He and his friend left in the morning. The year was 2009. His friend was older than Wilian and had traveled unsuccessfully once before. The friend led the way. They took a bus to Guatemala City. For the first time in his life, he saw people dressed in indigenous clothing. It was a big, strange city, but Wilian felt safe as long as he was with his friend. His friend had always protected him.

From there, they went to the border with Mexico. They had a difficult time at the river. A man nearby the river told them to pay him ten dollars to cross. But the ferryman exacted his own charge of ten dollars, and then on the other side another man demanded another ten dollars. Wilian and his friend explained that they had already paid, but to no avail. They continued north by *combi* (a system of paid transport in vans across southern Mexico). At Ciudad Hidalgo, not far from the border, they were assaulted and robbed. The bandits knew he was Salvadoran. I asked Wilian how they identified him as a Salvadoran migrant to be robbed. He thought about it and explained that Salvadorans are whiter than Mexicans. He thought the color of his skin was a giveaway. I pressed him a bit for more ways that these robbers, and later the Mexican authorities, knew he was Salvadoran. He paused again before admitting that he had forgotten to take off a belt that said "El Salvador" in decoration across it. A smile spread across his face as he remembered it.

Undaunted, Wilian and his friend continued their quest. A man approached them, offering his services as a guide. They gave him what money they had left, and he took them to a house. There, they were interrogated and intimidated, but despite the intense interrogation, both Wilian and his friend insisted that they had no relatives in the United States. In fact, his friend's mother lived there, and the young man's father was there as well, but they stuck to their stories. A big, scary-looking man spent the night in the next room, and the wall was flimsy, so they did not feel safe and did not sleep well that night. Wilian might have slept a little, but only because his friend stayed awake. Early in the morning, they escaped. They had to break out, because they had been locked in. After the escape, his friend told him stories about kidnappers posing as smugglers.

The boys explained their desperate situation to a Mexican woman whom they met while she was making tortillas. She gave them a bit of money, warned them to be careful, and advised them to take a combi to Tapachula, where they could look for work. They asked everyone for work at the Tapachula market. When one woman told them that she only hires Mexicans, Wilian became angry, but his friend urged them onward, explaining that it would be best to leave and not come back. Finally, they found another woman in the market willing to give them advice and money. She recommended that they had better get a place to stay for the night, as it was soon approaching. She told them about the migrant shelter. At first, Wilian objected to the idea, thinking that Mexican authorities must run the shelter in order to apprehend and deport people like him. But she explained that the Church ran the shelter. He agreed to go but remained suspicious. The kindly woman put the boys in a cab, and she instructed the driver that he must take them directly to the doorstep of the migrant shelter, not dropping them off anywhere but there. She paid fifty pesos for the cab. Even when they arrived, Wilian remained nervous.

They entered the shelter and answered the questions of the man who was registering arrivals. The next day, they helped in the garden, made beds, and cleaned; only then did Wilian begin to relax. The priest was kind and popular in the neighborhood. As it happened, they celebrated the priest's birthday with the migrants and local parishioners. The parish gave clothing and prepaid phone cards to the migrants. Both boys called their mothers, and their mothers wired them money, as is the common practice along the transit route. However, the priest warned them that gang members and kidnappers liked to hang out at the corner across from the shelter. The priest also warned them not to tell anyone, including other migrants, about family members in the United States, because kidnappers send people into the migrant shelters to get that kind of information. The man who monitors the shelter door cannot always detect these informants. In this way, Wilian understood that he could not trust other migrants; it was dangerous to share any information with those he met along the route.

Despite their mothers' pleading to return home to El Salvador, he and his friend used the money sent by their mothers take another combi north. They had planned to go to another migrant shelter, but the police stopped them as soon as they arrived in the next town. The police asked why they were carrying backpacks. The boys claimed to be Mexican, but the police knew better. They took the boys to the police station in Tapachula for questioning, and the police told them that they did not talk like Mexicans. His friend, who was very light skinned, admitted that he was Salvadoran. Thus, Wilian also admitted to being Salvadoran, because could not imagine continuing alone.

There are no borders on the map Wilian and his friend drew (see Figure 2.1). The drawing's colors and patterns reflect the boys' first experience of the indigenous culture of Guatemala and convey their youthful sense of adventure. Perhaps the map reimagines the experiences of the boys as they wished it would have happened. Despite the cheerfulness of the map and occasional laughter in our conversation, Wilian shuddered as he recalled the journey's dangers.

Figure 2.1. Wilian's Map
A brief adventure shared by two boys who did not reach the United States.

After a year of visiting this family, I was surprised by talk of another trip. Wilian's father had disappeared again into the United States. With him gone, the meager flow of remittances the family received had dried up. Hauled away by the police after a drunken incident and accused of extortion, the oldest son Carlos was incarcerated indefinitely, with no clear date for a trial. The oldest daughter, a beautiful willowy girl with almond-shaped eyes, had begun to date a recruiter for the local smuggler. Yanira informed me that if her daughter managed to talk her boyfriend into taking Yanira to the United States for free or in exchange for a loan, she would go. Yanira would leave despite all the suffering the route had already caused her family. "God willing, he will take me."

One day the journey may seem unimaginably difficult; the next day, people may find themselves traveling on the road north. Wilian swore in earnest he would never again brave the route. However, after listening to many such declarations, I too have learned to entrust the future to fate. Several people broke their promises of not returning, leaving after outbursts of violence or worsening, material hardship in El Salvador which unexpectedly drove them from home. Several people swore they would not return to the United States after being deported, only to find themselves migrating once again and thus moving in a never-ending circuit. In February 2014, I returned to El Salvador and searched for this family. I learned that the eldest son had been murdered after returning to the community from prison. Her neighbors knew only that Yanira had fled to another town with her three remaining children. I have not found them. Like Karla, whom we met in the introduction of this book, Wilian may even now be moving north on the route to the United States, despite his initial rejection of such plans.

However, even if Wilian does not attempt to cross the border again, his aborted journey has already played a small role in weaving together a transit corridor from El Salvador through Mexico. Whether they succeed or fail, hundreds of thousands of Central Americans reinvent the social and material infrastructure of migration across Mexico every year. Their movement knits places together with a shared imaginary and material reality of migration. Because they may wander Mexico indefinitely, successfully cross into the United States, or return to Central America empty handed, the route does not have many tidy beginnings or ends.

At the Borders of Anthropology and International Relations

By walking in their footsteps, we come to see that the shadows cast by clandestine migration, criminal violence, and migration policing extend from home to the destination, creating a borderland spanning several nation-states. We also acquire a more expansive perspective on politics as it is negotiated in everyday practice. Finally, by retracing the migrants' footsteps, we learn to acknowledge the limits of what we know about spontaneous social processes that adapt without self-conscious and intentional coordination. As social scientists, we might discern larger patterns of violence and continuity in migration flows. However, at the level of practice, that macrolevel information offers migrants little guidance as to how to make choices at specific moments during the journey. In fact, the view "from above" tends to gloss over and thus obscure the dynamic and unpredictable social realm "below."

Borrowing methods employed in the anthropology of flows and clandestine activity,[25] this approach offers a window onto globalization that has been overlooked by many scholars of international politics. These methods involve immersion by the researcher in a field structured by false binaries: mobile/ immobile, legal/illegal, insider/outsider. By definition, this social field is a world of disguise and concealment, both hidden from official surveillance and common knowledge at the level of practice. As such, it cannot be understood from a single vantage point, and it must be interrogated through this immersive experience.[26] As a source of knowledge, this immersive experience can be judged as successful to the extent that it enables us to identify political practices important to local people.[27] In this sense, a focus on the practice of transnational migration does not simply fill a gap in mainstream IR scholarship; it is a disruption of the boundaries of politics—in itself a political act.[28] Furthermore, this ethnographic lens offers a nuanced vision of globalization from below. It emphasizes unanticipated changes in the state-society relationship and highlights the contingencies of that process. Thus, my analysis points to otherwise overlooked political practices and also challenges both optimistic and pessimistic predictions about the potential for territorial control in a globalized world.

A Conceptual Framework

Despite the fact that their destinations often remain elusive and their future indefinite, Roberto and other migrants imagine *el Camino*, the route to the United States, as a definite place. Despite its clandestine and liminal character, el Camino represents a way of life; it is a series of everyday brokerage practices, known as *coyotaje*, which become the lifeblood of the communities through which migrants frequently transit. The word coyotaje derives from *coyote*—human smuggler—but it is a social process much larger than the individuals who guide migrants across terrain. In his study of Northern Mexico, David Spener defines coyotaje as a variety of strategies and practices that facilitate clandestine movement, including but not limited to the tactics and protocols that migrants, their friends, and family members use to locate, hire, and negotiate with smugglers.[29] Participation in coyotaje extends through migrant sending and transit communities across the Americas and does not only involving smugglers themselves.

Thus, durable and sustained migration practices constitute *el Camino*. These practices leave visible imprints on the physical and socioeconomic landscapes, just like the migrants' footfalls cut trails through desert and mountains.[30] Cultural and economic communities orient themselves toward the movement of people across the landscape, and both supporting and predatory activities cluster along prominent paths. These ruts carved by migrants and their smugglers become a *transit political economy* where entire communities spring to life along these burgeoning trade routes.[31] Human movement along a trade route is like a river, carving a path through the society it traverses and depositing the physical and cultural sediment of people along its current. The routes through Mexico have thus created a transit political economy that participates in a mobile culture.

The weaving of places together (to paraphrase Michel de Certeau) gives rise to material transformations that have their counterpart in the human mind. The coyotaje routines of the pathway become fixed expectations and social identities, just as the physical terrain of the pathway becomes adorned with signposts for the initiated. As a *culture of migration* emerges, sustained movement wears grooves in the social imaginary. In this social imaginary, where strategic expectations, causal attributions, and normative commitments fit together, a mobile culture takes shape, sometimes uneasily creating gaps to be exploited.[32] A culture of migration develops when geographic mobility becomes omnipresent in the everyday practices of a community, such that the decision to migrate becomes a socially sanctioned (and even expected) means for achieving economic goals.[33] Such transit communities also become both socially and economically oriented to the passage of people.[34] The material path that these people traverse shapes the social imagination, making a particular route appear self-evident, becoming a spontaneously created knowledge-based artifact, embedded in and imbued with social memory.

As the social sediment of passing people accumulates along the path, the cultural landscape changes, ultimately broadening the social imagination. An exchange takes places, as migrants and smugglers from diverse parts of Central America track the social practices that constitute everyday life into the cultural space of transit communities and destinations. Migrants and their smugglers create and come to rely on transnational ways of speaking with mixed dialects, combining Salvadoran, Guatemalan, Honduran, Mexican, and American slang into a syncretic dialect, along with exposure to unfamiliar foods; methods of negotiating; and the adaptive tactics for overcoming obstacles and challenges along the way.

This exchange occurs among migrants and smugglers moving along the route and other people living in communities of origin, transit, and destination. They make friends, create enemies, and form sexual partnerships along the way. Most of the everyday world of food vendors, bus and taxi drivers, hotel owners and landlords, and employers does not directly involve smuggling, but these people contract with migrants and smugglers on a daily basis. They thereby rely on the transit economy for their livelihood, and through their economic practices, they become enmeshed in social relations with migrants and smugglers. Because of their ongoing daily interaction with migrants, settled citizens along the routes play an integral role in the production and transmission of coyotaje. These citizens do so without ever leaving home.

In this way, the routes become what Abraham and van Schendel call an "underground" of "legally banned but socially sanctioned and protected" practice where information mediates entry.[35] Recognizing this, there are two primary ways of accessing this social space to encounter coyotaje—what I call *route terrain* and *migrant flow*. The route terrain is the places and things that form the material infrastructure of the route. The migrant flow is the collective body of people and rituals that form the social infrastructure of the route.

The analogy with "flow" should not give the impression of free mobility, however. Being caught in a current can limit movement as well as facilitate it. The experience of being trapped, forced to move involuntarily, or immobilized by poverty and immigration policing is part and parcel of the migrant flow as it eddies.[36] The flow also cuts a terrible undertow, potentially pulling people backward from their intended trajectory.

Nevertheless, these are the social institutions of the route, constituted by the practices of movement, as well as state attempts to suppress that movement. As they travel, migrants and smugglers shape places, unintentionally and intentionally, leaving traces of their passage behind in physical artifacts. The places they thus create become gathering points for those who follow.

Route Terrain

The route terrain is the places and objects, ranging from messages scribbled on the walls of shelters to scattered water bottles and altars in the desert, molded by daily social activity that thereby becomes part of the material culture of el Camino. As *knowledge-based artifacts* emerge when smuggling and migration routines become widely shared, they are the physical monuments and institutions of transit. In his study of long-distance trade, a process bearing many similarities to the transnational smuggling route, Avner Greif follows F.H. Hayek by explaining how "institutionalized rules aggregate private information and knowledge and distribute it in compressed form."[37] Similar to social rules, the material evidence of practice is a compressed form of knowledge: it is the physical manifestation and embodiment of patterned migration and sustained smuggling. In his groundbreaking analysis of material traces of crossings, Jason De León demonstrates how such artifacts can be used for archaeology of borders.[38] In his evaluation of the wear patterns and modifications made to objects by migrants, the physical remnants of crossings reveal the invisible suffering of undocumented migrants and help to demonstrate the consequences of border militarization.[39] Here, I am focused on how such artifacts become knowledge resources for other migrants.

Migration and smuggling practice shape these objects both deliberately (what De León calls *modifications*) and incidentally (what De León calls *wear patterns*), conveying information to successive migrants and smugglers as they subsequently encounter these physical remnants along the route. Of course, these knowledge-based artifacts also (and quite unintentionally) transmit information to bandits and police.[40] By revealing widely shared practices for all to see and thus generating an expectation of repetition, these knowledge-based artifacts create geographic points and social situations in which migrants and smugglers are acutely vulnerable.

In this case, unintended knowledge-based artifacts include train tracks and footpaths, as sustained movement reconfigures terrain that orients subsequent travelers. Many migrants leave home without money or knowledge of geography; they know only that when they arrive at a train yard, they will find the route north by moving with the human tide. Those migrants who cannot afford the door-to-door smuggling service also realize that they will eventually encounter a coyote within that human tide. The terrain itself becomes an instrument of coyotaje, as migrants leverage knowledge-based artifacts to locate smugglers. It is worth noting, however, that this terrain can also be turned against migrants, as the State deploys the dangers of desert and sea in a policing strategy meant to increase risks during migrant journeys.[41] Nevertheless, in this instance, migrants depend on the train yard as a signpost to lead them to smugglers.

After passenger service was discontinued, the only people (aside from the conductors) that traveled the Mexican trains were unauthorized. For decades, every morning in southern Mexico, hundreds of Central Americans would swamp train yards and the rooftops of train cars. Since the summer of 2014, a Mexican police crackdown on the trains has diminished migrants' capacity to board and to ride safely. These migrants must now pay gang members who control the train fees for passage, and their odds of escaping apprehension on this means of transport have diminished. However, riding the freight trains has never been safe, and now the risks and uncertainties of that transport have multiplied. Thus, fewer migrants board the trains as a vehicle for movement. Nevertheless, these migrants still rely on the train tracks to lead them north or to locate migrant shelters for humanitarian aid and underground activities. In this way, migrants use the train tracks, artifacts of the legally sanctioned movement of commodities, as a compass needle for unauthorized movement and coyotaje contacts. They co-opt the train yards, key sites in the legal economy, as a staging ground for moving north. As explained by a Salvadoran man who was too poor to hire a paid guide early in his journey, "The train is the guide. You just follow the tracks and they get you there."[42] Similarly, footpaths emerge around migration checkpoints, to and from shelters and train yards, and across borders. Once worn into the land, these footpaths direct movement to, through, and around these sites.

For this reason, movement in the legal and illegal economies is often symbiotic. At the macroeconomic level, free market policy and the growth of the illegal economy in Latin America are closely related.[43] At the microeconomic level, legal traffic facilitates illegal traffic by camouflaging clandestine movements and weakening the capacity of the State to control unwanted trade.[44] The physical infrastructure of border crossings and roads can be harnessed by both legal and illegal traffic. Busy urban environments camouflage illegal transactions.[45] However, legal economic practices do not just conceal information from police; they provide information to those engaged in illegal activity. In this case, migrants orient themselves to the legal traffic through the tracks and highways as a guide from the periphery to the economic core. They may also collect information about smuggling services through the networks forged while consuming or working in the legal economy. The boundaries between legal economic practices and coyotaje blur, as migrants leverage their social and economic contacts with employers, coworkers, and other service providers to locate and hire smugglers. Legal economic practices contribute to an informational infrastructure that may also be exploited by migrants and smugglers through reimagination and improvisation.

Intentional knowledge-based artifacts include efforts by organizations, smugglers, and migrants to convey knowledge to the people coming after them. Migrants sometimes leave notes with addresses of other safe places and resources on the walls of shelters. Migrant artists paint detailed murals conveying their experiences of the route. Family members post flyers bearing the photos of missing migrants. Gang members, many of them involved in smuggling and black or grey market activities, mark their territory with graffiti and mark their bodies with tattoos. Kidnappers and gangs demonstrate their brutality by mutilating and dumping human bodies. Government agencies post wanted signs, warnings, and propaganda. Human rights agencies and organizations make maps and print brochures describing the route's dangers, migrants' legal rights, and safety precautions. However, like unintended artifacts and the places where migrants congregate, these messages can cut two ways, both transmitting vital and security information to migrants and exposing migrants to harm by publicizing the nature of migration and smuggling practices to potential predators. And as migrants and smugglers are fully aware, these messages can also be instruments of misinformation.

Clandestine sites along the route also convey information by facilitating social encounters. As migrants move over terrain, key places emerge that provide an excellent environment for coyotaje. These places of coyotaje, such as shelters, train yards, overlooks with a view of the border, brothels, flophouses, and cantinas, both heighten and lessen migrant vulnerability to violence. These clandestine sites are "hidden but known";[46] they consist of space routinely and publicly used for purposes outside the law. Because they persist over time, these places become increasingly visible to a variety of actors. They are oases where information surfaces in an informational desert, and again, like oases, they are necessary both for the migrants' survival and as a sustained market for smuggling services. But they also attract predators. As their visibility increases, these sites become focal points in a struggle over information.[47] Migrants, state authorities with a variety of official agendas (ranging from public health to law enforcement), kidnappers, smugglers, corrupt authorities, humanitarian workers, activists, religious leaders, family members of missing persons, potential employers, journalists, and academics vie for information. Not coincidentally, I visited many of these places during fieldwork; I, too, found them essential. Migrants and smugglers, in response, devise tactics for maintaining secrecy. Eventually the overuse of such sites makes many migrants leery of visiting them, and the sites suffer periodic purges or decline into ruins scattered across terrain.

Migrant Flow

The migrant flow eddies in these places, transmitting information through both observation and social learning: what is popularly known as the *wisdom of crowds*.[48] By merely observing the behavior of others, the presence of or movement in a crowd can trigger an information cascade.[49] Within the migrant flow, information also diffuses among strangers by word of mouth. While serendipity plays a role in all human affairs, casual meetings in these crowds are usually more than random encounters; the material, socioeconomic, and sociopsychological landscapes shape opportunities for these exchanges. These roving crowds constitute the social practice of coyotaje as sustained movement. To paraphrase Emmanuel Adler's discussion of *communities of practice*, migrants and even competing smugglers are, at times, informally bound by a shared interest in learning and applying migration practice.[50] They follow the flow in search of information and the physical and emotional security found in numbers. Sometimes there is an explicit agreement to travel as a collective, as people form cooperative groups along the route and smugglers collaborate. At other times, people just move in the same direction, in the same way.

Nevertheless, these flows do not necessarily produce a sense of community, even within travel groups organized by smugglers. Depending on the specific circumstances and social practices, socialization may lead to suspicion and animosity between migrants, rather than trust, reciprocity, and obligation. In order to obtain information about potential victims or clients, kidnappers and smugglers often move within these crowds disguised as migrants. Most of the time, migrant flows mix community and hostility. Put another way, they do not necessarily become transnational communities of practice with institutionalized moral expectations,[51] but they may. Along the route, some groups dissipate after a short time, either breaking up as the migrants flee danger or simply wandering off on their separate ways. Other groups develop solidarity through shared emotional experiences; by learning how to migrate within the context of a social group, they may reimagine a new collective identity as migrants, using "somos migrantes" as a rallying cry.[52] They may even openly reject or co-opt derogatory terms, like *cachuco* (a racial slur against Central Americans in Mexico) or *guanaco* (a slur based on Salvadoran national origin that has long been co-opted by Salvadorans to demonstrate their patriotism in the face of xenophobic hostility), thereby explicitly claiming their migrant identity.

Importantly, community is not the only context for exchanging information, even in dangerous situations. In the anonymity of the flow, there is little or no expectation of repeated interaction or durable ties of reciprocity. Encounters between migrants do not necessarily produce much social capital, and smugglers may not rely on market reputation. Nevertheless, migrants and smugglers convey and process vital information, and they engage in simple forms of mimicry. Casual meetings of strangers are invaluable to the people involved.

Many kinds of face-to-face encounters occur in these places: veiled warnings, small talk, storytelling, sex, bragging, commiserating, joking, singing, evangelizing, speculating, complaining, interviews, begging, selling, and trading. Sometimes people intentionally transmit information to strangers and, at other times, the information exchanged is incidental to other social purposes. Misunderstandings and misinformation (i.e., intentionally conveyed misunderstandings) are common. Migrants are motivated to share information for many reasons, ranging from boredom to material self-interest. Sometimes there is only the mutual need for information. At other times, the motive behind information sharing is neither clearly instrumental nor altruistic. People often engage in conversation for their own entertainment or to relieve loneliness. Sometimes people overhear information conveyed to others; eavesdropping is very important. Finally, the information exchanged often has very little to do with what is actually said, let alone what was intended.[53] Speech is certainly not the only form of communication; people also interpret situations and strangers, including potential smugglers, with their eyes.

People watch and mimic strangers along the route. They look for spontaneous collective actions, like the sudden dispersion of the crowd as a sign of impending danger, rapid movement to the train yard as indication of impending departure, or the presence of a large group of customers waiting to depart with a guide as a signal of good reputation. And smugglers watch other smugglers, looking for ideas and tactics that might help move along the route.

Finally, migrants and smugglers observe others in order to discern their intentions. Membership in *imagined worlds*, such as those constituted by nationality, religion, street gangs, class, and gender, provide interpretive frames for judging strangers.[54] These memberships can be inscribed on the body, as well as verbally revealed or claimed. And information about them is an invaluable asset for the migrant. These identities define roles that people might perform and thus the ways that they might pose threats, offer assistance, or be vulnerable or valuable to criminals.

The ability to conceal identity can also be invaluable. For example, Central Americans study and then mimic Mexicans living along the route. The value of mimicry is high because the ability to pass as a Mexican citizen provides greater safety from both state authorities and criminal predators. Central American migrants thus learn to dress and speak like Mexicans as a form of camouflage and are sometimes coached by their smugglers on how to do so. Smugglers, on the other hand, learn to pass as Central American migrants to enter shelters alongside their clients or to look for new clients. Other kinds of mimicry arise unconsciously, as new expressions, accents, and mannerisms become habitual through interaction between Mexicans and Central Americans along the route. In so far that they are advantageous, such adaptations become a form of *cultural capital*.[55] Some Mexicans unwittingly take on the cultural tells of Central Americans. Indeed, urban Central American street culture, generally associated with the spread of gangs from Los Angeles to El Salvador in the 1990s, has become a hybridized panoply of transnational urban practices, speech patterns, and styles of representation.[56] These are now common among all nationalities along el Camino.

On the one hand, this cross-cultural exchange can be a distinct disadvantage for Mexicans because it enhances the likelihood of wrongful deportation and other abuse. Some Mexican people along the route traversed by Central Americans are, for all purposes, undocumented in their own country, because they lack papers and because Mexican squatter settlements along the train tracks sometimes have an ambiguous legal status.[57] Indeed, human rights activists deplore the impunity with which Mexican officials abuse their own citizens, let alone migrants. For these already marginalized Mexicans, the adoption of Central American cultural traits can be doubly dangerous. For example, in the context of a racialized nationalism that has failed to fully incorporate indigenous identities into the Mexican polity, Rebecca Galemba argues that the securitization of ethno-nationalist border between Mexico and Guatemala has made Mexican citizens' lives more precarious.[58] The cultural markers shared with Guatemalan-born indigenous people render indigenous Mexicans subject to illegal detentions by migration authorities.[59]

On the other hand, such markers may be an advantage by allowing them to participate in a community of practice shared with migrants who also inhabit their everyday world. Ironically, the increased difficulty of entering and staying in the United States has created a fertile social field for communities of practice along the routes. Because so many people make repeated attempts to enter the United States, migrants and smugglers may encounter each other several times. Aggressive migration policing and deportation policies in the United States have encouraged the emergence of bands of Central Americans who rove the routes through Mexico for months at a time. Some migrants have, in fact, simply adopted transit as a lifestyle. Unwilling or unable to return to the poverty and criminal violence they left behind, but equally unable to make a home in the United States, these young men roam the railways like hobos.[60] Indeed, migrants who wander aimlessly across Mexico are sometimes recruited into street gangs and/or as guides in smuggling networks (and/or more sinister kidnapping networks). In this way, border control has spawned a transnational class of vagabonds, and with it, a more durable community of practice with links to professional smuggling networks. Hang out in any migrant shelter or train yard along the route, and you will begin to recognize their faces in the crowd.

The familiarity that endless migration produces cuts both ways for these vagabonds. On the one hand, they benefit from their ties to settled Mexican citizens, transnational street gangs, and professional smuggling networks. On the other hand, their faces become increasingly recognizable to others along the route, making them a potential target for criminals or authorities. As they become recognizable, they can no longer claim that they are "legitimate" migrants searching for a better life. As a consequence, Church-run shelters may deny them assistance because they suspect that they are guides or gang members. In many situations along the route, the best strategy is to pass incognito.

Therein lies the central problem of information along the route. Information becomes most accessible and most visible as practice takes on the form of social rules and reputations that bind communities or in the form of material artifacts that give meaning to places. However, the very visibility of information often diminishes its utility for migrants and smugglers, who must navigate a dynamic and violent strategic environment, as patterned behavior generates vulnerability. In the context of criminal violence and immigration enforcement, a well-worn path or overused strategy can be disastrous. For that reason, information about survival tactics, paths forward, or people alone cannot guarantee safety.

Coping with the Informational Paradox of Route Terrain and Migrant Flow with Improvisation

The significance of information lies in how it is used by migrants, smugglers, and their foes and largely depends upon their capacity to use it in novel ways that involve imagination and improvisation en route. Similarly, in his study of border crossing, David Spener documents imaginative ad hoc tactics employed by Mexican migrants in the desert; he identifies an ingenuity born of hope under conditions of economic injustice that extends to hybrid Chicano cultural formations, as well as the material tactics for clandestine journeys.[61] I find that the makeshift tactics described by Spener are not limited to Mexican/ Chicano cultural forms. In a study of Central American migration through Mexico, Wendy Vogt also mentions the "makeshift" quality of migration, because it is a nonlinear process. Migrants must respond to unforeseen obstacles, changing their trajectory and tactics unexpectedly, sometimes retreating before advancing or choosing circuitous ways of moving without knowing the next step forward.

Such processes require imagination. Beyond the boundaries of the thinkable, imagination is largely unconscious, only revealing itself in fragments and generating connections "not by conscious choice or deliberate selection, but by a mechanism over which we do not exercise deliberate control."[62] The imaginary provides a normative and geographic orientation to migration, but without depicting an explicit grid. As migrants move along the route, the social imaginary becomes transnational as people from different cultural backgrounds meet and exchange habits, ideas, and tall tales.[63] The creative capacity of the social imaginary redoubles by moving within this clandestine crossroads of cultures.

Paradoxically, however, the social imaginary also reifies common sense.[64] To better understand this Janus-faced quality of innovation and reproduction in the context of coyotaje, we must first understand improvisation.

Stephen Greenblatt defines improvisation as "the ability to both capitalize on the unforeseen and to transform given materials into one's own scenario . . . the opportunistic grasp of that which seems fixed and established."[65] By this definition, improvisation does not imply the absence of rules, maps, scripts, or prior preparation.[66] It is, instead, the co-optation of whatever symbolic or material tools might be at hand without respecting their original or conventional purpose.

Conscious planning alone cannot produce improvised adaptations.[67] Neither migrants nor their professional smugglers can perfectly plan their routes as they confront and evade a proactive State and bandits. As a rural Salvadoran community leader explained (and many migrants echoed in interviews), "no one is ever prepared" for the unknowns that attend the route; no one knows exactly what the journey will entail before they leave home, because "every trip is different."[68] To hold stubbornly to a route chosen before the journey begins would be suicide in a context of rapidly changing patterns of violence. To mindlessly follow established conventions of travel would only lead migrants and smugglers to their destruction. Like lemmings over a cliff, they would march unwittingly into the clutches of predators. However, migration practice is not solely spontaneous either. Migrants and smugglers do not summon their tactics from thin air, but instead improvise through reflexive reinterpretation in specific social and strategic situations. They must be both flexible and determined when confronted with the possibility of detentions, deportation, prosecution for smuggling, robbery, rape, or even death. Violence structures coyotaje, such that the routes exist because of violence and not simply despite it. However, repetition of these social routines also drives their transformation in unpredictable ways.[69]

Firstly, migrants improvise identities, changing the very basis of social interaction along the route over time. Initial social contacts between strangers are negotiated within a makeshift mosaic of imagination. In this vein, Erving Goffman provides what is perhaps the most complete sociological theory of the practice of face-to-face interaction. He reminds us that, in the absence of full information about another individual, we tend to use "cues, tests, hints, expressive gestures, status symbols, etc.—as predictive devices."[70] Goffman famously argues that each social meeting requires a performance to make the situation recognizable to its participants and, in fact, recognizable to themselves. Each performance requires a social role reenacted through a script, the repetition of which constructs a coherent (if momentary) sense of self despite an individual's competing identities. These "bad faith" performances mollify the conscience into believing our actions are determined when other possibilities actually exist.[71] Along the migration trail, migrants, kidnappers, smugglers, and border patrol agents may even become convinced that certain situations are inevitable and thus tolerable. However, the intelligibility of these scripts and their cues to all parties in a social meeting is not guaranteed. As we will see, mismatches occur, sometimes through honest misunderstanding and sometimes through deception and fraud.

These roles originate in the social imaginary that migrants bring from their home communities. Their scripts become subsequently melded into coyotaje through personal stories of departures, returns, and longing for family and home, as well as long-distance symbolic and economic linkages, such as remittance flows and popular media.[72] Sometimes life imitates art. Central Americans are inundated by movies, songs, internet sites, television programs, radio reports, and newspaper articles describing previous journeys. In fact, films like *El Norte* (The North) (1983), *Tres Veces Mojado* (Three Times a Wetback) (1989), *La Misma Luna* (Under the Same Moon) (2007), and *Sin Nombre* (Nameless) (2009) have become cult classics. Each of them illustrates encounters with various types of smugglers and situations en route, crafting migrants' expectations for the journey ahead. Spanish-language news programs on television and Central American newspapers now publish almost daily reports of migrant abuse. The U.S. Border Patrol (USBP) sponsors a public relations campaign in Mexico and Central America that uses these mediums in order to warn people of the dangers of migration. And, of course, the singular, most important book for the transnational social imaginary of Central American migrants is the Bible. Narratives from all these sources support archetypes of people, places, and things that migrants expect to encounter along the route.

As they move along the route, migrants listen intently to stories about the journey of others. In the ephemeral communities of practice that arise from time to time, migrants exchange information through campfire stories, anecdotes, songs, jokes, rumors, sermons, and *testimonios* (a tradition of stories that describe the experience of witnessing and surviving). These narratives circulate among many other people besides migrants: bandits, kidnappers, police, townspeople, smugglers, activists, journalists, and academics. Migrants recognize that these stories are often a mishmash of truth and untruth as people err, exaggerate, bluff, boast, entertain, and just plainly lie.

But in a dangerous and uncertain context, no information can be entirely dismissed. People listen most intently to tales about events that have occurred in places in which they are located or where they intend to travel next. But even when stories are fantastic, new images and ideas seep into the imaginary. These images and ideas may surface again as they improvise tactics and strategies in novel situations.

In this way, the route becomes a *place*, and coyotes become legends inhabiting this place constructed by stories told before, during, and after the journey. And people become their performances, as they imagine themselves in the various social worlds along the route. Within these imagined worlds, migrants and smugglers perform a variety of competing and complimentary social roles with varying degrees of sincerity: migrant and smuggler (categories which are not mutually exclusive), and also friend, lover, wife, mother, gang member, informant, and activist. The possible scripts are legion.

Imagination reconciles scripts with unfamiliar situations. These scripts are not behavioral imperatives but are the infrastructure for improvisation. Improvisation, in turn, is not pure innovation but is a rethinking of roles and alternatives that involves tinkering with available symbolic and material resources. Scripts guide tentative social interaction along the route the way a theme might enable a stand-up comedian to confront hecklers or a mood might inspire a jazz musician in a new ensemble. Flexibly altered to fit specific situations, social scripts aid the self-presentation, interpretation, and organization of face-to-face social interactions under conditions of uncertainty.

While performances of identity always have at least some ritualized aspects, interaction among migrants, police, and criminal predators constantly revises and reimagines the sometimes mundane ceremonies on which identity is presented and claimed. For this reason, we can say that identity is a makeshift prop, rather than an essentialist personal characteristic. In highly uncertain situations, identity loses some of its utility as an enabler of solidarity or indicator of vulnerability the moment it becomes common knowledge. Put another way, as identity becomes predictable in social relations, it simultaneously enables passing across a variety of identity categories (such as gender, nationality and other membership groups) and thus loses some of its informational value for people in social interactions, because migrants, police, and criminals can manipulate these identities.

Central Americans and their smugglers adopt, rework, and re-create the instruments, practices, and customs of coyotaje, including the identities that shape social interaction.[73] In so doing, they change Mexican and U.S. culture more broadly. As will be discussed in Chapter 4, when female migrants and female smugglers leverage feminine wiles and patriarchal norms to overstep traditional roles as well as immigration law, they alter understandings of gender. When Central American migrants pass as Mexican citizens to avoid detection by immigration authorities and Mexican coyotes pass as Central American migrants to enter Catholic shelters or avoid prosecution for smuggling, they erode the reliability of national stereotypes. In a shift that in some contexts might be called corruption, migrants and smugglers improvise upon the practices and rules of the State and legal economy. Such is the handiwork of brokerage practices.

Secondly, during the journey, people often usefully employ things and ideas in a manner that their creators or authors never intended. Empty plastic bottles are fashioned into a makeshift raft or a life vest. A mango becomes a hiding place for money. The words of a national anthem or the dates of a national holiday become an impromptu citizenship test at a migration checkpoint. An ambulance hides contraband. A tattoo marks the nationality of a body for the government bureaucrats who ship that person home to Central America. This improvisation of material encounters reshapes the physical terrain over time.

Of course, physical terrain does set some limits on migration. Looking back at contraband shipments from the nineteenth century to the present, we can see that three physical terrain features encourage smuggling practices by conferring an advantage to those who intimately know the terrain—including the location of borders and natural choke points and the characteristics of urban environments.[74] Even in the age of globalization, coyotaje is constrained by the social and physical landscape, a landscape that it nonetheless shapes with sustained passage.

Conclusion

In conventional migration models, information is gathered through reciprocal relationships among family or community members.[75] These models assume that information about past journeys can reach the home community before it becomes obsolete and that information is a thing that can be possessed and exchanged without losing its value.[76] Despite their utility for explaining the durability of informal institutions of hometown coyotaje, the underlying concepts of social capital and interpersonal trust networks underestimate the flexibility of migration.[77] Because networks dynamically emerge and disappear along the migratory route, I explore a strategic environment in which the reliability of information almost immediately expires. Durable knowledge of a dynamic and unpredictable route simply does not exist. And nevertheless, people like Roberto migrate. To understand how they do this, we need new concepts, such as improvisation, which has large consequences for the State.

Improvisation obviously characterizes all human life, but it essential to survival at the margins. The homes of the poorest people (such as Roberto's) in Latin America are often improvised out of recycled materials: discarded tin, tires, cardboard, mud, extension cords that tap borrowed sources of electricity, fallen tree branches, and trash bags.[78] Their livelihoods are similarly patched together, with odd jobs and hustle. Indeed, the migratory journey is part of a grand improvisation of living that begins at home, long before the decision to move has been made. In this sense, the journey is a continuation of physical insecurity and economic marginalization that requires improvised tactics for survival.

Nor does migration or improvisation end upon safe arrival in the United States. Despite being the object of intense longing, the destination often offers only a temporary respite from wandering. Migrants constantly face deportation and therefore must continually anticipate and reimagine the possibility of another journey.[79] Clandestine spaces emerge within the United States, including footpaths around highway checkpoints; the locked safe houses in Los Angeles and Houston where smugglers demand final payment before releasing migrants to their families; the seasonal circuit followed by immigrant agricultural workers; and the urban street corners where immigrant day laborers await employers in daylight and trafficked women await customers at night.[80] With migration policing intensifying at bus and train stations, a smuggling industry now exists within the United States as well as the border. Indeed, during my fieldwork, it cost just as much for a migrant to travel with a guide from McAllen, Texas to Houston as it did to cross the U.S.-Mexico border.[81]

To return to the story that introduced this chapter: By the time Roberto finished his map, he had begun to think that the time to make another journey might be approaching. After sharing his meager portion of beans and tortillas with me, Roberto asked me if I would be willing to help him find a job in the United States.[82] In that moment, I realized that Roberto had navigated our interviews with the same performances of humility and reciprocity that had helped him survive encounters with strangers along the route. In our conversations, he had not only been describing how he navigates the route; he *had been* navigating the route. He had been laying the groundwork for an uncertain future, imagining and improvising a new transnational relationship with the resources at hand. The muddy path from his one-room, mud-walled home was a tributary of that route, and as he stood in the doorway, he had already embarked on it. With some surprise, I recognized that I, too, had unwittingly become implicated in that transnational social space, and my own experience of the route had come to mirror the improvised journeys of discovery made by migrants. I had to move in new intellectual directions to keep up with the migrants whom I met.

As ethnographers with higher stakes, migrants update their information along the way, and this information often prompts them to change tactics, and even goals. Smugglers, for example, may be hired at any point during this journey, and the location of the contract between smuggler and migrant influences its content. Strangers interact. Interpersonal trust networks are forged and dissolved. Along the way north, migrants respond with ingenuity and agility to unexpected situations. As they move across a terrain, they come into contact with new practices and their artifacts, mimicking other people in order to survive, improvising—sometimes unconsciously—upon social repertoires, and adapting material objects to their needs. As they do so, migrants reshape the social and material terrain of nation-states.

Everyday people leading private lives rarely merit attention in the great histories of nation-states. Their names will not likely be memorized by school children hundreds of years from now. Even in this book, which acknowledges their role in reshaping possibilities for transnational politics, Yanira, Wilian, Roberto, and the other migrants remain anonymous. Their stories transit through the pages of this book and disappear without warning; in this sense, the text mirrors the semi-anonymous transitory environment of the migration corridor. Many details of their lives are missing: questions left unasked during interviews, answers not given by migrants, people who may or may not have arrived at their intended destinations but with whom I ultimately lost contact. Nevertheless, wherever they roam, Yanira, Wilian, and Roberto will have a profound and largely unintended impact on the social and political landscape of North America as they weave a region together.

Chapter 3

The Cast of Characters

Actors and Their Relationships en Route

Introduction

As they cross the southern border of Mexico, Central American migrants are acutely aware of the dangerous path that lies ahead. The way forward is obscured by ambiguous social relationships. Social groups and their allegiances reorganize rapidly. Territory changes hands among competing criminal gangs without warning. Kidnappers disguise themselves as migrants or smugglers. Authorities collaborate with criminals. New violence emerges suddenly and spectacularly. As people reflect on their experiences or past events, even the hindsight of violence seldom provides clarity. Rumors compete with official versions of events. Instead, the unearthing of anonymous mass graves, the transience and disappearance of migrants, a lack of faith in the capacity of governments to prosecute the culpable, and rampant conspiracy theories heighten a sense of uncertainty along the route.

El Camino became less predictable in the aftermath of the drug war since 2005. Mexican bandits have long assaulted Central American migrants. For over three decades of mass migration, beginning with the northbound wave of refugees in the 1980s, corrupt officials have robbed and raped them, and tricksters have posed as smugglers to defraud and then abandon them along the route. Those dangerous characters remain on the scene today. However, organized actors capable of orchestrating mass kidnappings of migrants for ransom have joined the repertory of crimes along the route. The emergence of these new predators and the subsequent reordering of social relationships, norms, and routines create uncertainty for the migrants who attempt to cross Mexico.

This chapter describes the gauntlet of organized crime that migrants run as they move through Mexico. It explains how relationships among organized criminal groups along the route have changed over time, with deleterious consequences for migrants. I trace the evolution of the cast of characters along the route over three historical periods. First, I examine the route traveled by Central American refugees in the 1980s, and the relationship between the route's *coyotes* (human smugglers) and the migrants who followed them. Second, I describe the intensification of immigration enforcement in the 1990s to 2001 and the manifestation of a new face of villainy: transnational street gangs, known as *maras*. Third, I discuss the contemporary relationship between kidnappers and smugglers in the 2006–12 drug war era, known in Mexico as the bloody *sexenio* (six-year term) during the Calderón administration.

The discussion of each of these three historical periods follows a travel story from a migrant. I selected these three stories as exemplars of the changing personae dramatis of the route in each epoch, but the reader should be advised that there is no "typical" journey. I have chosen stories that resonate as reliable in this chapter, but I caution that these narratives represent performances in themselves, with silences and scripts crafted by interview participants who have their own motives. In conveying these stories in three acts, I hope to give the reader a sense of the violent, unpredictable, and dynamic context of migrant journeys and its cast of characters. I also hope to convey the importance of image making to these characters, as they build on and manipulate the legends and lore of the route that accumulate overtime.

These are the players in the human security tragedy along the route. The relationships among these players define the social structures through which migrants must pass on their journey. Clearly, the characters are not mutually exclusive. Shakespeare is quite right that "one man in his time plays many parts" and our roles evolve over time.[1] Indeed, the actors along the route may unexpectedly shift their roles and betray their allegiances. Adversaries have the potential to recombine into allies, giving them the quality of dangerous chimera. Fluidity characterizes the relationships between corrupt officials, coyotes, mareros (defined later in this chapter), and criminal terrain bosses. Furthermore, in this transient and semi-anonymous environment, people may not be who they seem to be. These fluid relationships and ambiguous roles, leading sometimes to unexpected changes in territory and organizations, generate uncertainty for migrants as they contemplate their journey.

Refugee Flow: First Period (1979–1992)

A consensus among migrants, human rights activists, and police suggests that both uncertainty and risk were less during the refugee crisis of the 1980s than in later periods of migration. Migrants encountered fewer police and control points across Mexico and along the U.S. border. Criminals that preyed upon migrants were generally less well organized and, for those who had money to travel, easier to avoid given the many options for unmonitored routes. Smugglers were relatively cheap. That said, it is important to remember that violence and vulnerability were already an integral part of the migration experience, even in those earlier days. A story of an evangelical minister illustrates how the collective sense of the route has changed since that time.

A Story from a Bygone Era: The Minister

We met at a popular local church in rural El Salvador. A mutual friend had referred me to him. The evangelical minister, Marcos, wore his hair in a short, military style.[2] A faint scar marked his left cheek. He had been counting the Church's finances when I knocked on the door. A notebook, a pile of pennies, a dollar, and a few rolls of coins were strewn across the table in front of him the first time we talked. Despite being preoccupied by this task, he agreed to share his story with me.

Marcos left El Salvador in 1989 during the civil war that ravaged the country from 1980 to 1992. It was a period when hundreds of thousands of

Salvadorans and Guatemalans traveled north, fleeing the violence and economic dislocation wrought by the war.[3] As he spoke, the minister returned again and again to the fact that the days of an easy journey north were gone. Neither the rules of conduct along the route nor life in the United States were what they had been when he traveled:

> Back then, the United States was a land of opportunity. Now, it is only a false hope. . . . False promises, sometimes by the coyote. False hopes. They [migrants] enter something like a trance with the dollar. They can only think of the money. It is all they see. They don't think about the risks, the impact on their family. It is a sickness.

Marcos explained that only the people who left early and established lives in the United States could build big houses in the rural Salvadoran town. The big houses perpetuate the illusion of opportunity.[4] But, the minister warned, the young people leaving now are not going to build big houses, because the epoch of opportunity ended in the 1990s. I asked what advice he gave his congregational members when they make migration decisions, and Marcos explained that the Bible is central to his advice to them. While I have found no empirical support for his claim, Marcos tells me that the spread of evangelicalism in El Salvador slows the flow of migrants north:

> Faith generates a feeling of security to stay. It does not matter where you live when God gives you his blessing. You will receive that in El Salvador. If an evangelical does go, he has lost his faith. Evangelicals have faith in God, not faith in the United States. They have real hope, not false hope in the United States.

Despite Marcos's clearly negative attitude toward emigration, I met people from his congregation who chose to make the journey. However, as their pastor, Marcos claimed to counsel them to remain home. As he explained, he tends to the spiritual needs of young people, not their material needs. Using his faith as the pillar of this counsel, he warns them of the potential disintegration of the family in the wake of migration and that breaking the law is a sin, both of which, in Marcos's estimation, constitute threats to their spiritual life. Marcos also advises them that their eternal salvation need not happen in the United States. Indeed, salvation can only be found in the Bible. Thus, he does not rely on his own experiences along the route to offer ad-

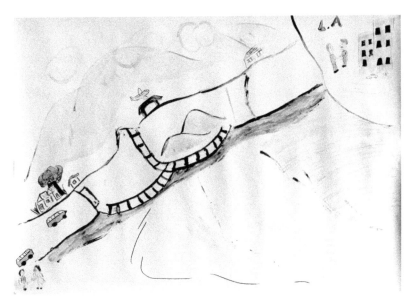

Figure 3.1. The Soldier Who Became a Minister
This map describes the journey to the United States made by
a former soldier during the Salvadoran civil war.

vice, because Marcos thinks these experiences are no longer relevant for the younger generation. Only the wisdom of the Bible is timeless.

Marcos joined the Salvadoran army at the age of fifteen. After his first two-year enlistment, he re-upped for two more. He was in the army in the mountainous Morazán department, the stronghold of the guerilla fighters, during the worst years of the war, from 1985 to 1989. But the leftists discovered that he had volunteered to reenlist, and they assumed he did it because he wanted to serve the government. Since Marcos was not a forced conscript, they threatened to kill his pregnant companion and their toddler son; once his enlistment contract ended, his family urged him to leave for their own safety. Despite the fact that she understood why Marcos had to go, his mother cried when he told her that he was leaving. His father was already in the United States and saved the $1,500 to hire a smuggler. The map Marcos drew of the experience shows him leaving home with a backpack that did not survive the journey (see Figure 3.1).

The left-hand side of the map shows his mother crying as he left home. On the right, Marcos reunites with his father in Los Angeles. The map also shows how he took a bus from El Salvador to the Guatemala-Mexico border. Marcos, his coyote, and the other migrants disembarked the bus to cross that border. After entering Mexico clandestinely, the coyote purchased a tourist visa for him, and they flew by airplane to Tijuana. Marcos traveled the length of the journey with the same coyote. He explained that he had a very good coyote:

> A good coyote is well connected. He knows who and how to bribe. That is his job. He also can talk like a Mexican and pass. Those are his skills.

Community Coyotes: Hometown Heroes and Neighborhood Con Men

We will return to Marcos's story, but before so doing, it is worth pointing out that his story illustrates that the coyote has long been a central character in the drama of Central American migration. The coyote is the guide to both the natural terrain—orienting migrants to the desert and watching for the movements of the U.S. Border Patrol—and the social terrain—negotiating the bribes to authorities and fees to criminal bosses necessary for safe passage through Mexico. The coyote also coaches the migrants about Mexican culture, helping them "pass" undetected among the citizens. However, the very experience and social connections that permit coyotes to negotiate bribes also link them to nefarious networks, a potential source of corruption and threat to the migrants who contract with them.

Even in these early days of mass Central American migration, the coyote represented a dual personality, rendered both useful and dangerous by the capacity to transgress terrain and the social contacts that come with such capacity. Coyotes facilitate escape from the horrors of war and poverty and also potentially trick, abandon, or abuse clients.[5] As Amparo Marroquín explains,

> In this flight there is a central character. In many cases, he has been the difference between life and death, success and failure. He is an obscure character loosely portrayed in the media: the forger of roads, the speaker of riddles, the knower of passwords and secret handshakes that open borders and close the doors to extortion and kidnapping. Alternately respected, feared, invoked and conjured: he is the coyote.

This duality intensified in the 2000s, when some coyotes became involved in an organized system of mass kidnappings in collaboration with Mexican criminal terrain bosses. In the 1980s, however, a coyotes' breach of contract posed perhaps the greatest danger to migrants en route. Coyotes could abandon their charges in dangerous places such as the desert.[6] Coyotes often squeezed profits out of the travel costs by reneging on the purchase of promised hotels or food during the journey. In this case, the minister was fortunate. His coyote did neither. His father, already waiting for him in the United States, had found him a guide with a solid reputation. According to the usual protocol for such transactions, the father paid half the money in advance and expected to pay half on arrival. These pay-on-delivery arrangements built on Mexican traditions of coyotaje, providing mechanisms for enforcing contracts in the absence of a third party.[7] These protocols and social ties developed around the networks established by the earliest movers from the region. In this case, Marcos's father had left to look for work in the United States before the civil war.

Despite the potential duplicity of the early Central American smugglers, they generally maintained a direct relationship with their clients, which anchored (however imperfectly) both social and reputation mechanisms in the market for smuggling services. If and when a calamity occurred during the journey, the families at home knew whom to hold accountable. In the 1980s and 1990s, smuggling and migration had not yet been criminalized in migrant home countries. In El Salvador, migrants could contact coyotes through legitimate travel agencies that openly advertised trips to the United States "with or without visas."[8] While some unscrupulous tricksters would accept money for travel services and abandon their clients en route, the legal framework in Central America provided a slight, highly imperfect degree of protection before smuggling became outlawed. In 2001, however, El Salvador passed legislation that criminalized smuggling— punishable by eight years in prison—and since that time, several new rounds of legislation have increased that penalty. Migrants and their family members could bring fraud charges against tricksters or irresponsible smugglers in a court of law. Such charges were usually settled out of court, but the law provided clients of smugglers with some leverage when dealing with conationals.[9] When the state failed to punish an irresponsible guide, migrants and their families sometimes took the law into their own hands.[10]

Perhaps for these reasons, some observers have called this period "the era of the heroic coyote." Some home communities embraced this generation of pioneering migrants and coyotes, and by the early 1990s, an emerging patriotic discourse extolled their contributions to the national economies of Central America. Tales of suffering and adventure saturated song, film, newspapers, and even monuments, transforming migrants and their guides into celebrated public figures.[11] Indeed, a successful career as a hometown coyote in Latin America might even pave the way to the mayor's office.[12] Then as now, the clients of coyotes generally did not view them as "good or evil," but as the provider of a potentially dangerous—but necessary—service.[13] Despite the fact that governments, and sometimes nongovernmental organizations (NGOs), vilify coyotes, blaming them for the suffering that befalls people during their journeys, a trustworthy and competent coyote was (and is) invaluable for a migrant.

Border Policing and Border Crossing

In the 1980s and early 1990s, immigration control concentrated on borders. Throughout the period, the U.S. Border Patrol militarized its southern border, drawing on military tactics and equipment and launching a series of high-profile campaigns that pushed migrants into the most isolated, dangerous terrain.[14] This U.S. policing strategy, adopted explicitly in the *Border Patrol Strategic Action Plan: 1994 and Beyond* and continuing into the present, borrows from low intensity conflict (LIC) doctrine in an attempt to increase risks and thereby deter migrants from attempting the passage.[15]

Farther south, Mexico acted in tandem. Beginning in 1983, as the Central American refugee crisis worsened, Mexico restricted tourist visa (FM-T) availability to Central Americans, making it nearly impossible to cross Mexico legally on the way to the United States.[16] Mexican policing and deportations of Central Americans escalated throughout the period.[17] In 1993, the Mexican federal government established its first dedicated immigration agency, the National Institute for Migration (INM), to oversee these efforts, and sent more migration personnel to its southern border zone, including instituting a series of checkpoints in Chiapas throughout the decade.[18] By 2000, there were twenty-five migration stations established, most of them in the southernmost state of Chiapas.[19]

As a result of this emphasis on policing at the geographic margins of both the United States and Mexico, the border is the focal point of migration narratives from this period. In fact, the U.S.-Mexico border was the point of the most acute danger. Even in the early days of Central American migration to the United States, the aboveground desert and underground tunnel crossings across that border were becoming prominent symbols of death in popular culture. At the border, human bones and debris had already begun to accumulate along the paths through the wilderness traveled by migrants into the United States.[20] As early as July 1980, thirteen Salvadoran migrants died together while attempting to cross Organ Pipe Cactus National Monument in Arizona.[21] Coyotes would sometimes abandon their clients during a difficult border crossing; migrants suffered the elements and died from exposure.

The plot of Marcos's story also climaxes in the drama of the U.S. border crossing. After he flew in an airplane from southern Mexico to Tijuana, as illustrated in the map that he drew, Marcos and his coyote arrived at the staging ground just to the south of the U.S. border. There was an area at the border that had been off limits to both the Mexican and U.S. border patrols:

> You can stand in this zone and see the patrols on the mountains on either side. There's a big market that sells lots of food. People chat. The coyotes shepherd their groups through. It is safe and harmonious. You can relax before the next part of the journey. The coyotes chat. They watch the hills for the right moment. Then they set off in small groups along their routes. They take different routes and stay in small groups. . . . You don't get to this place alone.

In that no-man's-land, coyotes had friendly relations among themselves.[22] Marcos did not see them argue. His description sounds more like a picnic than the beginning of a potentially deadly trek through the wilderness. There, he crossed the desert, and he likened that experience to the song and movie *Tres Veces Mojado* (Three Times a Wetback), which was written by and starred the Mexican norteño band *Los Tigres del Norte*. His travel group included an old woman who had hurt her leg. Despite the fact that she slowed them down, making them vulnerable to capture, they could not leave her behind to die. After all, "in the trip, people become what happens to one happens to all." They band together. His group of ten travelers came from many different communities across El Salvador, and they became friends during the journey. They had to carry the old woman.

They slept in the desert overnight, but they were captured by the border patrol outside San Diego. When they saw the U.S. Border Patrol approach, they huddled together to hide under a bridge. The patrol surrounded them, and an agent pushed him onto the ground. The agents had their guns drawn, but the minister was not scared. Others might have been scared, but Marcos had been in the war and knew that they were not going to harm him. When they arrested him, one of the agents taunted him in Spanish, "Bienvenidos a los Estados Unidos, cabrón" (Welcome to the United States, bastard). Marcos laughed coldly remembering it, but from the look on his face and the tone of his voice, he clearly did not laugh because it was funny.

Bandits and Corrupt Officials

Marcos, like many migrants, encountered rough handling and rudeness by U.S. officials at the border. Human rights organizations have documented extensive, and in some cases fatal, use of excessive force by U.S. Customs and Border Protection.[23] Scholars have documented corruption and numerous sexual assaults of migrants by officials on U.S. soil.[24] I interviewed one man who reported receiving a severe beating by U.S. Border Patrol agents and several others who reported verbal or emotional abuse, both at the border and in immigrant detention facilities.[25] Two people reported the denial of vital medical services that they are entitled during their detainment, and one of them urged me to investigate the death of a friend that resulted from the denial of these medical services.[26] The humiliation of detainment and deportation from the United States is extreme. Nevertheless, the encounter with U.S. migration officials is generally traumatic for its potential to end in official detention and deportation, not for its potential for criminal victimization, when compared to interactions with Mexican authorities.[27] Despite the degradations inherent to detainment and deportation procedures, many migrants reported professional behavior from U.S. officials.

Encounters with Mexican authorities, by contrast, were almost always accompanied by the extortion of bribes and sometimes assault or rape: "the corrupt [Mexican] police beat you and leave you robbed. The others [in the United States] arrest you and deport you."[28] In fact, migrants *expect* corruption and criminal violence from Mexican officials, whether they are dealing with federal, state, or local police or migration authorities. During the early period of Central American migration, encounters with Mexican authorities usually occurred in border towns. Corrupt Mexican authorities perpetrated many crimes against migrants. It is therefore no coincidence that border towns were criminally dangerous. While migrants suffered fraud and banditry across Mexico during this period, the U.S. border itself constituted the most visible and dangerous segment of the route. As another Salvadoran man who flew to Tijuana explained,

> There was always danger. The border was always dangerous in the past. . . . At the U.S.-Mexico border, it was always like that, risky.

This is not to say that danger and violence were limited to that border space. This Salvadoran man, like the minister, could afford luxury; he traveled by airplane across a large portion of the route through Mexico.[29] However, many Central Americans, lacking the funds or contacts with well-connected coyotes, had to make the land journey by land in its entirety, sometimes requiring weeks or even months of sacrifice to arrive in the United States, if they arrived at all.[30] Despite the relative ease of passage through Mexico in the 1980s when compared to later decades, the journey could still be very dangerous. Even in the halcyon days, bandits and corrupt coyotes raped, robbed, and assaulted Central American migrants with impunity.[31] Many people who traveled across Mexico by land, even those who did so with a visa, reported some form of criminal victimization or threats.[32] Indeed, criminal victimization of migrants has been integral to the route through Mexico since this early period. The Salvadoran minister Marcos was lucky that he did not meet with corrupt Mexican authorities or bandits at the border.

U.S. Entry: Legal, Economic, and Social Integration

During this early period, the U.S. Border Patrol practiced "catch and release" policing; they bused Mexicans immediately across the border and released them to try their luck again.[33] For this reason, many Central Americans attempted to impersonate Mexicans to avoid beginning their journey again from home. For a time in the early 1990s, however, Mexicans began to impersonate Central American political refugees who might be eligible for protected entry to the United States, released into the country to await asylum hearings, or granted temporary status.[34] There was no charade for Marcos. The U.S. immigration agents knew he was Salvadoran. They looked at the passport he carried. After he explained that he was a military veteran fleeing persecution, the border patrol released him.[35] His father paid several hundred dollars in bail money, roughly equal to what he would have paid as a final installment to a coyote.

Eventually, Marcos received Temporary Protected Status (TPS). TPS is a provision established by the Immigration Act of 1990, which followed on the heels of a decade of activism and a series of hard-won legal judgments that also opened possibilities for Central American asylum seekers.[36] Under this provision, the Secretary of Homeland Security may temporarily provide legal status to citizens of certain countries with vulnerable populations, such as people fleeing war or natural disasters, thereby granting a short-term, renewable stay to such foreign nationals in the United States.

Even after receiving temporary status, Marcos had trouble finding work in the United States. Until that point, his only experience in life had been carrying a gun. Despite eventually landing a factory job, he never really adapted to the U.S. lifestyle; in words that echo many other unsatisfied Central American migrants, Marcos complained that too much "pressure" permeates daily life in the United States. With persistence and hardship, he felt that he ultimately met with financial success, but Marcos remained socially isolated and missed the country he loved. As soon as the war ended in 1992, he returned home. By that time, though, his companion and two children had moved on with their lives.

Marcos bought his current house with money he saved in the United States, and he began a new family. He explained, however, that nowadays many people take loans to travel to the United States and lose their houses as a result. The interest on these loans can run as high as 30 percent, and coyote services are much more expensive now than during his journey. Some people who traveled in this period paid as little as a few hundred dollars to the coyote, and at the time of the interview, far less comfortable journeys could cost as much as $7,000. Following the 2008 economic recession and intensified immigration enforcement in the United States, many people returned home poorer than when they left. A failed journey or abrupt deportation could set families back financially rather than improve their situation. Indeed, his brother wanted to take an $8,000 loan against their father's property to pay a smuggler; the brother could easily lose their family homestead. Marcos had warned him not to go, that times have changed, but his brother is an adult. If he wants to go, there is nothing to be done about it.

Then and Now

Beyond differences in the legal and economic context in destination communities, Marcos's travel story points to several key differences between the route in the early days of mass migration from Central America to the United States and the post-2006 journey. In the 1980s, when the refugees from internal conflicts in El Salvador (1979–92) and Guatemala (1960–96) began moving north en masse, professional smugglers generally maintained a more direct relationship with their clients and often accompanied them for the entire length of the journey. Relations among coyotes, while not always amicable, alternated between collaboration and market competitiveness, as opposed to combat. While women often suffered sexual coercion during the journey, loyalty within travel groups was the expectation. Con men sometimes posed as smugglers to defraud migrants, but prices for coyote services were thousands of dollars less than today's prices. Many people simply relied on experienced relatives to guide them. Some Central Americans had ventured north in search of work before the civil war, and the refugees relied on these transnational social networks for assistance during migration.[37]

The journey, while dangerous, was easier than the passage that confronts migrants today. Before the implementation of new technologies and stricter control at the border, some people could cross U.S. Border Patrol checkpoints hidden in the trunks of family friends' or relatives' cars.[38] Most importantly, however, migration control largely stopped at the borders. For either very daring or very poor migrants, it had been easier for Central Americans to travel the length of Mexico without a paid guide, as internal immigration enforcement through Mexico had been more lax. Bandits attacked migrants, and corrupt authorities extorted money from migrants, but fewer checkpoints within Mexico made a relatively wide range of travel options available to avoid crime, as migrants did not have to travel so circumspectly. Thus, even while acknowledging the violence that has always permeated the route, the early days of mass Central American migration to the United States were less risky and uncertain than later periods.

Intensified Border Enforcement: Second Period (1992–2005)

Throughout the 1990s, the risks of the journey increased in tandem with the expansion of migration policing from the U.S. border zone to the entire length of the route through Mexico. Mexican migration authorities established checkpoints along the northbound highways and began to inspect major transit points, such as bus terminals. The United States also implemented interior checkpoints and inspections. Gilberto Rosas traces this *thickening* of the border to the 1986 Immigration Reform and Control Act (IRCA), which invoked fears of immigrant criminality and set precedents for immigration enforcement in urban zones within the United States.[39]

In the years following this legislation, migration policing intensified. Both Mexico and the United States adopted more punitive laws for convicted smugglers. The United States also criminalized illegal entry, giving prison sentences to migrants who cross the border repeatedly, and adopted laws to make it easier to strip legal permanent residency from convicted criminals, even for minor offenses. The U.S. Immigration and Nationality Act (INA), revised in 1990, grants the U.S. Border Patrol warrantless searches and seizures a "reasonable distance" from the border that has been interpreted as one hundred miles from all external boundaries.[40] Throughout the decade, apprehensions of undocumented Central Americans both at the border and within the United States increased, and under the 1996 Illegal Immigration Reform and Immigrant Responsibility Act (IIRIRA) the category of deportable crimes widened, dramatically increasing the deportations of previously documented migrants from the United States.[41]

These deportations carried new cultural practices to Central America, including (but not limited to) the protocols, language, and styles of immigrant street gangs from Los Angeles. These practices soon spread along the train corridors of Mexico as a new generation of Central American migrants, with experience and extensive social ties in the United States, traveled the route again and again. Migrants continued to move despite the intensification of migration policing. They also continued to move because of it, motivated by the desire to return to the United States after deportation. The civil wars that motivated the refugee flows ended in El Salvador in 1992 and in Guatemala in 1996, but people continued to move to reunite with their families or search for work. This continued migration momentum clashed with the increasingly restrictive U.S. policies. As a result, the deportation circuit established in this decade generated a permanent transnational transience along the routes, in which migration became a lifestyle with an indefinite beginning and end. In so doing, it also produced new criminal opportunities and actors along the route. For this reason, we mark the beginning of the new period with this shift from refugee flow to labor and family reunification flow as well as the permanent transience that accompanied the changing policing environment. Alberto's story, a migration adventure that spans two epochs, illustrates this transience.

Home and Back Again, and Again: The English-Speaking Man

Alberto had spent enough time in the United States that he preferred to speak English in our interview.[42] Unlike Marcos, the minister, Alberto had embraced his life in the United States, and he longed to return to it. For that reason, I met Alberto in a migrant shelter in Saltillo, Coahuila, Mexico. In the summer of 2010, Alberto was on his way north through Mexico yet again, hopefully for the last time.

Alberto was originally from a community near the shores of Lago de Yojoa in Honduras, but he started riding the freight train through Mexico at the age of seventeen. Unlike Marcos, who crossed most of Mexico by plane, Alberto lacked the money for such expensive smuggling arrangements. The first time Alberto crossed through the southern state of Chiapas in 1998, migration agents raided the train in the dark of the night. From the next wagon over, other migrants warned him not to talk and to stay hidden. Then he heard a loud scream. When the train stopped five miles later, the conductor told him that someone had died and warned the migrants to be more careful. Alberto did not see what happened that time, but he has witnessed many assaults during his extensive time on the route. This time, in 2010, he witnessed a fall from the train:

> The police came while we were waiting [for the train at the station]. They chased us. We went too far away from where the train is slow near the station. We asked people if it was slow enough to board, and they said it was slow. But it came fast. I said, "If you guys can't catch it, don't even try it. . . ." The third guy fell. He tried again after falling. My cousin told him no, but he tried again. He put his legs under the train wheels, and it cut the legs off. I saw him flying. Someone shouted, "Hey! He don't have legs no more!" I was in shock. I couldn't jump [off the train to help him]. I wanted to, but it was moving too fast and someone stopped me. My cousin was behind with him. When my cousin got to the next station, he told me what had happened. The police came and the Red Cross. He will be in the hospital three months. Hopefully, he gets fake legs. That is the most horrible thing to have happened. Horrible.

Bandits

Returning to that first trip in 1998 in Chiapas, close to Tapachula (where the train line used to begin near the Mexico-Guatemala border), Alberto recalled that the train stopped with its head in the city and its tail concealed in the bush. Thirteen migrants, including Alberto, lingered alongside the tracks waiting for it to depart. They pooled their money to buy a soda pop, and they sent Alberto to the store. When he returned, his twelve travel companions were naked. Three Mexican thieves with firearms had assaulted them. They stole everything. They hit them. One of his companions had a purple eye. Alerted to the robbery, Alberto hid in the bush, and when the assailants left, they walked right by him. Such incidents, often committed by opportunist locals living nearby, regularly occur in the train yards and walking paths that lead through the wilderness around highway migration checkpoints in Mexico. Importantly, while locals may be opportunists, their opportunity to prey upon migrants can be traced to the bordering practices of the nation-state in both Mexico and the United States. These bordering practices produce vulnerability for migrants, as well as the criminality of delinquents who target them, as both groups find themselves pushed to the margins of neoliberal frontiers.[43]

Mareros

Alberto claimed that the thieves were Mexican, but he also said that there were Central American gangs around. To reinforce this point, he told me about yet another harrowing ordeal on the train:

> There used to be a lot of MS-13 [a prominent Central American street gang] on the train. I caught a wagon once. Inside the wagon were seven guys play-ing cards, each with a machete and tattoos. "We're MS-13", they said, and they threw the signs [hand signals]. I threw the signs too and pretended to be one of them. They gave me some food. They talked about all the stealing and rap-ing they had done, bragging. They asked me what I had done. I played along. They told me to go collect money and food and come back. I didn't come back. Thank God I never saw those people again. Those gangs used to be Hondurans.

Beginning in the mid-1990s, these Central American street gangs, whose members are known as *mareros* in Spanish, boarded the cargo trains that the poorest migrants ride through southern Mexico to rob, rape, and sometimes murder. The two most prominent transnational street gangs are the Mara Salvatrucha (MS-13) and Barrio 18 (M18). Members of the MS-13, in partic-ular, frequently demand fees from migrants and coyotes to ride and some-times throw uncooperative migrants from the train. Armed with machetes and pistols, they also stalk migrants in train yards, bars, and hotels in transit towns in Chiapas, the southernmost state of Mexico on the border with Guatemala. In communities along the routes, they engage in extortion, drug shipments, and dealing, and have deadly disputes with rivals. The gangs generally include street kids and young adults from Central America, some of them with experience in the United States. The most sophisticated gang members issue orders, by word of mouth or cell phone, from the inhumane, overcrowded, and uncontrolled prisons system in Central America.[44] However, individual cliques may only be loosely affiliated and not entirely controlled by this imprisoned leadership. The control and coher-ence of the gang has fluctuated dramatically over time and varies across different countries.[45]

The history of both of these gangs is inextricably tied to human migra-tion. Barrio 18 traces its roots to marginalized Mexican American youth who formed street gangs to protect their neighborhoods from local toughs in the 1960s;[46] it is named for Eighteenth Street in the Rampart district of Los Angeles, and it became one of the first multinational Latino street gangs. In the three decades that followed Barrio 18's founding, subsequent waves of immigration to these communities, coupled with conflict over control of local drug markets, violently splintered Latino gangs in Los Angeles.[47] In the 1980s, Salvadoran refugees created the Mara Salvatrucha to protect themselves from Barrio 18 and other hostile Los Angeles-based gangs.[48]

The initial spread of these gangs to Central America was an unintended consequence of U.S. migration policies. Elana Zilberg argues that U.S. incarceration of immigrant youths and their subsequent deportation forcibly transnationalized street gang and policing culture, linking Los Angeles and San Salvador in a *securityscape*: a transnational territory forged by interconnected, spatialized state practices, such as zero-tolerance criminal policing policies and immigrant deportation.[49] Having been fully acculturated into the street life of Los Angeles, many deportees felt like foreigners in their country of birth, expressing extreme feelings of disorientation and dislocation. Some of them barely spoke Spanish.[50] As cultural strangers and social outsiders in the country of citizenship, deportees created enclaves of urban U.S. street culture in San Salvador.[51] Over time, they crowded out most of the local gangs.[52] Nor did they passively accept exile; many attempted return along the route through Mexico, facilitating the unauthorized movement of drugs and migrants with them.[53] From San Salvador and Los Angeles, the gangs spread to Tegucigalpa and Guatemala City and then infiltrated rural areas across Central America.

These gangs, as well as other semi-organized criminal actors, flourish in the transnational circuit created by U.S. deportations and neoliberal economic dislocations, though the majority of members have never stepped outside their country of origin.[54] Despite the fears of the security community, survey research in Central America suggests that only a minority of gang members in Central America maintain transnational criminal networks.[55] Indeed, it may be that street gangs have fewer transnational contacts than other, more cosmopolitan sectors of Central American society. Most gang recruits share a position of what Sonja Wolf calls a "multiple marginality": a combination of socioeconomic exclusions that renders them incapable of seeking respect, status, and stability through other channels.[56] Shared routines and cultural repertoires, not necessarily sustained interpersonal networks, link these gangs across borders.

As Alberto's story suggests, these gangs developed cultural markers that distinguish membership with distinctive linguistic traditions and codes (including hand gestures), etiquette, artwork, and written symbols in graffiti, music, style of dress, mannerisms, and spoken history. Andrew V. Papachristos argues that these scripts and performances constitute the most powerful transnational dimension of the gangs:

> Globalization and street gangs exist in a paradox: Gangs are a global phenomenon not because the groups themselves have become transnational organizations (although a few have), but because of the recent hypermobility of gang members and their culture.[57]

Thus, these gangs are a collection of transnational practices that emerged spontaneously from the dislocation surrounding international migration and exclusionary policies. As cultural practices, they sit uneasily with national identity. For example, a Honduran man recounted an encounter with the members of a MS-13 clique that had surprised him. The gang members had benevolently explained themselves to terrified migrants on top a moving freight train, lamenting that they no longer felt Central American because they have lived in Mexico so long.[58] But, as these gang members explained, they were not Mexican, and they claimed to feel solidarity with their marginalized Central American brethren. In Mexico, this confusion is understandable given their transient transnational lives. The youth that roam the tracks frequently speak a mix of English, Mexican Spanish, Central American Spanish, and slang (known as "caliche" in El Salvador) among themselves, ingeniously employing mixed modes of communication incomprehensible to many outsiders.[59]

These young people move around a train like (from my perspective at least) it is most natural thing in the world to jump on and off a speeding locomotive or leap among the moving boxcars to defeat boredom, moving with grace and ease (with either real or faked comfort with the risks of doing so).[60] For many, ceaseless unauthorized movement has been their life, except perhaps when they have been imprisoned. They have faced extralegal extermination by cartels, vigilantes, and paramilitaries, sometimes in multiple countries. Many members, having lived in the streets since an early age, have substance abuse problems. At night, some of them huddle, cold and hungry, in the train yards. The gangs have norms and a hierarchy, enforced by violence. Orders can be issued from inside prisons and obeyed across great transnational distances, but leadership is frequently challenged and internal jealousies emerge; young people rebel. From the rumors of deaths and disappearances that circulated with some frequency through word of mouth or on Facebook, it would seem that their life expectancy is not long. In summary, *some* of the cliques along the route are not rigid, disciplined organizations.

Under these conditions of transnational transience, their cultural markers and protocols are meant to establish permanence of loyalties and inculcate a sense of belonging. To this end, both MS-13 and Barrio 18 have traditions of tattoos and the infamous "morgue rule" that promises only one way out of the gang—death. Despite these practices, membership and allegiances are continually challenged. While navigating a safe exit from these gangs is extremely difficult, some escape by fleeing their neighborhood or converting to evangelical Christianity.[61] As they engage in internal and external power struggles, gang members manipulate the norms and rules of their group, as well as the legal norms and rules of the state. Members of competing gangs may disguise themselves to infiltrate another gang. The State may sponsor impersonations of gang members in undercover police work. As suggested by Alberto's successful impersonation of a gang member, the signs of belonging cannot be fully relied on. Ambiguity persists despite these cultural markers.

In fact, the distinction between gang member and outside acquaintance is rarely as well defined as either the law or the gangs' own protocols would imply. Loyalty to the gang is supposed to be primary, even above family ties.[62] However, gang members inhabit a variety of other roles as parents, siblings, lovers, friends, migrants, and citizens; no one is *only* a gang member, subsumed entirely by a singular role. Despite the rituals of entry (often a beating or an assignment to kill), membership and mutual respect accrues gradually in a courtship period with new recruits, such that the social boundaries that demarcate membership have a gray zone of "sympathizers."[63] During a journey along the route, gang members and migrants (as well as migrants who happen to be gang members, and gang members who happen to be migrants) must shape-shift between competing social expectations and uncertain interactions, improvising scripts from all of these roles depending on the context.

Fluctuations in Criminal Control

These gang members can become more professional over time by acquiring skills and alliances with other criminal groups. Their control waxes and wanes along the unauthorized migratory routes. By most accounts, the presence of gangs along the route surged in 2003, when El Salvador and subsequently other Central American governments implemented a repressive policing strategy called Mano Dura (iron fist).[64] In El Salvador, Mano Dura in 2003 and its successor Super Mano Dura in 2004, both widely criticized by human rights advocates for overstepping civil liberties and protections for minors, initiated a series of punitive anti-gang legislation that detained suspected members and aggressively deployed anti-gang task forces.[65] Since that time, the militarization of the fight against gangs and their criminalization has continued to intensify. Caught between the Mano Dura in the south and zero tolerance gang policing in the United States, gang members began to roam the route indefinitely.[66] In southern Mexico, the presence and power of MS-13 diminished after Hurricane Stan in 2005. The storm damaged the railroad connecting Tapachula with Arriaga, halting the trains. Following the termination of train service along that segment, migrants dispersed and depended more heavily on buses, combi (shuttles), and foot to arrive in Arriaga. The dispersal of migrants to other routes undermined the power of the gang, devaluing their territory and cutting their transport line.[67]

During the 2006–12 upheaval among the Mexican drug cartels that previously controlled the routes, the MS-13 gang may have acquired new resources along the route. The cartels are criminal organizations that have arisen around Mexican trafficking routes and have been "paramilitarized" in the wake of Mexican government military operations against them.[68] Both forms of criminality have escalated in response to state repression and widespread socioeconomic dispossession that has accompanied neoliberal economic policy since the 1990s. However, despite the fact that the U.S. Treasury Department has labeled MS-13 a Transnational Criminal Organization (TCO) in common with prominent Mexican crime syndicates, the cartels are distinct; they are more profitable and economically diversified than the gangs and organized relatively tightly in a corporate-military criminal model.[69]

Nevertheless, in the throes of the territorial wars and internecine violence that accompanied the 2006–12 period, these Mexican cartels may have subcontracted limited tasks to gangs.[70] Previously, street gangs were deemed too unruly to be reliable partners, but in the destabilized drug war context, they became valued for their low risk; street gang members know little about the inner circle of the cartels or their liaisons in government, which poses little threat if they are apprehended by authorities. Furthermore, Central American migrants can be used as an expendable, replaceable resource in a war with no end in sight.[71] This subcontracting follows a predictable division of labor among criminal groups, described by Richard Friman, in which: "Native crime groups relegate immigrants to the higher-risk and lower value-added stages of criminal activities and exclude them from information about how their stages fit into the broader economic processes of the national criminal economy."[72] For MS-13, contracts with Mexican cartels could mean greater access to sophisticated weaponry, bigger profits from drugs, and less fear of predation by stronger crime groups.

During my fieldwork, rumors suggested that the railroad between Tapachula and Arriaga might reopen, thereby increasing the value of the MS-13's traditional stronghold in Chiapas and restoring their transport lines. This development, which at the time of this writing has not come to pass, would have hypothetically given the Central American gangs a greater bargaining position with cartels as the "caretakers" of train shipments of drugs and people. According to some accounts, new, more organized, professional gang members may have been moving north from their stronghold in Central America to take advantage of these perceived opportunities.[73] These new cliques may have displaced or taken over some the cliques of marginalized youths that roamed the route terrorizing migrants and community members since 2005. As explained by one official with field knowledge of the migration route, "Well, there's a little of everything."[74] By July 2013, gangs had again reasserted their control of the Southern train route, demanding payments of $100 per migrant from smugglers boarding the train in Arriaga and at other points along the route.[75] Meanwhile, Mexican officials, presumably aware of this symbiotic relationship between legal transport infrastructure and criminality, have more recently made the so-called modernization of the train line a new priority, to include constructing barriers, increasing the speed of trains, and installing dome-shaped covers on freight cars to make riding atop difficult.

Intensified Internal Policing

There were many dangers for a Central American in Mexico during the 1990s. Nevertheless, when Alberto had traveled while underage in that era, Mexicans also reached out to help him and give him money. He worked and made friends in Saltillo. Then, Alberto worked for six months in Piedras Negras, a border town straddling the United States and Mexico, before crossing the border with a few Mexican friends instead of a paid guide.

Unfortunately, Alberto was only in the United States for two months before he was deported back to Honduras. He made the mistake of riding the Greyhound bus through Arizona. In the 1990s, migration agents began extensive surveillance of bus and train stations in search of migrants. In 1992, political pressure for migration enforcement mounted in the United States.[76] Beginning in 1993, the U.S. Border Patrol launched a series of high-profile operations to deter migrants from attempting the crossing and began construction on a wall at the border.[77] Section 287(g) of the Immigration Nationality Act (INA) of the 1996 Illegal Immigration Reform and Immigrant Responsibility Act (IIRIRA) established partnerships between state and local police and migration enforcement. The same legislation increased criminal penalties for smuggling and illegal reentry,[78] and it contained provisions for the deportation of permanent legal residents who commit even minor offenses. Originally, this legislation applied retroactively to migrants who had pleaded guilty to offenses, making many people eligible for deportation for crimes they thought had already been resolved and for which they had already been punished. In 2001, the U.S. Supreme Court ruled that the law could not be retroactively applied to migrants pleading guilty before 1996.[79] However, the ruling came only after many legal permanent residents had been returned to their countries of origin. The U.S. Border Patrol also established seventy-one interior checkpoints along highways inside the United States as a second tier of defense after the border.[80]

Migration policing and deportations also intensified south of the U.S. border.[81] In 1990, Mexico criminalized human smuggling, making it punishable with ten years in prison.[82] In a post-NAFTA "de facto bilateralism" agreement on the issue of border security with the United States, Mexico intensified both its internal and border policing.[83] In 2000, Mexico's National Institute of Migration (INM) maintained twenty-five migration stations, most of them congregated in Chiapas, near the Guatemalan border.[84] In 2001, President Vicente Fox launched *Plan Sur*; that established two internal control belts, with highway inspection checkpoints, across the Isthmus of Tehuantepec.[85] Between 2003 and 2005, Mexican migration authorities reported a dramatic rise in the number of migrant apprehensions across the country, a fact that Rodolfo Casillas attributes to their increased resources and personnel deployed in that time period.[86] By 2005, the INM had expanded operations to fifty-two migration stations across the length of the country, and not only at the border.[87]

Under pressure from the United States, Central American home countries also began to criminalize smuggling.[88] El Salvador outlawed human smuggling in 2001, coupling trafficking and smuggling under the same law. Peter Andreas labeled this shift to internal and transnational policing, with cooperation between destination, transit, and home countries, a "thickening" of borders.[89]

To return to Alberto's story: He did not know the specific legal and policy changes that ushered in this new era of migration policing, but he had experienced it. And he felt confident in his capacity to navigate this intensified policing. In part because of his extensive experience and the kindness of Mexican and American friends he met during his many journeys north, Alberto proudly explained that he had never been caught by migration authorities, whether Mexican or United States, at any border: "I know they don't catch me. They never catch me at the border." After his earlier deportations, Alberto had learned not to ride the buses. However, as migration policing extended and deepened along the length of the route, so too did criminal violence against migrants, and it was the ever-growing threat of crime that frightened him more than the possibility of apprehension by border patrol.

Coyotes: Subcontractors

In this challenging environment of growing banditry, extortion, and policing, coyotes diversified their tactics and raised their prices. After his capture while riding the bus and his subsequent deportation, Alberto immediately returned to the freight train through Mexico, and a nephew paid $400 for a very inexpensive coyote only for help to cross the U.S. border. In the 1990s and early 2000s, door-to-door smuggling service from Honduras might have cost as much as $5,000, and he could not manage it. By that time, the freight train had become the symbol par excellence for the dangers of the journey, as migration policing funneled the poorest migrants toward the tracks.[90] The bus routes had now become off-limits for anyone incapable of negotiating a series of bribes for passage through the checkpoints, and migrants with sufficient financial resources often paid for expensive passage in hidden compartments in trucks. But the hidden compartments are not without their own risks.

Hidden Compartments

A Salvadoran man, Gabriel, described his harrowing experience in 2000.[91] During his journey with a coyote, he and his travel companions were trapped inside a hidden compartment in a truck until Puebla. He heard the migration officials outside, asking "You carrying any pollos [chickens—slang for migrants] in there?" and banging on the walls of the hidden compartment. The officials walked loudly over the top of the compartment, but everyone inside sat silently. Gabriel had curled into a small ball with his head to the side. He could not shift his weight. The migrants urinated on one another, but the guides had given them a pill to keep them from defecating. They passed the migration checkpoint, and when the coyotes dragged them from the compartment, none of them could move. The coyotes pulled their ankles or legs and dumped them onto the ground like bags of potatoes. People would fall and lie immobile, as the blood returned to their limbs. Gabriel estimated that it took thirty minutes before he could move.

Another man, Jorge, told of strikingly similar experiences during the same era.[92] On his first adventure in a hidden compartment, Mexican migration police had rescued his travel group at a checkpoint. Without the intervention of law enforcement, they would have suffocated. However, the close call with death did not prevent Jorge from attempting a second ride in a hidden compartment from Mexicali to the border:

We got into another hidden compartment to be taken to the border. When I got out, I couldn't move. My body was asleep. I had a fat woman on top of me the whole time. I had been one of the first in. They had to drag me out by the arms and legs and toss me under a tree. Helicopters were circling overhead. It took an hour before I could move my body again. I was numb. The guide said not to move, but I was worried the police would come and everyone would run. I would just be laying there.

These men's experiences are not isolated events. Many others tell similar stories and describe the crippling, humiliating, and near fatal conditions within hidden compartments.[93] In what journalist Jorge Ramos called "the worst immigrant tragedy in American history," nineteen Mexican and Central American migrants, including one small child, suffocated in a trailer after their coyote abandoned them at a truck stop in south Texas in May 2003.[94] Smugglers hid the migrants inside the truck trailer in order to pass the inspections at the interior migration checkpoint in south Texas before reaching Houston.[95]

Coyote Accountability

These dangers increased as coyotes adopted business models that complicate accountability in the wake of such tragedies. In response to intensified policing and criminalization of smuggling, some coyotes began to outsource risky segments of the journey to other guides.[96] Coyotes specializing in high-end door-to-door service from Central America to the United States, in particular, increasingly subcontracted to specialists for each part of the route. Underling Mexican guides were easy to blame for the mistreatment of clients. Safe houses, the places where smugglers hide their clients en route, became increasingly overcrowded, as multinational travel groups merged there. Service deteriorated and migrants found themselves frequently locked inside houses under unhygienic conditions as they waited for transport to the next rest stop on the route. The safe houses, under the control of people with only distant relationships with the migrants' home communities, were not safe.

Over time, these arrangements began to erode some of the reputational and social mechanisms that enforced contracts.[97] Suffering became ever more normalized, an expectation of the journey. Migrants with close relatives in the United States continued to pay for premium services, in hopes of avoiding both the police and gangs stalking the routes. Some migrants also continued to rely on experienced friends and family members to guide them. Human smuggling through Mexico became an increasingly diverse collection of enterprises with packages to fit any customer's budget and risk profile.[98]

Then and Now

Alberto managed to stay in the United States for five consecutive years. By his account, he worked hard. He helped two brothers get to the United States. He married a U.S. citizen, and he tried to fix his legal status. However, an attorney provided poor advice. In reality, Alberto could not change his status until a ten-year reentry ban that he had received during his previous deportation expired. When Alberto went to the government office to file the paperwork, migration agents caught him and deported him again. Thus, in 2010 at the age of twenty-nine, he immediately began to travel again.

Alberto had experienced the dangers first hand during his last journey, and he knew that the route had deteriorated during his years in the United States. I asked him why he was willing to risk it all again to return. In response, Alberto explained that he had a three-and-a-half-year-old U.S. citizen son. On the phone, his son had pleaded with him, "Daddy come back home." With the sound of his son's voice in his ears, Alberto was ready to undertake any risk and uncertainty to arrive. His wife, born and raised in the United States, was frightened for him on this last journey, but she did not want to live in Honduras. She had a job in Minnesota.

The irony of his transnational life had not been lost on Alberto. He had achieved his original goals in the United States, but through his son and wife, now found himself tied permanently to a country to which he did not legally belong. He had first left Honduras because his family was poor. He and his brothers worked hard. They acquired nice houses, land, and a truck in Honduras, but his son was in the United States; "it is one thing or the other." Even so, Alberto lamented, "This is my last trip. I don't want to die." After all, since the 1990s, the migration route has seen the spectacular emergence of new forms of violence, and Alberto's migratory experience and social ties no longer guaranteed his safety. Indeed, on this journey to end all journeys, these very social ties actually rendered him even more vulnerable. If kidnappers were to learn that Alberto had family in the United States, they would demand a large ransom for him. I did not cross paths with Alberto again, and I do not know whether he was able to reunite with his family in the United States.

Bloody Sexenio: Third Period (2006–2012)

Between 2006 and 2012, the security situation along the migratory routes deteriorated precipitously. As the drug war escalated, contestation over territory and tributes paid to "plaza" (criminal terrain) bosses increased both risk and uncertainty for migrants. In Mexico, the discovery of anonymous mass graves and disappearances of migrants became more frequent. With the splintering of Mexican criminal groups, the protocols and relationships that formerly underpinned smuggling networks underwent a period of intense renegotiation. Allegiances could not be trusted. Drug cartels turned to kidnapping migrants for ransoms paid by U.S.-based relatives and coerced some formerly trustworthy coyotes into collaboration, blurring the boundaries between traffickers and smugglers. Nevertheless, migrants continued to embark on the evermore dangerous journey.

A Story of Betrayal: A Desperate Young Man

I met one such desperate young man in the office of the migrant shelter in Ixtepec, Oaxaca, Mexico. Edwin was from Tocoa, Colón, Honduras.[99] The first time he traveled through Mexico to the United States was in 1999, when Edwin was just fourteen years old. His mother had lived in the United States since he had turned one, and he had never known her. His grandparents sent him away after a street gang killed a family member. His aunt in the United States told him to come quickly to avoid the violence. Edwin left suddenly, without a guide. His family gave him US$1,000 to cover all his travel expenditures, and in Chiapas he met a cattle farmer who brought him north. The rancher was connected to organized crime, but he became a friend, willing to adopt the fourteen year old. However, Edwin chose a reunion with his mother over the adoptive father. The rancher accepted his decision and helped him on his way. A smuggler friend of the rancher took him in a hidden compartment of a truck to Mexico City. This friend stole cars for a living, and Edwin stayed with him for ten days before the rancher arranged for a second smuggler friend to take him as far as Monterrey. Again, the rancher asked him to stay and offered him a job, but still, the boy was determined to join his mother. The rancher took him to Reynosa, Tamaulipas, where Edwin's aunt came to help him across the border.

Edwin lived in Houston for nearly a decade, acculturating to his community there and embracing life in the United States. By his own admission, he felt more at home in Texas than Honduras. In Houston, however, a cousin started a fire in their apartment and police falsely accused him of his cousin's crime. Understanding that he was taking a fall for another family member, a second cousin paid a lawyer for him. But, in order to receive parole, the lawyer advised him to sign a paper with an admission of guilt. The desperate young man followed this advice only under duress; Edwin had never been incarcerated before and felt utter desperation to be released. However, after accepting the guilt, the court sentenced him to two years in state prison; three months later they sent him to the migration authorities. It was October 30, 2008, when they deported him. The deportation papers bore both his name and his cousin's name.

Edwin began the return journey to the United States in November, as soon as he landed in Honduras. There was no internal debate, no moment of indecision, about the choice to return. His work was in the United States, as well as everything he owned and everyone he cared about. Edwin could not stay in exile in Honduras.

A friend from Honduras accompanied him on the return journey. This friend had a friend who lived in Veracruz, Mexico, and who had taken him north last time without a problem. The last journey with this friendly contact was safe, comfortable, and inexpensive. The contact offered to take them from Coatzacoalcos, Veracruz, to Houston, for $3,500. From Central America to the United States, smuggling services can cost more than double that sum. The young men called their relatives in the United States to arrange for the contract and payment. After some negotiation, his cousin offered to pay for delivery when they arrived in Reynosa. However, the two migrants did not know that their "friend" in Veracruz was now working for the Zetas.

The Zeta Franchise: "You Know the Letter"

We will return to Edwin's story, but first it is important to explain that the daily humiliations and crimes of opportunity committed by mareros, tricksters, bandits, and corrupt officials continue, as in the previous period; however, between 2006 and 2012, the specter of the *Zetas* overshadowed them in the contemporary imagination of migration. Smugglers, humanitarian workers and migrants all agree that human security of migrants and smugglers deteriorated with the arrival of the Zetas on the scene. Systematic mass kidnappings of migrants crossing Mexico were virtually unheard of until after 2005. The policy of "decapitating" organizations through kingpin killings and prosecutions incited violent power struggles within drug associations as well as among them. During President Calderón's tenure in office (2006–12), perhaps as many as fifty thousand Mexicans and an unknown number of undocumented migrants died in drug war violence.[100] In August 2010, the Zetas allegedly committed a highly publicized mass murder of seventy-two migrants in Tamaulipas, Mexico.[101] In the years following this massacre, Mexican authorities discovered other mass graves of migrants, and many of the corpses exhibit signs of torture.[102] On May 13, 2012, Mexican authorities discovered forty-nine mutilated corpses, many of them missing heads, arms, and feet, in Cadereyta, Nuevo León. The government of El Salvador and human rights activists worried that the dead could be Central American migrants, but the bodies had not been immediately identified.[103] Despite an arrest in the case, the massacre remained shrouded in fear—fear that provoked ambiguity and became the subject of endless rumors instead of a sense of justice. In such situations, the Zetas were often the official suspects, but one can never be sure. One shelter staff member answered the question of when violence began to escalate against migrants in this way:

> Three years ago, I came to work in the shelter in 2007. There were painful stories about suffering back then, particularly in the north, in the desert. But in 2008, Veracruz became worse. Then the stories from the Istmo began. Between 2009 and 2010, it has been continuous violence, stronger every day. . . . It has been getting worse since the Zetas. In the past, it was common thieves. Of course, the migrants *say* it is the Zetas. I do not know. The Zetas cause so much fear. People used to say "maras" and now they say "Zetas." They are so feared because they are organized and strong. They can stop a train and take

everyone away and there is nothing that can be done. Many thieves might say they are the Zetas. The real Zetas are more organized than all the shelters combined. . . . But those thieves that steal 200 pesos. . . . Why would a Zeta risk himself for 200 pesos? When they can stop whole trains? There must be thieves who claim to be Zetas. They must be common delinquents if they steal only 200. . . . All a thief has to say is "you know the letter" [the letter Z].[104]

I sought more information, but she demurred, explaining that she does not want to know more about the Zetas. Knowing less is better, safer. The original Zetas group likely formed when Osiel Cardenas Guillen, then boss of the Gulf organization, hired Mexican Army Lieutenant Arturo Guzman Decena as an enforcer in 1997.[105] In turn, Guzman recruited other soldiers. The Mexican Special Unit Against Organized Crime (UEDO) initially identified thirty-one former enlisted men working as "Zetas,"[106] of whom at least thirteen served in the Special Forces Airmobile Group (GAFE).[107] These men formed the original "core" of the organization behind Guzman, and their penchant for dressing in black uniforms and driving dark suburban vehicles with tinted windows quickly became part of the their legend.[108] The group recruited ex-military (including Guatemalan special forces), ex-police personnel, and corrupt officials into its ranks.[109] The military origins of the group have become a form of cultural capital, part of an intimidating mythos.

The Zetas' break from the Gulf cartel and the subsequent war with the cartel precipitated the more aggressive entry of this group into the kidnapping industry. Indeed, the capacity to franchise these kidnappings, granting the right to commit them in the Zetas' name, may provide an easy way to pay members of a very loosely connected extended network.[110] By 2012, the Zetas controlled much of the terrain along the Mexican border with Texas, collecting passage fees from coyotes.[111]

Very few of the original Zetas members remained alive, even halfway through the *bloody sexenio*. By 2009, they no longer constituted an exclusive, elite group of professional mercenaries.[112] Nevertheless, Zetas and their imitators went to great lengths to maintain their image of military efficiency, threatening journalists who wrote stories about their weaknesses and defeats.[113] They frequently made a spectacle of their black uniforms, high caliber weapons, and cavalcade of black Suburbans, as well as the torture and killings of their captives. The image-conscious Zetas pioneered the

practice of beheadings as "narcomessages," now part of the common repertoire of Mexican drug gangs. Zetas and their collaborators purposely spread
rumors of their own brutality. In chapter 4, we explore how migrants perform social roles to survive, but it is important to remember that a variety of
criminal predators also self-consciously and selectively *perform* their roles to
either intimidate or conceal their intentions.

Thus, the image of this paramilitary group came to personify kidnappings
and extortion of migrants. The Zetas and violence against migrants became,
during that period, synonymous in the public imagination, despite the fact
that the Sinaloa cartel also kidnapped migrants crossing its terrain.[114] Other
groups, including the Gulf, Juarez, and Tijuana cartels, did not provoke
the terror and spectacle of the Zetas, despite some forays into kidnapping
and trafficking as well as charging crossing fees from smugglers passing
their territory.[115]

As a result of the infamy of the Zetas, less well-organized, local groups
imitated their kidnappings. They used the infamous Zeta image and name
to incite fear in their victims. The extent to which the Zetas licensed the use
of their name or outsourced certain activities to local collaborators is open to
speculation, but it also seems to have become a common practice. Furthermore, unauthorized use of the Zeta brand and internal conflicts within and
among the various Zeta cliques rose as the Mexican government pushed back
against the Zetas. Competing gangs likely committed crimes claiming Zeta
responsibility to bring the attention of law enforcement personnel to Zeta territory; indeed, the investigation into the Cadereyta massacre was complicated by
a strange series of messages both owning and disowning Zeta responsibility.[116]

In the second half of this period, the boundaries of the group became unclear. Some observers heralded the fragmentation and decline of the Zetas,
though their obituary seems premature as cells regroup.[117] In previous years,
some evidence of the enforcement of Zeta name brand surfaced, such as in
2009 when a kidnapping band was killed in a Nuevo Laredo jail, allegedly for
using the Zeta name without permission.[118] However, these enforcement activities were restricted to a key territory. For this reason, Alejandro Hope reasoned
that the Zeta organizations were in disarray following arrests of leadership,
but that the violent and remorseless Zeta attitude and practice will continue at
the hands of new perpetrators.[119] So far, this prediction has proven prophetic.
Regardless of whether the Zeta organizations continue to operate, they have
initiated new protocols, practices, and tactics in the Mexican drug war.

Further complicating the attribution of blame, the term "Zeta" became a generic descriptor for organized and brutal kidnappers, thereby undermining the group's capacity to enforce its brand. I asked kidnapping victims how they identified their kidnappers as "Zetas." Some kidnappers claim to be Zetas, despite working in regions not known for Zeta activity; some claim to be Zetas, despite a poverty and lack of professionalism that contradict the gang's folklore. Nevertheless, migrants seem inclined to believe these claims. As explained by shelter staff, "They construct the meaning of the word [Zeta] along the route . . . as they move north, they feel their presence more."[120] In other words, migrants themselves use the name "Zetas" in a manner that changes its meaning, undermining the group's control of the trademark. The word became associated with cruelty and the costumes of any paramilitary criminals (such as the black or camouflage clothes), the trucks with dark tinted windows, and high-power rifles. When asked how migrants knew their kidnappers were Zetas, many people respond with a shrug—of course they are Zetas: "they were cruel and bad men." Indeed, the word for kidnapper became interchangeable with the letter "Zeta" in conversation. The transference of "Zeta" to mean "kidnapper" illustrates the ambiguity that confronted migrants. The infamous letter Z was just one of many phantoms that stalked the route in this period.

Corrupt Officials

For migrants, the difference between a *Zeta* and a *migra* (Mexican migration official), like the blurry boundary between rival criminal gangs, was also often unclear. When a freight train stopped for a migration raid, few migrants would wait around to identify or to check the uniforms of those who had stopped the train. In the confusion and the dark, people screamed, pushed, and fell from the train. Everyone ran. Families sometimes became separated. People hid. Afterward, few people knew with any certainty whether the migrants captured had been kidnapped by criminals, or detained by officials, or both. In an interview in the chapel of a now-defunct migrant house in Lecheria, a Honduran man explained:

> In San Ramon [on the train route between Arriaga, Chiapas, and Ixtepec, Oaxaca], there was a truck that drove along the side of the train. From the

truck, they stopped the train using the break tube. The truck was white with two people in it. . . . The two were armed and they caught like thirty [migrants]. Some say it was migra and others say it was Zeta. I did not have time to figure it out. I escaped in the corn.[121]

The man guessed that he witnessed a kidnapping, but there is no way to be certain. Even when Mexican authorities wear uniforms, migrants cannot be certain whether they will carry out official duties or corrupt activity. Sometimes officials simply extort bribes. At other times, they work more intimately with organized crime.[122] Such criminal activity is common enough that encounters with law abiding Mexican police and soldiers come as a surprise to migrants. Thus, migrants attempt, with limited success, to develop frames for understanding the intentions of state authorities.

For example, a Honduran migrant explained a rumor about secret codes in Mexican police uniforms.[123] He and his friends had met a mysterious group of well-armed men, some in uniform and others in plain clothes, on a trail through the wilderness leading around a migration checkpoint. At first, he thought they were kidnappers, but the well-armed men claimed to be protecting the migrants. They warned the migrants of the known locations of bandits. In retrospect, the Honduran migrant reasoned that they must have been "real" police, because Zetas who dress in Mexican police uniforms, "go about with the insignia on the opposite side," or so a friend told him.

These migrants were understandably nervous when approached by any armed person, whether they wear a uniform or not. Despite the belief of the Honduran man, clues like subtle alterations to uniforms are not a reliable code to understand intentions. Indeed, even if *real* Mexican officials detain migrants, there is a chance that they end up in the hands of kidnappers, or beaten and robbed, rather than deported home. Migrants do not necessarily know whether the police approaching them are kidnappers or serving in their official capacity, and either way migrants are likely to try to escape before they need to find out.[124] In 2011, Mexican migration officials allegedly apprehended 120 Mexican, Central American, and Chinese migrants traveling north by bus and gave them to the Gulf cartel.[125] In that year, the National Institute of Migration (INM) registered 230 reports of corruption.[126] Between January 2006 and December 2012, the INM removed 883 agents from their posts for "irregular conduct."[127] Furthermore, kidnappers sometimes evade capture, because they receive advance warning about Mexican officials' plans to raid their drop houses.[128] Of course, collusion between Mexican officials, including police and military personnel, is particularly blatant in kidnapping stories in which victims must be transported across the country to captivity in the northern border towns. Some victims of these kidnappings reported, both in interviews I conducted and in interviews conducted by human rights groups, that officials at highway checkpoints interacted with their kidnappers.[129] For example, a Salvadoran man, Miguel, described his kidnapping and collusion between kidnappers and Mexican police:[130]

> A friend from Honduras said, "let's go have a beer. . . ." In the park, close to the church and the Casa de la Caridad [shelter], there were two taxis, and we went five and five in each. The plan was to [later] take the train to Nuevo Laredo, but it didn't go like that. We were kidnapped by the Zetas. . . . There was a group of twelve, well armed and dressed as civilians in three trucks, like what the Padre has [small SUVs]. They hit us. They took our money. They killed my friend and another. . . . .

I interrupted to ask, "Why did they kill him?"

> His error was that he didn't tell them that he had a wife and children in the United States. The boss told me, "I cooperated with the killing of the seventy two." I said I had family that would pay. And I told them I was looking for La Güera in Nuevo Laredo [a coyote]. The boss said, "We're the same." So, he took us to a neighborhood in those cars. I thought, "Why don't my friends call for help?" There were people around. But it was because of fear. This was Saturday. On Sunday, three friends' money came. The ransom came. They were released. I had to wait eight days. . . .

I asked about the ransoms, and he explained:

> They asked for $5,000 [for] each one. One Nicaraguan friend had an aunt in Costa Rica who sent $6,000. Every day they hit us. At ten to seven he took us in a car for the money. When they moved us, they passed a patrol and the police talked to the murderer. The law is corrupt.

Miguel's quote illustrates the potential for collaboration between coyotes, police, and Zetas, as well as its dire consequences for migrants. Kidnappers released Miguel after his sister in El Salvador sent $3,000 to save his life.[131]

A brother in Las Vegas did not help. Instead, his sister took out a high interest loan to pay the ransom. Debts acquired to pay ransoms are potentially catastrophic for families, because the rescued person is not delivered to the United States where a job might be available to help pay them. For this reason, kidnappers sometimes need to torture victims or kill their travel companions to extract contact information about family members from migrants. Kidnappers also sometimes audibly torture migrants during negotiations with family members. The sacrifice made by his sister, who earns $238 dollars a month in a Salvadoran clothing factory, drove Miguel to contemplate suicide. Instead, he embarked on the journey again, desperate to find work and pay the debt or die trying.

Coyotes vs. Zetas

While collusion between coyotes, police, and Zetas was common, the relationships among the different groups of actors along the route change over time, and these changes reshape the physical security of migrants in transit. During the 2006–12 period, the most violent crimes against migrants were not committed by coyotes, but by cartels. Indeed, since that period, migrants have paid coyotes largely to help them negotiate the tributes to organized crime, rather than evade capture and deportation by migration authorities. As explained by Alberto in the shelter in Saltillo:

> I don't plan to go by myself, alone, because of the kidnapping. The coyote pays the Zetas $300 for each individual. So you have a license to walk from here to the border. The price of a coyote [only from Saltillo, Coahuila to cross the border] is $2,000. They charge you to be in this territory. . . . A friend told me . . . A friend came in bus. In Veracruz, the *migra* stopped him and said that for $300 we let you go and be sure to call this number. It was the Zetas, and you have to pay and they gave him a pin [a password]. They said if another Zeta catches you, give him the pin. He once gave the pin to the police, and they let him go. They're together, the police and the Zetas.

Alberto's friend had traveled in 2008. The story makes evident important changes in the route since Alberto's earlier adventures on the train. Migrants hire coyotes, not primarily to avoid immigration enforcement as they did in the 1990s, but to avoid the possibility of kidnapping. Organized criminal groups, who charge fees for passage, often seem more capable of controlling passage than law enforcement officials. By the time they reach the shelter in Saltillo, migrants like Alberto overwhelmingly believed that to travel farther without a connected coyote would be tantamount to suicide.

> Don't take the train after Saltillo. You take the train, you'll get caught by either migration or the Zetas. Big organizations—a chain—cross fifty people at a time. That's why they [the Zetas] respect those people [big coyotes]. They [the coyotes] pay to let them work.

This man and his travel party decided to rely on a cousin who had traveled to the United States three weeks before they did to choose a coyote. They hoped that the record of the coyote in his recent dealing with the migrant's family member signaled reliability, but the danger was always that the coyote would sell them to the Zetas rather than deliver them to the United States. Given how quickly criminal territory and relationships changed in the 2006–12 environment, past dealings with the coyote offered no certain outcome for future contracts.

Indeed, the relationship between kidnapping groups and smugglers alternated rapidly between conflict, coercion, and collaboration.[132] Likewise, the "Zetas" and mareros had a sometimes adversarial, sometimes cooperative relationship. In the northern part of Mexico, the Zetas and other organized groups fought over territory,[133] and factions within the Zetas fought among themselves.[134] As explained previously, the Zetas did not control use of their brand at all times and places, and other, smaller bands of kidnappers capitalized on their symbolic resources (with or without permission). For these reasons, the criminal threats to migrants were multiple and fluid, depending on changes in the relationships among these actors and the territory they controlled. This complicated the relationship between the Zetas who controlled terrain and the coyotes who wished to pass clients across it.

Several stories of Zetas torturing, threatening, or murdering coyotes came to my attention during fieldwork. These stories underscored the potential for conflict between smugglers and kidnappers. In interviews with migrants describing their own kidnappings, two types of criminal violence against guides have surfaced: punishment and coercion. Criminal groups tax movement on the routes north, and guides who have not paid the requisite fee may be killed and their clients held for ransom. During kidnappings, Zetas also tortured migrants to identify paid guides within travel groups, presumably with the knowledge that each paid guide has a smuggling boss with money to ransom his worker and clients. A middle-aged Salvadoran woman, Mery, whom I met at a shelter in Arriaga, recounted the story of the kidnapping of her travel group in Tierra Blanca in 2009:

> At first, the Zetas did not know the Guatemalan was the guide. There was a Honduran, a Guatemalan, and my husband. They beat all of them. The Honduran fingered the Guatemalan as the guide. The Zetas know that when there's a guide, there's a boss. They knew this Guatemalan had a boss who would pay. They told him to call his boss and tell him he needs to pay $5,000. The boss paid and we ended up at his house in Nuevo Laredo where there were about ten Central American guides and that Mexican boss. . . . Migration gets paid $300 for each migrant, like the Zetas. . . . In Monterrey, migration stopped the trailer. The boss paid to get us through to Nuevo Laredo. No problem. We did not know where we were going. When we got there, we knew we were in Nuevo Laredo. . . . The boss insisted that we pay $2,800 per person.[135]

Her Mexican "husband" endured a terrible beating by the Zetas, leaving him "black and blue all over his back and chest" and barely capable of walking.[136] Since the coyote boss paid the ransoms to the Zetas, the woman and her "husband" became his chattel in Nuevo Laredo:

> Well, I was in the hands of those people, a band of coyote. They wanted $2,800 for each of us. . . . They said that we had to work for them, if we could not pay. But we escaped. The guards were drinking and then fell asleep. They forgot to lock the door. . . . They wanted him to work as a coyote, and they wanted me to work as a housekeeper, helping the woman of the house. My husband is Mexican. The boss threatened to turn him over to migration, and he said, "Go ahead. I will go to migration myself. I am not going to work for you." . . . The boss bargained with them: "OK, how about $800 for the food and shelter that they used en route [from Tierra Blanca to Nuevo Laredo]?" But my husband refused to pay. . . . And he said "I am Mexican." He was not going to be bullied by them like the Central Americans get bullied.

Despite this woman's insistence that she had escaped and now desired to return to El Salvador, rumors that surfaced during interviews with other migrants indicate that she continued along the route and might actually have been working for an abusive coyote. While drunk guards forgetting to lock a door is a plausible story (one that appears in multiple kidnapping narratives), the escape may have been a fabrication to hide the woman's complicity with illegal schemes. In other words, this kidnapping might have forced migrants to become smugglers or forged a new collaboration between smugglers and kidnappers. The coyote boss in Nuevo Laredo presumably learned he must pay Zetas, just as he pays migration, to get his people through their territory. And clients who cannot pay their debts become "his people."

Indeed, with a little coercion, Zetas turned the capture of guides into new business arrangements that blurred the line between the kidnapping and smuggling industries. With the shifts in territory caused by leadership change and criminal reorganization in the wake of intensified policing, kidnapping became a method for making contact with human smugglers; it was a form of communication with potential business partners, a means to begin negotiations over a new system of tributes. Smugglers were then forced either to pay tribute to the plaza boss or to find victims for kidnappers with false promises of travel services; when they cooperated with kidnappers at the expense of their clients, they were no longer smugglers, but tricksters.

In the process of establishing their independence from the Gulf organization, the Zetas launched an immense effort to co-opt guides and control the taxation of movement along the routes. In the migrant shelter in Saltillo, a Honduran kidnapping victim, Maynard, reiterated the claim that the coyotes must pay $300 per client to pass Zeta territory or pay with their lives. When I asked him how he knew that, Maynard shrugged, "All the world knows that."[137]

Independent coyotes face a twofold threat. First, the guides fear apprehension and prosecution by state authorities. In Mexico, the government has criminalized smuggling and adopted highly punitive policies. Second, independent guides fear punishment and coercion from nonstate violent groups. As violent criminal groups proliferated, human smuggling became more difficult; tribute demands also proliferated, and, when territory changed hands, new and often dangerous first social contacts were required. As explained by Steven Dudley in his analysis of migrant kidnappings and organized crime:

> Which group he [the coyote] paid depended on what was happening in the area. Responsible coyotes, therefore, may carry extra cash on hand for any

unforeseen circumstances. No matter what the system, confusion about who has paid how and when remains a strong possibility. Moreover, in a shifting landscape, it is difficult for coyotes and their representatives to properly identify a given criminal group's role and informants.[138]

Furthermore, organized criminal groups have distinct characteristics, resources, and strategies, such that changes in territorial ownership among them have consequences for patterns in violence.[139] Given their reliance on coercive business practices with smugglers, the Zetas presented a special safety challenge to coyotes and their clients. Indeed, a smuggler based in El Salvador claimed that things would be much better for Central American migrants if the Gulf cartel won its fight against the Zetas and reestablished its domain.[140] In Monterrey, Nuevo León, during the summer of 2011, when fighting between the groups still erupted in the area, locals whispered in hushed tones that they longed for the old criminal bosses, because the Zetas obeyed no codes of conduct.[141] One Salvadoran migrant chose to travel through Piedras Negras, Coahuila, rather than Zeta territory in Nuevo Laredo, because he had not heard negative reports from returning migrants from that location and he knows that "it is the cartel of El Chapo there [the Sinoloa cartel], and that is the best of the cartels."[142] However, since that time, despite major setbacks and loss of territory for the Zetas, neither the Sinoloa nor the Gulf cartel have proven capable of putting the lid back on the kidnapping box. Codes of conduct, once broken, are difficult to reassemble.

Smuggling vs. Kidnapping

The Mexican human smuggling industry and the migrant kidnapping industry overlap, each with an intimate effect on the business opportunities in the other, but the activities should not be conflated, as they often are in media reports. The migrant kidnapping industry grew from a common practice in the human smuggling industry: payment on delivery. For Central American coyotes, payment of half the travel fee prior to the journey and half on successful arrival within the United States is still the norm. Migrants are then held hostage until family members pay the agreed-upon final installment; it is a guarantee for payment. Importantly, migrants do not consider this to be "kidnapping," *unless* the smuggler unilaterally changes of the terms of the contract and demands more money than expected. In some cases, the journey north may have accrued unexpected expenses and the smuggler may attempt to recoup these expenses by changing the terms of the oral contract after departure. From the perspective of the migrant, changes made after departure may constitute an unfair business practice, or worse, a kidnapping. Extreme violence and torture does not generally accompany this type of smuggler-kidnapping, probably because the perpetrators remain tied to a travel service business that depends on attracting future clients.

However, smuggling and kidnapping share a common insight: family members waiting for migrants in the United States have money to pay the border crossing guides. If they have a long-distance coyote that takes them all the way from Central America, and not just a border crossing guide, the family members have even more money waiting for the migrant's arrival. Brian Roberts et al. summarized various survey estimates of the U.S. border crossing for Mexican nationals and found a range in averages to be estimated between $1,305 and $1,845 and rising over time.[143] Of course, that money only covers the short distance of the U.S. border itself. Healthy adult Salvadorans paid between $5,000 and $7,000 for door-to-door service from El Salvador to destinations within the United States in 2010. At that time, special services from a reputable coyote for small children and pregnant women who cannot cross long distances by foot could cost as much as $10,000. Unauthorized travel from McAllen to Houston, once inside the United States, cost as much money as the border crossing. Prices vary according to the services and length of segments included in the travel package. For high-end long-distance arrangements, a protocol from an earlier era of migration remains intact: half the money is generally paid at departure, and half the money is paid on delivery.

Therefore, kidnappers generally ask for the amount expected by the average smuggler on delivery. In the 2006–12 period, this ranged anywhere between $2,000–$5,000 in ransom from U.S. family members. Sometimes family members can negotiate the ransom down to a few hundred dollars. But we should expect the prices in the two industries to influence each other. As fees for smugglers increase under pressure from immigration policing, so will the ransom demands of kidnappers. Kidnappers will continue to assume that the families of migrants have sufficient money to pay the guides.

If kidnappers do not receive payment, they may try to extract profit through forced work. This also happens when a family cannot pay a smuggler the agreed-upon fees at delivery. Women might be forced to prostitute or to do housework in the drop house. Men might be forced to smuggle. In the 2006–12 period, the Zetas forced some Central American migrants to work as spies, known as *rateros*, along migratory routes, identifying other migrants who receive remittances from the United States and setting them up for capture.

It is important to correctly differentiate between the types of criminal actors that travel the unauthorized migratory routes. Recent media coverage conflates smugglers and kidnappers to the benefit of the Mexican government's human rights reputation. Under pressure from human rights groups promoting the protection of migrants, the Mexican government and its associated media have been quick to call any interception of migrants en route a "rescue." The language of "rescue" began to appear with greater frequency following the publicity that surrounded the massacre of seventy-two migrants in Tamaulipas in August 2010.[144] Not all claims of rescue are valid. For example, on February 8, 2011, the military claimed to have rescued forty-four Guatemalan migrants in Reynosa, Tamaulipas, but the Guatemalan Foreign Ministry argued that the migrants were not victims of kidnapping, but rather paying clients of a smuggler.[145]

News reports about "rescues" provoked an incredulous reaction from human rights defenders. In particular, they argued that if the reported "rescue" occurs at a highway checkpoint, and migrants are pulled from a northbound moving van, it is possible that they were traveling in their chosen direction with their guide and not held against their will. Furthermore, a human rights activist pointed out that these so-called "rescues" provide a convenient excuse for military personnel to perform the duties of migration agents, a crossover prohibited by law.[146] Without testimony from migrants themselves, it is difficult to tell the difference between rescues and immigration raids, and few newspaper articles include such firsthand accounts by victims. Several cases have surfaced in the Mexican media in which immigration enforcement has likely masqueraded as human rights defense, making it difficult to evaluate government efforts to protect migrants. These cases illustrate the danger of conflating smugglers and kidnappers.

Kidnappers and thieves frequently disguise themselves as guides or coyotes. Furthermore, even reputable smugglers sometimes engage in extortion and other misdeeds (particularly sexual coercion or threats to enforce contracts),[147] but smugglers do not *necessarily* use violence against migrants or others; the primary source of their profit is the provision of a travel service, and the best guides treat migrants as customers, not cargo. By definition, however, kidnappers and thieves assault migrants, and the interests of these violent criminals are at odds with those of reputable guides engaged in the smuggling industry. When the Zetas declared their independence from the Gulf organization, clandestine spaces along migratory routes became more fragmented and fluid, with former alliances under continuous renegotiation and routes with shifting territorial control. This emergent social world challenged simple state-crime dichotomies.

Coyotes: Traffickers or Smugglers?

Of course, the boundaries between actors are not fixed, and frequently one actor has many roles depending on the place, time, and people with whom they are engaged. For example, the low-level guides and the coyote that I met during fieldwork did not engage in smuggling as a full-time or lifetime career. At many levels of the smuggling enterprise, it seems necessary to "keep your day job," with smuggling only supplementing other income or occurring as the opportunity presents itself. Consistent with David Spener's study of Mexican coyotaje,[148] I found that many experienced Central American migrants also pass in and out of the category of smuggler along the route; sometimes and in some segments, they guide friends for altruistic reasons, and at other times, they ask for a little financial help in return (often to finance their own unauthorized migration north). While the era of the "heroic coyote" might be over, human smuggling remains a diverse cluster of social processes; no single crime group controls all Mexican human smuggling routes. Nor did smugglers respond to danger in a homogenous manner. Guides adopted a variety of strategies for dealing with risk and uncertainty, frequently combining tactics of collaboration, subversion, and conflict.

In addition to subcontracting schemes, an even more decentralized system has emerged to cope with increased violence: a chain of people who buy and sell migrants.[149] The smuggler in the community of origin receives the first payment for recruitment of the migrant. After crossing the first segment of the route north, the smuggler then sells the human cargo for a small sum of money. As delivery payoff gets closer and risk of apprehension decreases, the price of the migrant increases, and the human cargo changes hands many times. This system mirrors how investors deal with risk in commodity and financial markets; it is a form of hedging against the increased risks posed by intensified policing. Indeed, migrants hire smugglers because they can often better judge risk. Consistent with Mexican migrants' experiences with coyotes crossing into the United States, coyotes who cross Mexico are "risk managers."[150] By complicating the attribution of blame when violence occurs and distancing social relationships between client and service provider, both of these schemes undermine the reputational and personal mechanisms that could enforce a smuggler-migrant contract. This tactical displacement thereby exacerbates the insecurity of migrants en route. Over time, practices developed by migrants and smugglers to evade immigration control have exacerbated migrants' exposure to violence perpetrated by criminal gangs. Both risk and uncertainty have increased.

In other words, a smuggler is not an immutable social category, but includes people who engage in a transient practice that overlaps with other social practices, including activities motivated by both reciprocity and economic profit. Likewise, "kidnapper" is not an immutable social category, but a transient practice that overlaps with other social practices, including smuggling. In some social contexts, officials may be corrupt, but not others. Finally, despite the youth gangs' emphasis on lifetime membership, fealty, and the indelibility of tattoos, it too represents a transient practice overlapping with other social practices and relationships. The key for understanding the human security of migrants is to examine the social practices that link the activities of these actors as they move across a violent landscape.

To Be Kidnapped

To return to Edwin: He discovered what happens to a migrant when they fall into the clutches of the Zetas, and he lived to tell about it. The friend in Veracruz, now under contract as their guide north, took them in trucks to another guide in Reynosa. But the contract suddenly changed. The new guide wanted another $3,500 in addition to the original bargain. The new guide began to negotiate with relatives in the United States, and Edwin and his travel companions were kept locked in a safe house with insufficient food. Edwin estimated that 140 men and 36 women were in this house. The guides, now acting as kidnappers, extorted money from relatives in the United States, and they repeatedly raped the women.

To celebrate Christmas 2008, the kidnappers drank heavily. Only two of the six armed men had been left to guard the house, and they were outside making fajitas. As they became aware of the lax security during the holiday celebrations, the migrants had an idea: they would escape as soon as the New Year's Eve festivities began. Edwin and his friend organized a group of forty captive migrants to escape.

Unfortunately, hunger overcame one skinny migrant, and he alerted the guards to the plan in an attempt to receive larger food rations. The kidnappers subsequently identified the four masterminds of the escape. When they first took Edwin and the three other plotters from the larger group of migrants, Edwin thought his relatives must have paid his ransom. He expected to be released. But very suddenly, they started hitting him with a pistol in the chest and head. They tied his arms behind his back and took him to a second safe house, where the kidnappers held another large group of migrants. Edwin slept that night with his hands tied uncomfortably behind his back.

One member of his group of four masterminds was a man from San Pedro Sula, Honduras. He was an evangelical Christian. They came for him on a Friday and said, "You are on the way to Houston." But instead, they took the Christian man to the Rio Bravo where they cut off his head with a machete and threw the body in the river. On Saturday, they showed the video of his beheading to the remaining three masterminds of the escape plot. They told Edwin that it would be his turn on Monday. Edwin knew he would soon be dead.

However, Edwin and his two coconspirators began to talk to the other migrants in the safe house. There were people from Brazil, Guatemala, Peru, Nicaragua, Ecuador, a few from El Salvador, and even a Chinese person. But most of the victims were Hondurans. All of the migrants had been tricked into thinking they were dealing with coyotes only to bring them to the drop house in Reynosa instead of the United States. Many people had been held captive for four to six months, and some had been there as long as a year. That Sunday, six Nicaraguan migrants agreed that it was time to escape. At five A.M., when it was still dark, they turned off the electricity, and everyone began to fight the kidnappers, wielding a pitchfork and anything else they could get their hands on. Edwin saw one person killed with the pitchfork. All of the migrants on the bottom floor of the house escaped. They broke the windows—smashed through them. Blood drenched the floor.

By seven or eight in the morning, the kidnappers had regained sufficient control to move over one hundred victims, including Edwin, from the top floor to a neighboring house. The kidnappers squeezed these people into three cramped rooms that already housed over one hundred people. Edwin estimated that the little house held around 340 victims. A Honduran kidnapper with a gun guarded the new house. Monday morning dawned, and four (presumed) Zetas arrived to take Edwin to his death. By this time, a desperate Edwin was thin and close to starvation.

At that moment, when the four Zetas arrived to take Edwin to his death, the military and police raided the house. The soldiers had beaten a kidnapper found in the abandoned safe house next door, hit him in the head with a rifle butt, and smashed his teeth to get information. He disclosed where the migrants were held. The military surrounded the house in a big circle so that no one could escape, but a few of the migrants ran. The migrants had made an agreement among themselves not to run when the police came, but to stay and give their testimony rather than evade deportation. Despite this agreement, Edwin ran and hid in the garage, where a soldier found him. Upon being discovered, Edwin gave a silent signal to indicate the hidden position of a kidnapper nearby. The soldier then discovered and beat the kidnapper, and Edwin rejoined the migrants, now in official custody.

According to Edwin's account, the police and military rescued him from the kidnappers on January 4, 2009. He and sixty other migrants gave their testimony in Reynosa, and then they were promptly turned over to the migration authorities. Edwin did not know about the Mexican FM3 visa (designed for victims of crime who give testimony) that he would have been eligible to receive. In 2007, the Mexican government acquiesced to human rights advocates and established these humanitarian visas.[151] Unfortunately, like Edwin, few migrants seem capable of accessing these visas or are even aware that they are entitled to them.

In fact, to Edwin's surprise, they turned Edwin over to the same migration officials who had visited the kidnappers' house. Edwin believes the officials were part of the same group of Zetas. Of course, neither he nor the other victims said anything, because they were afraid. Edwin reasoned that the migration authorities could let the Zetas kill them while they remained in official custody, because the police had only caught the guards at the safe house, not the bosses. Even the soldiers had their faces covered for their own protection, signaling the danger. Fortunately, a special police force and consular officials from some of the home countries accompanied the migrants during the deportation process.

Over a month after his rescue from the kidnappers, Edwin was deported from Mexico to Honduras with the same friend who had accompanied him throughout the hideous experience. His friend left immediately again for the United States, but Edwin could not. He had been beaten savagely, taking blows to the head. And he was so skinny. He needed medical attention and vitamins. Edwin rested in Honduras for a year before trying again.

In December 2010, when I met Edwin in the migrant shelter in Oaxaca on his third journey through Mexico, he felt confident that he now had better information about where the dangers were. The contours of these dangers had begun to take shape in his mental map. Edwin explained that MS-13 territory extends for some part and then the Zeta territory begins. He had heard rumors that the contact who betrayed him during the last journey is now an infamous boss of a clique of Zetas in Medias Aguas, Veracruz, which is the next stop north of Ixtepec on the western train route.

While Edwin expressed greater confidence that he could locate the dangers on a map, he had suddenly found himself more vulnerable to these dangers. He had come to know the route, but in the process, the *maras* had come to know him. As a result, he had to abandon his original plan to travel north by train. A friend had come through this Catholic shelter only three months before, and he reported that there had not been a gang problem. However, now in the shelter, he had come to believe that the gangs had infiltrated the place. Edwin watched gang members wander the grounds at night, and they returned for a meal during the daytime.

The gang's entry into the Catholic shelter made Edwin nervous, because a handful of gang members, armed with a knife, had attempted to rob him after he disembarked the train and walked toward the shelter. In response, Edwin and his friends had picked up rocks and threatened their would-be attackers. After that incident, the gang knew him and could recognize him as one of the migrants who resisted them. He feared that they might seek their revenge. In fact, he believed that they sent a man to spy on him:[152] "From street gangs to Zetas, there is danger on every side. Before, one could pass like it was nothing. . . . This time there is no social interaction. Now, I cannot confide in other people." Edwin lamented how he must now assume the worst of people, but he repeated that he had seen with his own eyes the man with the gang, who Edwin identified as a black Honduran who had attempted to rob him. Because of the likelihood that the gang would hunt him down for resisting them, Edwin received advice from the shelter manager about a little-known bus route; he lacked the anonymity necessary to travel the train route safely. Edwin had become known through his encounters with the gang and marked by his resistance to them.

Conclusion

This chapter describes the semi-anonymous, violent, and uncertain social context of migrant journeys. It charts the dramatic and unexpected changes in the relationships among migrants, coyotes, Zetas, mareros, and Mexican officials that have unfolded along the routes over three decades of mass migration. Despite this veil of uncertainty and ambiguity, we must not conflate the many actors involved in diverse clandestine activities along the routes. The relationships between coyotes and kidnappers vary between collaboration and conflict, with important consequences for migrant safety. People change their roles without warning; coyotes or police may become kidnappers. Friends and travel companions report to kidnappers. Mareros and Zetas may strike deals. When street gangs become a nuisance, Zetas would hunt them. Some so-called Zetas were imposters, and common criminals manipulated cases of mistaken identity to their advantage. Members of the same gang turned on one another, battling for control and collaborating with enemies.

In summary, loyalties are more ephemeral than the tattoos gang members wear. Loyalties are also crosscutting, as individuals who wander the route trespass across multiple social roles and identities, as well as across terrain. A gang member might be a migrant, a Central American by birth, an adopted member of a Mexican community, a man, a friend, a boyfriend, husband, a Catholic, a father, an occasional kidnapper or bandit, and a part-time coyote. Pulled in many directions, these conflicted souls might collaborate with one another one day, and combat the next. As they wander, their own odysseys to the United States derailed, gang members struggle for power within their own cliques, as well as against competing gangs. The result is uncertainty and ambiguity for all migrants. In the next chapter of this book, we will begin to explore how migrants negotiate with these chimerical characters and navigate the migratory route.

ACT 2

Rising Action

Chapter 4

The Performance

Migrant Scripts and Roles

The eight-year-old Salvadoran boy, David, sauntered through the yard of the migrant shelter, showing off his capacity for Mexican language; he used an exaggerated "guey" (a Mexican colloquialism) at the beginning of each sentence and mimicked the melodic stereotype of Mexican Spanish in the cadence of his speech. Looking for attention from adults, he exclaimed, "I can speak like a Mexican!" David had been in Mexico for several months now, idling at the shelter while his family applied for asylum because they had suffered persecution by criminal gangs in El Salvador. While they still hoped to ultimately arrive in the United States, Mexican asylum would allow them to move through Mexico more safely and work for better wages along the way, blending into the citizen population without fear of deportation. However, social camouflage, not legal status, would save them from notice by criminal predators along the route north. David's performances in the shelter yard garnered him chuckles and smiles from his intended audience.[1] Nevertheless, he also demonstrated a potentially important survival skill that he was acquiring through play: the capacity to pass as Mexican.

The wider the range of identities through which someone can "pass," the safer a transnational journey becomes. Indeed, if David could have "passed" as American by speaking unaccented English, the border crossing into the United States would have been easier. His mother had considered borrowing the documents of another child and having her son pretend to be asleep as he crossed the U.S. checkpoint in a car, with U.S. citizens posing as his parents; but she worried that the border patrol might wake him.[2] Despite some tutoring he received at the migrant shelter and his father's fluency in the language, David's English would not have withstood even cursory questioning. Instead, he would have had to risk the dangerous desert crossing when they reached the border.

In this chapter, we will see that by walking in the shoes of this playful boy, we learn a great deal about the tenuous relationship between territory and identity. The narratives presented here demonstrate how unauthorized migration requires the negotiation of interpersonal encounters that are collectively reimagined by migrants, migration enforcement agents, humanitarian aid workers, kidnappers, smugglers, and other people living along the route through nationality and gender. The focus will be on the performance of roles derived from nationality and gender, because the boundaries between these two identities delineate victims and perpetrators of violence: foreigners and citizens, women and men.

Introducing Survival Plays

The empirical argument presented here is twofold, focusing first on survival strategies of migrants, and second, on the larger political and social effects of those strategies. As people move across an uncertain and violent social landscape, survival often requires a series of *performances*, both in good faith and bad faith. I call these performances *survival plays*. Erving Goffman defines a performance as an activity that alters the understanding of another individual within a face-to-face encounter; it is meaningful practice.[3] Migrants and the people they meet en route reenact a series of social roles, improvising on scripts to present self-idealizations and define situations accordingly. Strangers come to know each other and shape the context of their interaction through a series of performances—acquiring information about others and negotiating the terms of their relationship.[4] Criminals and police rely on gendered and national markers to distinguish between citizens and migrants. In response, Central Americans manipulate or conceal these tells to move across the terrain undetected. Mexican citizens engage in counterperformances, sometimes passing as Central American. Women and men play with femininity and masculinity to gain sympathy, exude charisma, or hide their intentions, thereby facilitating migration.[5]

Collectively, these "survival plays" constitute a dynamic transnational imaginary of Central American migration to the United States. This chapter traces the potential of migrant performances to destabilize seemingly fixed identities, highlighting the improvised nature of these categories. Under the conditions of violent uncertainty that characterize the migration route, people *improvise* on cultural tells and social scripts. Stephen Greenblatt defines improvisation as "the ability both to capitalize on the unforeseen and to transform given materials into one's own scenario. . . . the opportunistic grasp of that which seems fixed and established."[6] In this vein, the actors along the route must develop an opportunistic grasp of gender, racial, class, and national identities. For this reason, we can say that identity is makeshift. Like all information under conditions of strategic uncertainty, identity loses some of its utility as an indicator of solidarity the moment it becomes common knowledge. In other words, as identity acquires a predictable status in social relations, it simultaneously becomes a system for passing and loses some of its predictive value for people on the ground. Migrants, police, and criminal predators adapt.

A focus on the everyday processes of identification, misidentification, and misdirection that accompany illusory national and gender categories is fruitful for understanding the difficulties of territorial control.[7] The very possibility of "passing," or improvising on cultural tells and social scripts in order to go undetected, destabilizes the social boundaries used by state authorities to police territorial boundaries. As Linda Schlossberg explains:

> Because of this seemingly intimate relationship between the visual and the known, passing becomes a highly charged site for anxieties regarding visibility, invisibility, classification, and social demarcation. . . . If passing wreaks havoc with accepted systems of social recognition and cultural intelligibility, it also blurs the carefully marked lines of race, gender, and class, calling attention to the ways in which identity categories intersect, overlap, construct, and deconstruct one another. . . . The passing subject's ability to transcend or

abandon his or her "authentic" identity calls into question the very notion of authenticity itself. Passing, it seems, threatens to call attention to the performative and contingent nature of all seemingly "natural" or "obvious" identities.[8]

The long, dangerous journey through Mexico illustrates this point. To navigate violence, men and women *pass* in two senses. First, they pass from Central America through Mexico and the United States. Second, they pass across identity categories, posing as Mexican and performing gender scripts to survive. By describing this fluid process of identity switching, I show how state and nonstate violence structure the social terrain of the route—over 1,800 km across the interior of Mexico from the southern border to its northern limit. People collectively make sense of their journey in the performances and counterperformances of both national and gender identities. Improvisation on this imaginary shapes violence, future prospects for passage, and ultimately, the possibilities of the nation-state.

Performing Ethnography

Arriving at these insights required a methodological position open to understanding interviews *as* performances, not just data collection *about* performances. By taking a performance approach to ethnography, both inside and outside the interview context, migrants' survival plays take center stage in our analysis. Migrants are not the only actors in the performance of gender along the route. A large cast of smugglers, gang members, street vendors, taxi drivers, train conductors, migration officials, soldiers, police, hotel clerks, bartenders, food vendors, humanitarian workers, activists, and consulate officials populate the route. Academics and journalists also play a part. A long tradition of feminist scholarship makes this point.[9] Without this methodological position—one I arrived at only while in the field and actively conducting interviews—I would not have noticed how performances among strangers became a resource for migrant mobility, and ultimately, a source of cultural mobility.

Because this chapter demonstrates neatly how this methodological approach led to novel findings, I use this opportunity to call for studies of transit migration and border crossings to become "a riotous theatre of transgression," in which researchers self-consciously analyze the performances co-improvised with migrants.[10] In an interview setting, migrants do not simply retell their experiences. Nor do migrants necessarily view researchers as an objective and passive audience, but a potential ally for their own purposes: for material gain or information; a platform for making political statements to a broader public; an opportunity for altruism; a vehicle for self-projection or self-aggrandizement; potential friendship, camaraderie, or sexual interest; and/ or simply the entertainment of talking. The narratives coproduced in these interviews are themselves survival plays as people negotiate an uncertain and potentially violent social terrain. By listening to the interviews as such, I illustrate subtle improvisations on gender and nationality that facilitate migration in real time. Thus, we discover survival strategies that would be otherwise overlooked, and we can trace the larger effects of these strategies on the social imaginary that constitute the migration route. For this reason, this chapter makes a methodological argument as well as a substantive one.

Road Map: Nationality and Gender

The rest of this chapter will look at the performance of national and gender scripts, respectively. Gender scripts are the masculine and feminine conventions and cultural codes that people draw on, consciously and unconsciously, to craft their actions.[11] National scripts are the ethno-belonging, the legal and cultural conventions and codes that people draw on, consciously and unconsciously, to craft their actions.[12] Migrants draw on both gendered and national scripts as they perform dialogue with locals, rituals of camaraderie with fellow travelers, and protest repertoires with human rights activists. Survival plays on social scripts are a perennial survival strategy within societies where territorial or social mobility is restricted by race, class, and sex.[13] For example, in hostile migrant receiving communities, migrants may publicly perform assimilation, adopting the scripts of the dominant culture to avoid detection or discrimination.[14] Such survival strategies unfold through communities of transit as well. Over time, the expectation of such "passing" erodes unquestioned trust in traditional scripts as cognitive maps for navigating new social encounters.

An analytical coupling of performances of nationality and gender serves two purposes. Firstly, the national and gender roles that underpin migrant performances intersect, creating possibilities and constraints for improvisation.

As will be explained in greater detail in the ethnographic narratives that follow, gender mediates nationality and vice versa. This chapter illustrates interaction between these performances along the migrant trail, as well as discussing their class and racial dimensions. Secondly, by discussing gender and national performances together, this chapter illuminates a larger process of improvisation and its implications across multiple identity categories.

Nationality

Scholars describe nationality alternatively as a naturalized imagined belonging or a state invention.[15] Along the migration route, however, national identity becomes a makeshift collection of markers that cannot be completely trusted. Ascribed traits and the performance of narratives, not necessarily deeply ingrained self-images, constitute national identity and provide cognitive clues to the other actors in the drama.[16] All actors in the migration drama covet information about national membership as leverage for expedient deportation by authorities, identification for criminal predation, or a potential signal about worthiness for humanitarian relief. Central American migrants learn to conceal this information, imitating Mexican or American national traits to avoid deportation or criminal victimization. For example, they frequently impersonate Mexicans in order to pass undetected through the migration checkpoints and public spaces of the interior of Mexico. Meanwhile, Mexican citizens sometimes infiltrate the migration stream, playing a role in a variety of transnational practices.

Over time, the unchoreographed practice of clandestine mobility blurs the cultural boundaries that states use to enforce territory. The cumulative footfall of everyday folk undermines the policing utility of "virtual checkpoints," such as racial stereotypes and national tells.[17] If the state continues its attempt to impede flows using these virtual checkpoints, wielding violence blindly without reliable social profiles that coincide with its physical terrain, it does so at the expense of citizens and foreigners alike. The state risks targeting its own population in cases of mistaken identities, creating an underclass of "authorized but unrecognized" people;[18] the state thereby erodes its own legitimacy with native-born citizens within its territory.

A Brief History of the National Hustle

To survive, migrants must have an uncanny knack for the national hustle. Central Americans face detention and deportation when they encounter migration authorities in Mexico, but they must also evade bandits, street gangs, organized kidnappers who demand ransoms from U.S.-based families, and corrupt officials.[19] Due to this precarity, migrants prefer to be (mis)recognized as a citizen during the journey.

Precarity also characterized the experience of the hundreds of thousands of Salvadoran and Guatemalan refugees who fled their homelands across Mexico in the 1980s and 1990s.[20] Even in that early period of mass migration, the journey was dangerous, requiring Central Americans to exercise both courage and wit to evade authorities and violent criminals.[21] In 1983, Mexico more vigorously policed and deported the migrants within its territory; Mexican migration officials removed hundreds of thousands of Central Americans throughout the decade.[22] In response, many migrants in the country's interior "passed" as Mexican.[23] By the end of that decade, approximately two hundred thousand Guatemalans and five hundred thousand Salvadorans had made a temporary home in Mexico, with or without permission.[24] After the end of the Salvadoran and Guatemalan civil wars in the mid-1990s, an unrelenting stream of labor migrants followed in the footsteps of the refugees.[25] Thus, Central Americans have performed Mexican nationality on a massive scale for three decades, and the national hustle has become a common practice along migration corridors.

While this hustle is as old as nation-states, Central American migrants face new challenges in the contemporary context. Territory changes hands quickly and without warning among competing gangs, leaving migrants vulnerable to kidnappings and extortions by rival smugglers. Previously trustworthy human smugglers may defect from their clients, unexpectedly breaking contracts and selling their human cargo to another potentially unreliable carrier. The old codes of conduct for dealing with corrupt officials can no longer be relied on; bribes are often no longer sufficient to avoid brutality. Despite this upheaval, each year hundreds of thousands of Central Americans continue to flee the social disorder, economic malaise, and criminal violence of Central America.[26] While reliable data on unauthorized transit migration through Mexico is lacking, it is clear that over three decades, masses of dispossessed

Central Americans have moved continuously across the Mexican landscape. As we will see, the individual acts that constitute this sustained passage reshape society.

During these performances of the national hustle, the cultural tells that "out" migrants include language, ignorance of common knowledge shared by conationals, and physical appearance. Accents, grammatical constructions, and colloquialisms give migrants away. Any conversation can expose a foreigner, leaving them vulnerable to deportation or extortion. One man complained that he needed only open his mouth to order a bus ticket and "they will say that I am 'cachuco' [an ethnic slur for a Central American in Mexico] . . . that I am a wetback, an imposter."[27]

The content of conversation can also reveal national identity. National education systems inculcate a collective imaginary of the calendar (e.g., national holidays and work rhythms), symbols (e.g., recognizable flags, anthems, monuments, ethnic foods, and faces), and folklore (e.g., common historical narratives, events, and figures). Some given names, like Kevin, are more prevalent in Central America than Mexico. Tells include moments of hesitation that break the natural rhythm of a dialogue about places and people "known to be known" by any Mexican.

Racial Scripts

Racial scripts intersect with nationality, producing constraints and opportunities for migrants, depending on the color of their skin. For example, I asked a U.S. immigration agent to explain how he knew that a person was engaged in illegal activity at a port of entry, and he began to describe a sense or a gut feeling that agents develop with experience on line duty:

> But people develop a sense. It's like at the border. The agents can see a car coming from half a mile away. Maybe the mannerisms are just not right. It's just that something doesn't feel right. The agents have a difficult time articulating the probable cause. They just know who to stop.[28]

At this point in the interview, I stopped him to venture a naïve guess about the feeling he was describing, "We might call it tacit knowledge?" But he laughed at my idea. "In law enforcement, we call it profiling."

Indeed, both U.S. and Mexican authorities use racial profiles to identify migrants.[29]

In Mexico, some of this reliance on racial markers can be attributed to the fact that many citizens do not carry documents in their own country. However, more complete documentation of citizens cannot solve these dilemmas for the State. Fake documentation provides a helpful prop in migrant performances but does not alleviate the need to be a convincing Mexican. A poor performance of nationality will invite scrutiny, and failed attempts at passing with fake documents carry prison time.[30]

In Mexico, a country where the "mestizo" of mixed Spanish and indigenous heritage represents the dominant racial ideology, profiling renders black migrants most vulnerable to identification. Of course, since it standardizes practice in a dynamic strategic setting, racial profiling may also create opportunities for smuggling. Smugglers sometimes blend high-paying Peruvian clients into travel groups with indigenous Guatemalans, because of their similar phenotype.[31] The Peruvians pass as Guatemalan, and if they are captured, they only need to travel to Central America rather than returning to South America. This minimizes financial risks for the smugglers transporting them. Therefore, racial stereotypes can be harnessed, not only by state authorities, but by migrants and smugglers as well.

Like state authorities, criminals identify potential victims for kidnapping, rape, robbery, and extortion by trying to detect the accent, migrant clothing, and phenotype of Central Americans. In part because of racial profiling, Hondurans, and in particular black Hondurans, are most likely to rely on the dangerous train route where mass kidnappings and muggings occur with frequency, thereby avoiding buses that travel through migration checkpoints.[32] The proportion of migrants reporting Honduran nationality on the registration rolls of the shelters has been the highest of any national group since Hurricane Mitch in 1998, and often by a very large margin.[33] One rumor circulating among migrants suggests that organized criminal groups particularly seek out Salvadorans, who are known to be better connected to established families in the United States and thus fetch higher ransoms, than the poverty-stricken Hondurans, who throng the migrant shelters and crowd the most desperate routes to the United States.[34] Whatever the preference of kidnappers might be, *any* identifiable Central American nationality invites legal, illegal, and extralegal violence en route.

Class and Urban/Rural Scripts

Class and urban/rural differences also shape performances of nationality. The most visible Central American migrants wear a unisex costume, shaped by the physical demands of the cheapest way to the United States: denim pants, dark and dirty clothing, sneakers, baseball caps, and backpacks.[35] The style is comfortable for travel on the freight trains and treks through remote wilderness. However, in small transit towns, the style also makes migrants visible. For this reason, many migrants purchase local name brands and fashions at their earliest opportunity if they leave the train route behind.[36] The adoption of Mexican or U.S. dress and dialect facilitates survival when passing through densely populated portions of the route, such as the bus lines and urban areas. Migrants may also choose to travel without any identifying papers or possessions that might tie them to their homeland. The capacity to pass undetected through migration checkpoints along the highway saves migrants from the treacherous footpaths around them, where bandits frequently lie in wait. As explained by a transgendered Guatemalan migrant, a former circus performer who is keenly aware of the power of self-presentation:

> My advice, from my point of view, I have seen some people . . . it seems to me that if you go well dressed, man or woman, whatever . . . if you are a woman if you go very well put together: skirt, heels, very pretty in bus . . . they [Mexican migration authorities or police] will not take you off the bus. Avoid the train. They realize that one is undocumented if you go dirty, if you smell bad, if you come dressed in dark clothes, if you carry your backpack and tennis shoes particularly . . . if you come comfortable, more like those here [in the shelter]. . . . [37]

Indeed, this advice seems prudent if a migrant has the gumption and familiarity with Mexican national customs. People do travel in this way, passing through the citizen population. Sometimes Central Americans work and beg their way through Mexico on a meandering path over the course of weeks, months, or even years. However, there is no perfect script for all situations that will be encountered en route. To exude wealth also has its risks and can make a migrant a target for kidnapping in other circumstances.

Expressions of humility and other rural class markers, such as simple dress appropriate for outdoor labor, homemade items, simple speech, and expressions of religion, serve as a proxy for a lack of worldliness and unfamiliarity with social networks that could include transnational gangs. These markers also signal a shared goal and normative orientation to the journey, indicating a lack of exposure to worldly vices. These preferences are not without basis; there are innumerable performances of class-based solidarity, even across national boundaries. Many stories of poor Mexicans sharing their modest wealth with Central Americans and unexpected (even lifesaving) moments of hospitality circulate along the route. Finally, a "humble" appearance might also make migrants a less appealing catch for kidnappers, who gain the most from the extortion of those migrants with established family in the United States, who are capable of sending financial remittances. In an attempt to safeguard themselves, some migrants emphasized class-based tells to differentiate between humble campesinos (peasants) and potential threats:

> It's very easy [to know who to trust]. By their humility. If someone is very tattooed with eyes that [unfinished sentence coupled with a shifting of the eyes]. . . . One does not believe them. Look for simple, respectful people in whom you can see the desire to arrive.[38]

The tattoos and hip-hop styles popular with urban youth are read as stigmata associated with Central American street gangs, particularly when the individual fits the racial and class stereotype of gang membership. These gangs are best understood as a collection of transnational practice—in other words, a set of cultural markers apparent on the body of gang members (speech, fashion, etc.) as well as the violent protocols that structure their relationships—rather than tightly organized criminal networks.[39] Cultural markers associated with these practices have been criminalized in Central America under Mano Dura (Strong Hand) anti-gang legislation. Such cultural markers indicate exposure to a wider world and sometimes signal access to financial resources that enable the purchase of luxury goods. Urbanized and transnational fashions are an outward expression of the ways that migration has complicated traditional Latin American class relations. These cultural transgressions provoke (often unwarranted) fear and unwanted attention from police authorities across the Americas.[40] As explained by Gilberto Rosas in his analysis of delinquent refusals at the new frontier:

Popular discourses about cholos [criminalized urban youth] mobilize latent, historically constructed racial and social meanings of the contamination of a disorganized, unwieldy, and increasingly global mestizaje [cultural mixing]; and pulsating anxieties about unauthorized, pathologized hybridities of the impoverished across the Americas. Ideologues and commentators immersed in neoliberalism muster vile images and imaginaries of cholos in their attacks on impoverished, undocumented border crossers. Intensifying nightmares about cholos capture a mass-mediated, insidious, anxiety toward these dangerous, yet seductive, hybridized lumpen figures. . . . [41]

Indeed, the markers associated with gang culture represent a subversion of traditional urban-rural class boundaries through transnational cultural exchange. While Central Americans "dress up" in order to perform conventional Mexican class roles, passing through checkpoints along the route without the appearance of desperate poverty often associated with migrants, unscrupulous people "dress down" to perform a rural class role to infiltrate the route. Potential criminal threats do not only come from people dressed in stereotypical "gang fashion."

In fact, as soon as the association of class tells with trustworthiness becomes common knowledge, it becomes a resource to be improvised on, mitigating somewhat its power to predict loyalties or nationality. Furthermore, both naïve Mexican authorities (many of them drawn from the ranks of campesinos themselves) and Central American migrants frequently misread contemporary fashions, which can fluctuate wildly. For example, Elana Zilberg illustrates the fallibility of "fashion police" with a compelling anecdote:

The police were often barely literate in the semiotics of youth culture. Take for example, Weasel's first attempt to cross back into the United States at the end of 2003 when he was turned back in Mexico because of his clothing. . . . We laughed uproariously when he told me why he was one picked out of everyone on the bus as an undocumented Central American migrant passing through Mexico. When he asked the federale (officer) who apprehended him, "Why me?" the man explained that it was because he was wearing old-fashioned clothes that no Mexican wore anymore. Weasel was wearing, as he put it, "a very stylish [1970s style] retro shirt," and as such he was dressed in the height of urban youth fashion.[42]

Further highlighting how these class-based fashion strategies can back-fire, Jason De León describes how an attempt by migrants to dress up inadvertently led to their identification by Mexican authorities.[43] As soon as the means for passing are exposed, in this case by recently purchased clothing, they lose their utility to migrants; social camouflage only works if the predator is unaware of its possibility. Therefore, inflexible rules about whom to trust or distrust and *how* to perform class identities can produce disastrous mistakes. And migrants cannot always predict how their performances will be interpreted.

Anonymity and Relationships in a Transient Social Field: Resources for Performances

The prolonged nature of some of these journeys highlights how sustained relationships and guarded anonymity become double-edged resources for national performances. Because of the double-edged nature of social relationships and anonymity, continued immersion in a transient social field both empowers and endangers migrants. One Salvadoran man, Ricardo, interviewed at a midway point along the route, equated his strategy for *knowing* the route with the social relationships he formed during the journey:

> Here [in the migrant shelter] you cannot confide in anyone. You must be prudent. I will stay in the D.F. [Mexico City] for four months or so, and build relationships. . . . I do not *know* the route. It is necessary to meet and communicate with people.[44]

In the relative safety of a diverse and anonymous urban environment, where transience is not necessarily associated with unauthorized migration, Ricardo will adopt a strategy of selective social engagement. He compared the challenge to the way he navigated violence while working in his home country as a truck driver, transporting shipments of seafood along a dangerous route from the coast in La Union to the capital of San Salvador. While moving across the country with valuable cargo, the driver must recognize that "there are places you go around because you don't know the people. You cannot enter there." In those instances, anonymity complicates mobility. On the other hand, Ricardo thought unauthorized crossing of international borders was, in an important sense, easier and safer than trespassing the interior boundaries set by competing street gangs in his neighborhood, because at home he could be easily identified with a community. Sometimes knowing people and being known complicates mobility. Thus, learning new strategies works through an alternation of partial concealment and partial social engagement, both of which require artful performances as the migrant negotiates encounters with potential allies and enemies in a transient social field.

As migrants meander along the route for a long period of time or make repeated attempts to cross the border, anonymity erodes. Social networks, based on trust and reciprocity, may begin to emerge from their repeated performances along the route. The longer a person spends on the road, the more likely they fall victim to multiple violent events.[45] Thus, cultural and social capital does not accumulate a clear advantage, because the lack of anonymity and transgression of social boundaries produce a vulnerability to violence.

These wanderers begin to bridge Mexican communities and the transit flow. Their role as potential *enganchadores* (connectors) is both dangerous and helpful to other migrants. They might provide access to reputable smugglers or other useful information about opportunities and danger en route. However, using their contacts along the route, wanderers might also sell migrants to kidnappers or collaborate with thieves. This potential duality renders any advice they give to other migrants suspect. According to some migrants, the fact of simply knowing people along the route casts suspicion on a travel companion. When asked how to identify a "ratero," a spy for the kidnapping gangs, a Honduran migrant explained:

> They carry a cell phone. If they have a cell phone on this journey, they are bad people. Suspicious. What would a migrant need a phone for? Who in Mexico would they call? How would they pay for one? Migrants do not carry phones. Who would they call?[46]

Playing the Migrant

Mexican and Central American rateros, and a surprising variety of other people along the route, assume or maintain the cultural markers associated with Central American migrants. These counterperformances illustrate two important points. First, intentional counterpassing as a method of infiltration transforms the cultural markers associated with vulnerability into an asset for criminal predators. Second, unintentional counterperformances emerge in the wake of sustained transnational transience, and they also complicate the policing of territory. Taken together, these two points highlight the tremendous social ambiguity that emerges along the route.

Why would it serve to camouflage oneself as a member of the most vulnerable national groups along the route? Rateros befriend other migrants to find out who among them might be the most profitable targets for extortion, as they watch who receives remittances during their journey and gather contact information about migrants' families in the United States. These spies sometimes steer their travel group into ambush by guiding them to remote locations and then reporting their whereabouts to criminal accomplices. The shelters, train yards, hotels, and bars frequented by Central American migrants are full of these "orejas" (ears), some of whom were themselves migrants coercively recruited through kidnapping and threats into the ranks of criminal groups.

Along the train route, gangs with cliques, whether they are small franchises of organized Mexican crime groups or Central American street gangs, are often multinational bands of Mexicans, Salvadorans, Guatemalans, Hondurans, and sometimes Nicaraguans. Predators blend into the flow of humanity moving north and gather information and material resources along the route, learning about migrants by acting as one. A Honduran man repeated a common warning about rateros:

> They assault and kidnap. They come as a migrant and they spy on who carries money, who buys food. They hug like a friend, and they stick you with the knife. [He gestured the stabbing motion to illustrate.] You cannot confide in anyone, except the priest [in charge of the Catholic migrant shelter].[47]

Improvisation on the role of the migrant, a leveraging of the material and symbolic resources available only to people in transit along the route, can be an unpremeditated survival strategy. This survival strategy sometimes takes migrants themselves into the business of spying for kidnappers, other trickery (including but not limited to theft), or profit making from their travel companions (ranging from selling drugs to provisioning coyote services).

Racial Scripts

In contrast to the self-conscious manipulations of identity described above, some counterpassing is accidental and carries negative consequences for citizens. It is not unheard of for Mexican citizens to be wrongfully deported by Mexican migration authorities. I met a Mexican man of black Honduran heritage who, after receiving a savage beating that shattered his jawbone and being wrongfully deported, had been forced to return to his Mexican homeland alongside Central American migrants and to seek legal assistance at a migrant shelter to prove his nationality.[48] He had been traveling to visit family in San Luis Potosi when migration authorities intercepted him. Life along the migratory route as the Mexican citizen child or grandchild of a Central American can be an insecure existence, relative to other Mexicans. Abuse and harassment of citizens are the perils of racial profiling along a longstanding migration route.

Of course, abuse and harassment of citizens along the route is not wholly limited by race. Humanitarian workers and Mexican friends of migrants sometimes fall victim to accusations of smuggling by authorities, even though nonprofit assistance to unauthorized migrants has been legal in Mexico since 2008. More generally, among citizens, a sense of being suspect in the eyes of the State accompanies their interaction with migrants in transit.[49]

*Anonymity and Relationships in a Transient Social Field:
Resources for Performances*

To enhance security, the migrant shelters generally attempt to segregate Central American migrants, Mexican migrants, and nonmigrant homeless people, thereby creating fewer opportunities for infiltration by smugglers or kidnappers (or even accusations of such infiltration). Thus, many shelters discriminate in reverse, turning away down-and-out Mexicans. They often limit migrants' movement in and out of their compounds, accepting and releasing sojourners only during regulated hours and even locking people in their rooms at night. The shelters generally limit migrants to stays of three days and may limit the number of permitted visits.[50] And the shelters turn known people away if they cannot believably explain their repeated visitation. Shelter staff also watch for the cultural tells associated with gang membership.[51] During a registration process, the shelter staff looks for familiar faces, and recognition might lead to exclusion as a suspected smuggler.[52] Most shelters maintain a database with photographs that identify suspicious persons as well as aid in the identification of missing persons and dead bodies recovered along the route. To gain access to migrant shelters where many customers await opportunities to travel, enganchadores (connectors) must pretend to be migrants, earnestly moving north.

Thus, decreasing anonymity and the concurrent maturation of social relationships with locals is a mixed blessing for migrants who spend a great deal of time along the route. On the one hand, friendships and potential business partnerships generate resources for migrants. On the other hand, decreasing anonymity marks them as ineligible for many of the humanitarian resources dedicated to migrants in the route, because those that aimlessly wander the route are no longer perceived to belong to a deserving class of people who are attempting to better their lives. The narrative of migration motivated to provide for or reunite a family plays an important role in the Catholic Church's advocacy for border crossers. Transient people who no longer seriously seek to arrive in the United States may bear the stigma of criminality and homelessness, rather than appearing to be the heroic migrant that neatly fits the advocacy script. Furthermore, decreasing anonymity undermines their capacity to hide among the nameless and generates suspicion. As a consequence, their recognition enhances their vulnerability to violent retribution from rival gangs and accusations of smuggling that can result in severe legal penalties in the United States and Mexico.

The fact that smugglers, Mexican homeless persons, and spies for kidnappers impersonate Central American migrants is an open secret. The possibility that predators might "pass" as vulnerable migrants underscores the ambiguity of identity and the fluidity of relationships en route. People may slip from role to role depending on the performance, and anonymity facilitates such transformations. Social roles are not mutually exclusive, and people improvise on them under dangerous conditions: changing from smuggler to kidnapper, from migrant to smuggler, or from kidnapper to migrant. People in transit may have multiple or fluid motives for "being" a migrant. They may be moving north, but they may also be profiting from other activities along the way. The potential for hidden agendas sows distrust among migrants and heightens uncertainty along the route.[53]

An Undocumented Mexican in Mexico and His Honduran Guide

Importantly, the fluidity of social roles along the route also impacts Mexicans living within their own country. This ambiguity produces anxiety for citizens who must fear false accusations of smuggling or kidnapping. As sustained migration disrupts and reorganizes the cultural markers of nationality, citizens come to inhabit positions of vulnerability alongside migrants. A story from a migrant shelter in Coatzacoalcos provides an example of a Mexican citizen's experience of suspicion living along the route.[54] It also forcefully demonstrates how migrants and citizens come to occupy the same cultural markers, creating unintended consequences when state authorities attempt to control unauthorized migration:

The shelter in Coatzacoalcos was particularly dilapidated. Morale among the shelter volunteers was low, and one of the staff decried that the very migrants they served were criminals.[55] He accused them of selling drugs, assaulting their comrades, and smuggling from within the walls of the shelter. Fearing that someone would be killed at night, they limited their service to a short respite during daylight hours, and they evicted the migrants after a single meal. Indeed, a man with a gold-plated pistol, tucked into his pants but conspicuously displayed, lounged in the afternoon sun within the courtyard. There was no pretense by this man of playing the part of a migrant; the gold-plated pistol is a potentially deadly prop for the performance of the *narco* (i.e., a member of a Mexican drug cartel). The staff had resigned themselves to the lawlessness that pervaded the "refuge."

In this context, I met a migrant who freely admitted that he was not really a Central American. Miguel seemed older and more humble than his Central American travel companions. At first, he spoke timidly with a halting cadence that caused me to initially (and very incorrectly) doubt his intelligence, but over the course of the interview, he surprised me with his increasingly confident body language and well-spoken analysis of his situation.

Miguel was from Hermosillo in the state of Sonora, Mexico. I asked when he left home, and he shook his head:

I don't have a home, and I never did. There was never a house. I was an orphan. I live in the streets. Washed cars [as they pass, stopped at lights for pesos]. I did not even have grandparents. I always lived in the streets. . . .

As he continued, it became clear that Miguel had, in fact, once had a father and mother. But they began new families that did not seem to have a place for him. His stepfather became abusive and beat him with cables. As a boy, he would hide from his stepfather. He could not love his mother because she never protected him from this abuse, and he reasoned that the vast majority of street people share this background of domestic violence and neglect. Miguel thought that his grandmother might still be in a retirement home in Tucson, but it was too late to find her now. He sometimes lamented the loss of his family, longing for the opportunities that he saw other people enjoy. He knew that somewhere out there he had cousins, aunts, and uncles that he had never met. But for all intents and purposes, he was alone.

With a new appreciation of the depth of his homelessness, I rephrased my question; I asked when he left the city of Hermosillo. Satisfied with my new question, Miguel replied, "about a month ago," and he explained his motive for riding the trains along the route. He kept moving, because:

There is much discrimination here in Mexico, when one does not have a job. They don't respect you. They take your money, even your own police. The authorities take your money when you sleep in the street.

Later in the conversation, he returned to this issue:

Sometimes the Mexican authorities search your backpack and take your money, even if you don't have drugs or alcohol. When people see beggars, they call the police. But begging is not illegal.

The Central Americans and transient Mexicans share a vulnerability to harassment and abuse by Mexican authorities, and in response, his travel group pooled their resources. Miguel trusted his mixed band of Central Americans and Mexicans, even though he had only known his present companions for three or four days and they would go their separate ways soon:

When one goes in the street, when there is a multitude in the street, they unite to protect each other. . . . Mexicans help everyone. We beg together, eat together, share cigarettes, everything, like brothers.

While he felt at ease with his temporary band of brothers, Miguel described the discrimination that he suffered in the shelter system, on the basis of his Mexican nationality:

In many shelters, they discriminate against you, in some no. When I ask for money in the street, they [people in general] don't value me. I see how they look at me. I have had good jobs. . . . I arrived in a shelter in Tierra Blanca with much hunger, but it was purely for Hondurans and Guatemalans. They are not for Mexicans. They said I could not go there. I can travel without papers in all Mexico, but I also have necessity. I have never liked a shelter.

He had not yet mastered passing as a Central American migrant, but neither could he access his Mexican birthright. Miguel complained that many potential employers asked him for papers. Unfortunately, he had lost his identification card and had no idea how to replace it: "Now I am undocumented." I asked him what this meant for his relationship to the Mexican authorities.

Sometimes the authorities accuse me of being a pollero [human smuggler]. In Guanajuato, we were a group, smoking cigarettes, and migra [migration agents] arrived. They have a psychological capacity to tell who is Central American and Mexican. . . . They thought I was the pollero. One wants to help his friends, but it's dangerous. If I help, they think I am a pollero. I've lived with people from Chile, the United States, everywhere.

It was clear to me, at least, that Miguel, albeit an undocumented Mexican man, was not the smuggler in the group. Miguel's younger, tattooed Honduran companion Selvin made the decisions, signaling when it was time to go and indicating the direction. I interviewed this companion, and he seemed to be a more experienced traveler along the route than the native Mexican. Selvin immediately impressed me with an intimate knowledge, grinning broadly as he shared what he supposed were the sorts of criminal secrets that would help a fledgling writer: "That's good for your book, no?"

But I was more interested in his personal story. Selvin had grown up alone along the tracks in Mexico, leaving a broken home in Tegucigalpa, Honduras, at the age of eleven. On that first journey, his best friend had been thrown from the train. After many adventures and four years of living in Mexico, Selvin arrived in the United States, where he managed to stay for three years before being deported. He did not fear a second deportation from the United States to Honduras, because it would be an excuse for an interesting plane ride and then simply a new beginning of his travels. And if they put him in prison for illegal reentry, so much the better; at least he would eat well. But it was unclear whether Selvin would ever again arrive at Mexico's northern border. He claimed to be on his way north, but he was clearly leading a roving life through Mexico, probably involved in occasional smuggling or some other gray activity. Miguel confirmed that he and Selvin would probably head south together for reasons that remained mysterious.

As they lose their claims to the status of legitimate migrants and legitimate citizens, these wanderers enter a liminal position within the route. They are neither migrants nor citizens. As their faces become recognizable, rival smugglers and gangs may target them as potential competitors or enemies.[56] Authorities may target them as smugglers. They make both friends and enemies by lingering on the route. Mexican families sometimes de facto adopt these Central American men as sons, and Central American migrants may de facto adopt their Mexican comrades as brothers.[57] They may fall in love.[58] They may become fathers of Mexican citizens along the way.[59] They may become gang members or connect to smuggling networks. In the process, they bring news of distant events along the route with them. Thus, they embody both information and danger for others.

As Miguel's story of being undocumented in the country of his birth suggests, these improvisations on nationality diffuse along the route, merging national habits and obscuring cultural and racial boundaries while illuminating the arbitrariness of territorial boundaries. The national hustle and the ambiguities that accompany it have profound implications for the human security of migrants and citizens alike. For example, these ambiguities complicate the work of state authorities that rely on national stereotypes to carry out their official duties. Undocumented citizens may feel suspect in their own country.

Gender

The precocious Salvadoran boy, David, was at it again.[60] He had found a new way to attract the attention of the adults around him. This time, however, he was performing gender, rather than nationality. On the cement patio outside the shelter office, several people danced to Cumbia music, breaking the monotony of a long evening. The shelter's female attorney picked up a toddler and danced in circles with the babe in her arms, and a voluptuous Honduran woman took the eight-year-old Salvadoran boy as a partner. But the men gathered around the office began to shout to the boy that he should "stick her against the wall," and the scene morphed from a maternal moment into an overtly sexual spectacle. For her part, the woman seemed game to play along and suggestively shook to the rhythm. The boy, lacking in rhythm but not dramatics, lunged aggressively forward at her with his pelvis, pushing her against the wall as instructed by the male crowd. The grownups laughed, including the woman who was willing to let him try again and again. He was, after all, just a boy parodying male sexuality, not a "real" man. While this performance clearly lampoons gender for the laughter of an idle audience, gender scripts are part of the survival repertoire of all migrants confronted with violence along the route: male and female, adult and child. David was not just at play; he was practicing survival again, this time learning the expectations for male behavior and sexual aggression.

Gender can provide signals about trustworthiness, merit, and vulnerability that can either facilitate movement across the terrain or impede it, depending on the context of the social encounter. At some times, "acting the man" defines a variety of social encounters, negotiating respect while moving across terrain of gendered violence, and at other times, "acting the woman" enables identification with "safe" social roles replete with both material and symbolic resources for migration. People may consciously perform "gender acts" to convey these signals or they may simply exude such information as a consequence of an uncritically accepted identity.[61]

To discuss the survival and social implications of these gender performances, there will be a brief review of the literature on gender and transnational migration, highlighting the novelty of this approach to understanding human security in transit. Migration studies that focus on gendered social networks have missed an important resource available to the most vulnerable migrants: the encounters between strangers where no sustained ties or reciprocity emerge. Then, by examining the normative stage and improvised survival scenes that unfold within it, I will explain how the boundaries between female victims and male perpetrators of violence are not stable or certain. It will be clear that improvised performances and storytelling desta-bilize these boundaries and engender a new transnational politics of sur-vival along unauthorized routes through Mexico.

Gendered Vulnerabilities and Resources

Human rights workers, government officials, and migrants themselves al-most universally cite women as the most vulnerable group of Central Amer-icans in transit across Mexico to the United States. Smugglers have long been notorious for coercing their female clients into sexual relationships dur-ing the journey. Across the globe, migration has served as a gateway into sex-trafficking networks; traffickers pose as smugglers or labor recruiters, luring women away and abusing them as soon as they have left the protec-tive confines of their homes.[62] Many women must pay for passage with their body at various points—an informal sexual tax for crossing territory lever-aged by drug gangs and corrupt officials. Bandits lie in ambush, demanding to know how many women travel with each group and raping them within full view of their travel companions. A male Honduran migrant explained the incident that befell his travel group while hiking an isolated path in Los Pozos, Tabasco:

> Three attackers assaulted us and held us at gunpoint for two hours. They raped the two women who traveled with their partners. They did not want money. It was only to rape the women. Honduran women are known to be beautiful.[63]

Female migrants are vulnerable to a variety of special dangers during the journey north.[64] In this violent context along the migrant trail, gender per-formances facilitate geographic mobility, and ultimately, cultural change. On the one hand, predators manipulate nationality and gender to identify and exploit migrants. On the other hand, migrants both reinforce and subvert masculinity and femininity to survive these dangers and evade the confines of the nation-state. For example, women selectively perform femininity, thereby moving long distances, sometimes in defiance of traditional gender roles. Thus, as men and women perform migration, the transnational route becomes a social space that can reinterpret and reinforce gender in complex and unpredictable ways.

While violence against women provides a starting point for this discussion, a study of improvisation says as much about hidden sources of male vulnerability to violence as it says about women. Many forms of violence against men go unnoticed as gendered, when in reality they are shaped by ideas about masculinity. When confronted with violence during the journey, migrants' improvisations change what it means to be a man and rewrites the social script for women. The makeshift nature of these performances unmoors social expectations over time. This social ambiguity emanates outward from unauthorized routes and reorders possibilities and constraints for both men and women. Through these improvisations, vulnerability can be harnessed as an advantage, and advantages may become points of vulnerability.

Central American migrants' improvisations exemplify an instance where mobility tactics represent a form of vulnerability.[65] The state structures this vulnerability, shaping the liminal space of the migration corridor; Central American migrants experience violence, dehumanization, and ultimately their own commodification in such a space.[66] Men and women suffer this exposure differently. States' policing strategies thereby call gendered liminality and mobility tactics into existence.

A preponderance of sociological evidence documents how transnational migration is a fundamentally gendered process.[67] Migrating men and women are unevenly empowered with the potential to both overturn and reinforce accepted gender norms.[68] This migration literature often takes social networks as a starting place for the investigation of gender. Gendered networks rooted in relations of trust and reciprocity play an important role conveying resources to migrants before, during, and after their journey.[69] However, networks are not the only resource available to migrants. Ephemeral interactions among strangers may or may not give birth to new relationships of reciprocity, but they are nevertheless a resource for men and women in transit.

In fact, social networks may, at times, hinder survival. While networks carry helpful information, they also convey gossip that limits the capacity of migrants to improvise new roles for themselves. Gossip can reinforce traditional gender roles.[70] Given the stigma endured by rape victims, homosexuals, and promiscuous women, both the survival of sexual violence and the exercise of sexual freedom may require people to disconnect from existing networks.[71]

While the migration literature puts a great emphasis on the capacity of migrants to harness trust and reciprocity as a resource, anonymity can also be an asset. Insofar as the "in-between" nature of transit-spaces provides escape from gossip, the journey opens a space for reimagining the self. Insofar that gendered precarity provides a sympathetic victim-position for migrants, the journey also provides a survival script to perform within that liminal space. Therefore, to understand the relationship between gender, liminality, and mobility, we must examine how migrants craft survivable scenes in transit.

The Normative Stage and Improvising Survivable Scenes

Departure from the scripts associated with accepted gender roles provides an ex post facto justification for sexual violence, even among women's travel companions. Traditions, including limitations on travel to unknown territory, validate violence against women in Central America and Mexico.[72] In an extension of female travel restrictions accepted in many home communities, male migrants explained that women who travel without the protection of a brother, father, or husband invite abuse from coyotes or travel companions. Several men explained that without a close relationship to a female victim, a male hero would suffer extreme violence if he attempted to intercede on her behalf. Only fathers, brothers, and husbands or lovers, not the women themselves, and certainly not unrelated bystanders, have the right to protest. Several men, when confronted with a situation where a rape seemed imminent, ran away from the scene of the crime, complaining that they had no choice if they wanted to survive: "The guides treated the people well, except for the abuse of a few young women. Not all the guides abused the women, only some. . . . [But he does not know for sure, because] if you see something like that, you must run."[73] Despite a widespread belief that male guardianship is safer for women, husbands or fathers who attempted to protect their wives or daughters from abuse have been assaulted, raped, or killed.

Other men explained their hesitancy to protect female travel companions from sexually aggressive coyotes, because they believed that some women want to be coerced into having sex. One Salvadoran man, Herman, echoed a common sentiment, though rarely explained to me so directly. When I asked him whether the coyotes mistreated women, he responded with laughter before answering:

> Yes. Very humble women are easy to intimidate. But forceful women don't have a problem with their coyotes . . . The coyote might tell them that he will leave them, and then they go with him. But they don't really have to. They just *want* to do it. Maybe they like him or something. Some women just want an excuse.[74]

Whether he adopted this belief to justify his own inaction or whether he held this idea before beginning his journey, Herman did not view all coerced sex as rape. The virtues of women are suspect. For this reason, some men may not feel compelled to intervene to protect them. Norms that circumscribe the boundaries of accepted female behavior provide a convenient excuse for nonintervention by male witnesses.

Of course, in Mexico, sexual predators target Central American women, not only because they are women, but because they are migrants. Criminals profile potential victims as migrants according to national cues, such as phenotype, clothing, dialect, and accent. Mexican authorities notoriously perpetrate crimes against migrants in bad faith performances of their official duties.[75] For example, Mexican authorities sometimes pretend sexual assaults are an effort to check migrant women's genitalia for drugs.[76] As a Salvadoran man, Wakter, attests:

> I saw officials rape women. I don't know if they were private security from the railroad or police. They wore blue and black uniforms. They ordered all the women off the train. They raped them, and then they let the women on their way. If you try to stop the women from being raped, they'll kill you. That sort of thing happens every day.[77]

In this bad faith performance of official duties and other violent encounters, victimization is simultaneously anonymous and public. On the one hand, migrant women can sometimes hide their victimization from their family, such that the rape does not become common knowledge in their home. Distance provides deniability, sometimes shielding women from sexual stigmata and familial conflict.[78] Instead, they remain anonymous victims of a crime that everyone understands is endemic along the route. On the other hand, these rapes are witnessed by their travel party, rather than hidden behind closed doors. As a spectacle, this sexual violence sometimes takes extraordinary forms with life-threatening levels of physical abuse.

To survive this violence, women improvise on traditional gender roles. The availability of multiple scripts provides a key resource for migrants as they trespass across national borders and negotiate encounters with strangers. Firstly, women leverage traditional gender norms during their performance of nationality. To pass undetected by migration authorities in populated areas of Mexico, migrants mimic colloquial Mexican Spanish and dress. However, gender awareness is an integral part of any convincing performance of nationality, since expected national behavior, language, and costume varies by sex and rural/urban distinctions.

In interviews, several women discussed how femininity helped conceal their national identity. In one instance, officials boarded a bus and captured a Honduran woman's travel companions. In haste, the woman, Mirna, grabbed the arm of the young Mexican man sitting next to her, and with a coquettish glance, begged him for help. The young man whispered his consent and performed a supporting role as the Mexican boyfriend, holding Mirna intimately until the officials had disembarked. In this setting, it is difficult to imagine a migrant man finding such a ready collaborator. Mirna's travel companions, an uncle and aunt, had to pay a bribe before continuing on, but she escaped without one. Soon after, her uncle abused and abandoned her, and Mirna's family asked her to return home. Mirna refused. When I spoke with her, she was in the process of meeting new people, finding new partners, and continuing onward despite explicit instructions to return home. Disobeying her former guardians and finding people willing to accommodate her migratory goals, Mirna reimagined what it means to be a woman. Through a series of performances that enable her mobility, and in defiance of her social ties, Mirna created a role with greater freedom from her family and community—a new place for herself in society.

In another instance, migration authorities apprehended a Salvadoran woman, Gilma, traveling north with a Mexican man. As is custom, the male authorities addressed the man first, who pretended to be her boyfriend. He spoke for Gilma. Meanwhile, her shy silence was construed as normal, rather than what it was: an attempt to hide her accent and lack of knowledge of Mexico. Had Gilma been a man, the quiet submissiveness would have been

Figure 4.1. He Spoke for Gilma
Map structured as timeline: Gilma's journey to the United States.

remarkable, and her Salvadoran identity would have been revealed. However, the couple managed to escape without even paying a bribe. Her map illustrates this scene, among others (see Gilma's map in Figure 4.1).

Secondly, when guarding themselves from harassment within their travel groups, female migrants sometimes self-consciously perform gender scripts of virtue; they might dress conservatively and pray auspiciously, such that they demand the respect of their travel companions through an enactment of feminine worthiness. They may seek the support of older, nonthreatening males in the group to play support in this role. In this way, they may perform chastity.[79] One woman, Lisa, recounted how a man in her group, knowing that she was a religious woman, pretended to be her husband, and thereby saved Lisa from a rape at the hands of her smuggler. Several men told stories about protecting *deserving* women—those who had demonstrated a pious and humble demeanor. Women like Mirna or Lisa sometimes substitute a performed tradition of femininity for strict obedience to a tradition of feminine immobility. They thereby generate opportunities to travel without their husbands or fathers.

Thirdly, women may perform ostensibly masculine scripts. This survival strategy may include the improvisation of dress, manner, and habits commonly perceived as male attributes.[80] In a more subtle performance than passing as a man, women may signal sexual unavailability through posturing and bluff. A woman explained the advice she gave to her daughter:

When you are on the road, you must be strong. I had heard that coyotes some-times sexually abuse their women clients. I think that happens to the humble, delicate ones. If you have strength of character, you will be OK. I never showed any weakness, never complained. That is the advice I gave my daughter: never show any weakness, be forceful and strong, have strength of character. My daughter is very delicate, very feminine . . . I told her not to be scared. No one is going to touch you. If you shake with fear, tell them you are shaking with anger. Shout. Be forceful. If it is time to run, be the first to re-spond to the command. Run faster than the others. Never show weakness. If they try to touch you, dare them and threaten them. Tell them you don't need a man to protect you. And that's what she did. The coyotes tell the women, if you sleep with me, I'll protect you and make sure you get there. When the man said that to my daughter, she said, "My mom is paying my trip. So, you will protect me and get me there. I don't need you."[81]

This bravado does not protect against victimization by gangs, corrupt of-ficials, or kidnappers. The safety produced by such a performance is noth-ing more than smoke and mirrors. However, this posturing may scare away the most timid sexual aggressors among a woman's travel companions; pre-vent milder forms of sexual coercion by guides; and provide women with a sense of empowerment, strength, and calm to cope with emergencies. Un-fortunately, such bravado also deteriorates quickly into blaming the victim, thereby reinforcing the misconception that women that have coerced sex with guides do so voluntarily.

Fourthly, some women enter temporary partnerships with guides or travel companions. Wendy Vogt argues that smuggling is an exploitive form of "in-timate labor" that structures gender in the protective services provided by men and the sexual payment expected from women.[82] Indeed, as is the case with other relationships of convenience under conditions of scarcity and violence, such arrangements often work to the relative disadvantage of women, exacerbating preexisting inequalities. However, some guides do not sexually exploit their clients, and some women desire their travel companions. In one instance recounted during interviews, a teenage girl cried inconsol-ably after an older coyote rejected her advances as improper. Furthermore, some of these partnerships may be more equal than others, and the woman's primary function in the relationship may not necessarily be sexual. A Hon-duran man explains why he partnered with a woman to travel north, rather than a man:

I don't have money for the bus. But thanks to her, we can go in "puro ride" [only hitchhiking]. With her along, people don't have as much fear and stop to give [us] a ride. With her along, we can eat. If I beg for food, they don't give me anything. If she asks, they give us food. . . . You cannot trust in male friends. . . . but a woman is different. Yes, there is more risk. But they give food to her. When we ask . . . when a "hembra" [woman/hen] asks. She supports me. I had a thorn in my foot and she took it out for me. On the road, women suffer more.[83]

It would be naïve to think that his female companion's sexual services might not have played a role in the partnership or possibly provided occasional payments for the rides in private cars that he has enjoyed during the journey. However, a long list of qualities makes traveling with a woman desirable to men, many of them tied to archetypes of the innocent young woman or the caretaking mother. Begging, in particular, is a form of street theater that plays on gender stereotypes for financial gain.[84] Regardless of where we draw the boundaries of consent under such deprivation, it would be equally naïve to think that women do not leverage stereotypes to achieve their goals and manipulate their travel companions.

Finally, some women become predators. In fact, some women play vital roles in smuggling and trafficking networks, leveraging the innocent and maternal identities associated with their sex to recruit women as clients or pass authorities inconspicuously as couriers. Women sometimes play the role of bait, luring male victims to ambush with the promise of sex. Women generally tend the drop houses of both smugglers and kidnappers along the route through Mexico and perform the traditional feminine labors required to accomplish criminal activities: cooking, cleaning, and other caretaking. Some female smugglers use their gender as a selling point to attract female clients who fear sexual assault by their guides. Nevertheless, trusting a smuggler on the basis of her gender can lead to a disaster. As scholarship on prostitution rings acknowledges, female victims of sex trafficking sometimes rise through the ranks to play a role of madam, blurring the boundary between victim and perpetrator in complex ways.[85] In so doing, they subvert feminine ideals of innocence and transform the social reality, rendering women (in the perspective of other migrants) untrustworthy. Faced with their own precarity, women leverage traditional gender roles in smuggling activities, and in so doing, they defy the victim/victimizer binary.[86]

Thus, in the context of escalating violence against women across Mexico and Central America, we should not conflate this destabilization of traditional gender roles with an emancipatory social process. On the one hand, the reenactment of gender scripts creates opportunities for women, and the selective presentation of femininity may provide the means to disobey social and territorial restrictions on women. In so doing, they rewrite their role in society. On the other hand, new forms of sexual predation have emerged along the route and the traditional protections afforded to wives and daughters may be undermined. The outcome of the myriad of survival plays along the route is social ambiguity, not a clear-cut path to a new femininity or masculinity.

Masculinity and Hidden Vulnerability

Migrants reimagine femininity, but they also reimagine masculinity during their journey. Both femininity and masculinity provide resources for migrants. And even as human rights groups heighten visibility of female vulnerability, men continue to face hidden risks along the route. While sexual violence is a real and clear danger to female migrants, it is unclear that women are more vulnerable than men to many forms of violence, ranging from deportation to homicide. Indeed, some men also suffer rape, but with the additional stigma of homosexuality, they may be even less likely to admit to such victimization.[87] If women have difficulty recounting stories of sexual assault when it is widely recognized as a sad reality, many episodes of male rape may simply be unspeakable.

Furthermore, there are several dangers specific to male roles. These dangers arise from a normalization of an aggressive masculinity. Prevalent notions of masculinity in El Salvador naturalize violent behavior, alcohol abuse, and sexual promiscuity as biological traits.[88] Regardless of whether men conform to this construction of masculinity in reality, its first consequence along the route is the vulnerability of male migrants to accusations of being a rapist and subsequent attack by local lynch mobs. All men are rendered suspect for their sexually aggressive tendencies, but foreign wanderers may be particularly suspect.

In July 2008, a mob overran the migrant shelter in Ixtepec, Oaxaca, with gasoline, a tire, rocks, and sticks when a rumor circulated that a Nicaraguan had raped a local child. The crowd of townspeople, accompanied by local authorities, went as far as threatening to burn the priest who refused them entry, but eventually dispersed without bloodshed. Rumors and local newspaper stories that accuse migrants circulate frequently. Communities along the route fear the roving bands of men in transit, complaining that "they drink, drug, and lack respect," bringing prostitution, criminals, and contamination to the city. The attack in Ixtepec was not an isolated event. In July 2012, locals in Lechería in central Mexico attacked migrants and successfully demanded the closure of a migrant shelter.

As a Mexican community member sympathetic with the migrants explained, "the most serious thing is the rape of a girl. It is the worst rumor that you can make. There have been many victims of this type of rumor." I paused her and asked if someone intentionally generates the rumors to harm the migrants. She answered, "Yes. But the funny thing is that they invent it, and at the same time, they believe it."[89] Migrant men, whether or not they behave according to the masculine stereotypes embodied in such gossip, are vulnerable to these rumors and the possibility for vigilante justice that lurks within them.

Secondly, male migrants face the possibility of being trafficked as combatants in the drug war. Staff at one migrant shelter claimed that competing drug gangs recruit migrant men as assassins, sending them to clandestine camps for training. Some of this alleged recruitment is done via a personal invitation, not coercion. Sometimes they select young men, Mexican or Central American, living on the fringes of society, because they embody the qualities of toughness and cleverness. It is rumored that men with military or police experience are particularly sought after. Some recruits may reject an overture to join the ranks of a gang and live to tell the tale, as long as they withstand intimidation and persuasively deny any loyalties to a competing criminal group. However, failed recruitment by a gang can end tragically for the migrant. In the absence of reliable survey data, it is impossible to know how many forced combatants fill the ranks of warring gangs in Mexico. Furthermore, similar to the partnerships of convenience between male and female migrants along the route, the relationship between a gang and its membership often exists in a gray zone between coercion and choice. The level of compulsion in this relationship fluctuates over time, and attempts to renounce Central American street gang membership may be punished with death.[90]

Thirdly, masculinity may generate pressures for risk taking and belligerent behaviors: drinking, fighting, womanizing, gambling, joining gangs, and other acts of daring can earn men respect among peers. If anyone is at greatest risk of violence, it is the migrants (usually men) who drink in excess during their journey or seek drugs; migrant men who stumble from the notorious bars along the train tracks in Mexico regularly receive machete wounds in robberies committed by either locals or transnational street gangs. In Ixtepec, Oaxaca, migrant shelter staff estimated that such attacks come to their attention about once a week. These male victims do not fit neatly in the moral discourse reproduced by human rights organizations. These hidden dangers challenge a gendered dichotomy between victims and perpetrators.

Why do men continue to perform such a dangerous identity? For one, gender roles pervade the route from home communities through destinations in the United States and tend to be deeply internalized as identities. The social penalty for male noncompliance with violent masculine stereotypes can be perhaps more dangerous than the risks faced by women. Of course, a variety of gender and sexual scripts remain available to men, and this ambiguity presents an opportunity for improvisation.[91] Indeed, one version of the masculine archetype is the man with the strength and chivalry to safeguard his women. However, as mentioned before, men who attempt to reenact this guardian role may suffer violence themselves.

Men incapable of convincingly performing heterosexual scripts face special challenges. Some LGBT persons or males who do not conform to masculine stereotypes also migrate to escape violence in home communities.[92] The plight of LGBT refugees has only belatedly, and problematically, received recognition in U.S. asylum practice.[93] Along the route through Mexico, "feminine" gay men and transgendered persons are subjected to harassment, even inside the safe space of the shelter. While tolerance of sexual minorities exists in many communities along the route,[94] and we should not ascribe an unchanging sex/gender code to all of Latin American culture,[95] the punishment for male transgressions of gender stereotypes and heterosexual mores can be terrible. Meanwhile, assertive, heterosexual men and boys reap respect and camaraderie by demonstrating their masculinity through their escapades with women.

Finally, some performances of manhood can be "all talk." Boasts, bluster, and sexualized joke telling and yarn spinning around a campfire provide a relatively safe way to establish masculinity and its associated authority.

A gendered authority—a man's character—as constructed through story-telling can be a resource for migration. As Matthew Gutmann points out in his study of multiple Mexican masculinities, "for some men today, 'the macho' is also a playful role they can perform on demand."[96]

Performing Masculinity, Performing Interviews

The power of self-presentation is perhaps best illustrated with a story about a man in a wheelchair whom I met in the shelter in Ixtepec, Oaxaca.[97] Juan and I established a rapport, joking together about our respective physical weaknesses: he had titanium rods in his legs since polio crippled him as a child, and I have suffered problems with the metal rods along my spine since an accident as a young adult. Juan teased that if only the train had magnets, we could both ride easily north to the United States: "We could just stick ourselves on and go." I laughed at the image of us pegged awkwardly to the side of the train. The man in the wheelchair had a habit of making people smile, and I was not immune to his charm. Alas, in real life, there are no magnets and the train is not so easy, but he was not worried for himself. Juan only expressed concern about his girlfriend's safety, not his own.

Whenever Juan talked in the dusty yard of the shelter, an audience would gather—mostly people curious about how someone in a wheelchair navigates such dangers: "How do you go?" He had traveled before and knew this journey well. Juan had made eight trips and arrived successfully in the United States four times.

Before he made the first journey, Juan had always warned his family in Honduras that he would leave, but only God knew when the time would be right. But then, the news arrived that an uncle had abandoned his sister and an underage cousin in Guatemala. No one else was willing to go to help them. So, being a selfless man, Juan volunteered. After all, he tells me, "Man proposes, God disposes." Juan began his journey in the role of his sister's guardian. He found her in Esquipulas, Guatemala (near the border with Honduras), where the uncle had left her. But even with the help of the Guatemalan police, he could not find his cousin. The cousin was deaf and mute. Finally, a tip in a shelter in Guatemala led him to his cousin. They even located the derelict uncle, who agreed to lead them north again.

During our conversation, Juan's girlfriend sauntered over to us and reminded him to tell the story of the time a Salvadoran tried to sell her. Juan agreed. *That* Salvadoran worked in a car wash, near where their travel party slept for a night. Juan overheard the Salvadoran from the car wash plotting with a man from a whorehouse, and the next day, the pimp showed up to take her away. She said no, but the pimp insisted. Juan had to intervene: "She goes with me and I am not leaving her." I interrupted the story, puzzled by the fact that the woman seems more physically capable of putting up a fight than a man confined to a chair. "Wait. What gave a stranger at a car wash the right to sell her?" This time his girlfriend replied, "Only because I was a migrant." The pimp tried to talk Juan into leaving her, and they told one of his travel companions to reason with him. But Juan was adamant that he would not give her up. She would still be trapped in a brothel if not for his loyalty.

After this tangent, Juan, perhaps thinking of his sister, returned to the story of his first journey north. The uncle had been hanging around drug-addled men. They pulled a pistol on his uncle and said they were going to rape his little male cousin, but his sister saved him. She told them to rape her instead, and they did.

At this point in the story, his girlfriend gasped, "Where was it? La Arrocera?" A Salvadoran man guessed, "Before Lechería?"

"No, it was in Coatzacoalcos," on the other side of the tracks from a migrant shelter in a remote place where the uncle had gone to look for drugs. Juan had not been there to protect her. He had gone by bus while the others continued on the train. But his sister told him about it when they reunited in San Luis Potosi. There his uncle hired a coyote to cross his sister into the United States. It cost her $2,000. I asked, thinking that it must cost even more for a disabled man, "how much did it cost you?"

"Me? Nothing. I did not use a guide. I had faith in God." Everyone in our little circle paused for a moment, stunned at this claim. I broke the silence to ask, somewhat incredulously, "But whom did you cross with?"

"No one," he replied. He explained that he wheeled himself through a kilometer of desert across the Nuevo Laredo–Texas border. From the shelter in Laredo, one can see the first town in Texas. He could see the river that marks the border and where he had to go. While telling the story, he spread his hands in front of him so that I could imagine him looking at the view from the migrant shelter. He showed me how he rolled himself through the desert.

To pass the river, migrants must pay a fee to the ferrymen, but he did not. He made his own boat. By now, the audience was listening raptly, astonished. He took many empty plastic soda bottles and strung them together like a raft. From other interviews, I knew that poor swimmers sometimes wrap themselves in water bottles as an improvised life vest to cross the Rio Bravo, but the idea of a makeshift raft for a grown man in a wheelchair seemed far-fetched. So, again I stopped him to ask for clarification, "How did you know to do that?" He knew one bottle would not sink, and he tested the bottles to see how many were necessary. It was a thoughtful strategy for a rational, intelligent man.

After the river crossing, he wheeled himself over a slippery mountain and to the highway where he could catch the bus. In the wilderness, he happened on a man who was so impressed by him that he agreed to be his lookout for migration officials, exclaiming, "You've got balls!" The bus stopped at the highway. The bus driver tried to turn him away, because the bus had no ramp for a wheelchair. But he would not accept no for an answer. He climbed aboard and hauled his wheelchair up behind him.

Juan had been interviewed before, of course. He bragged that a Florida newspaper ran a profile of him once. After he finished with the story of his journey and bragged about his fame in Florida, Juan transitioned into the performance of a Christian-inspired rap song about migration. Before we disbanded, his girlfriend prompted him to add one more story. There was a time when the Guatemalan police were after the two of them for a bribe, but he saw them coming and shouted "Get on! Get on!" She climbed on the back of his wheelchair and they sped down a hill to escape. Everyone still listening laughed, probably imagining the unlikely getaway and admiring her unlikely protector.

Nothing in this story was achieved through the manipulation of pity for his physical condition. This man did not beg. Juan might have been unable to walk, but his strength of will, faith in God and tremendous "huevos" were enough to see him through the journey. Did anyone believe Juan's story about his lone crossing and self-reliance? Maybe. I did not—at least, not entirely. Such partly true stories play an important function for the teller. For that moment they were captivated by the storyteller's voice; the audience members reimagined him as a capable and authoritative man, the lead character

of his own drama. His performance, his quick wit, and his capacity to retrieve a laugh even under dire circumstances established him as a man with
uncanny charisma. He was someone worth getting to know. As Juan explained to me, "People orient you. You must chat with people. You must be
sociable." In this manner, he guided his group through Mexico, keeping them
cohesive and optimistic and reminding them of his ability to lead. He did so
despite his physical handicaps, or because of them, improvising on these material challenges. He converted his crippled body and wheelchair into props
for a superbly resourceful persona, temporarily suspending our disbelief. Indeed, the reshaping of his own story through its retelling may even suspend
his own disbelief, bolstering him for the treacherous journey ahead. He improvised on his disability and his gender to create a new role for himself. Such
storytelling makes visible surprising possibilities for an individual, for the potential of a disabled man, and for the route forward.

At the same time, the believability of the story also signals a high level of
vulnerability suffered by women. Listeners and performers of this story found
it perfectly reasonable that a disabled man in a wheelchair could protect an
able-bodied woman from sexual predation; never mind the fact that she is
more physically capable to defend herself. The normative stage and its accepted gender roles, rather than the material attributes of the actors, dictated the scene. Such a performance makes visible surprising violence,
danger, and social restrictions on a woman.

Juan's story illustrates three important points. First, it shows how gendered
performances among strangers become a resource for mobility. As a handicapped man in a wheelchair and without financial resources, we might expect Juan to be immobile. However, his charisma and storytelling won him
a following among other travelers who came to play important roles in his
migration. Second, Juan's story demonstrates how performance can reorder
or reinforce traditional gender roles. As a physically handicapped man, Juan
might have easily been cast into the role of invalid or victim along the migration route, panhandling to move forward. However, his artful performances demonstrated his authority, courage, and resourcefulness, recasting
him as a leader to be followed. In the process of accepting his leadership,
Juan's audience had to become open to new ideas about what it means to be
a man, beyond the brute strength and physical prowess that often constitute
the role along the migration route. Third, Juan's story shows the importance
of reading interviews as performances. In that interview, I was not listening

to Juan's stories of past journeys, I was watching Juan make his journey in real time. Had I taken the story at face value, as a literal telling of migration events, I would not have seen the ways that performance becomes a resource for mobility.

Silences that Speak

Within interviews with women, I also came to recognize ways that the interviews themselves became performances for survival rather than a strict telling of migration-related events. For example, despite intense and sustained immersion in the local context, I did not receive any first-person accounts of rape from victims themselves during formal interviews. In one instance, a woman approached me outside the interview setting, seeking medical attention immediately following her rape. Rather than analyze the situation as a performance or engage in an interview, I helped her access medical care. Thus, despite the analytical benefit of a performance approach to ethnography, a note of caution is necessary. Absent critical engagement with our own role as researcher, the metaphor of performance may also obscure violence. The theatrical language of *scripts* and *plays* may normalize victimization. Reading interview interaction as a performance risks negating the embodied experience of migration, as well as the embodied relationship between researcher and migrants. There is, after all, a time and place to step beyond the curtains and take action. A tradition of feminist and critical scholarship has long wrestled with the ethics of such relationships.[98]

In two instances, I interviewed women who (according to other reliable sources) had, in fact, been raped during their journey. In many other instances, both male and female migrants, as well as their advocates, told horrific third-person stories that sometimes included mutilation of genitalia or penetration with foreign objects. Some of these stories were eyewitness accounts of atrocities, and others were rumors that had attained the status of urban legend. I received many first-person reports of nonsexual assault, sexual harassment, and attempted rape. Most migrants suffered at least a robbery during their journey.

This juxtaposition of violence and silence signals how the stories people tell about themselves serve a survival purpose. Similarly, based on her fieldwork during the Guatemalan genocide, Linda Green suggests that silences provide a means to cope with lives fractured by violence, situations where survival requires the acceptance of incomplete or inconsistent narratives.[99] Indeed, some victims of rape may have transformed their personal experience into third-person accounts of violence suffered by "a friend" to avoid directly talking about their own experiences. Others may have shared their first-person narratives as close calls ending with a miraculous rescue. The plot turn of the close call recurs in the interviews; several women escaped rape at the last moment through an incredible turn of events. Given the stigma and emotions triggered by sexual victimization, optimistic adaptations of narratives are understandable. These selective silences are a means for surviving violence, protecting reputation, and redefining identity in its wake. Escape stories may be a way for victims to indicate the existence of violence without painfully casting themselves in the role of the victim during their interview performance.

This silence also reminds us that interviews themselves are performances where two strangers craft a relationship.[100] The researcher comes equipped with a script, including introductions, consent protocols, and questions, and this script is adapted to the context and course of the conversation. The stories told by participants are usually a mishmash of truth, exaggeration, wishful thinking, and lies, but the telling of each story nonetheless reconstitutes identity and emboldens beliefs. As they conduct interviews and make observations, researchers collaborate with migrants as they reimagine the route, making sense of the violence and suffering during the journey. The sensitivity of ethnographic method to performances, both inside and outside of the interview scene, reveals otherwise ignored survival strategies.

Conclusion

Drawing on experiences and interviews along the route, this chapter explored how actors improvise on the social scripts associated with nationality and gender. Each performance confers information about the actor and defines, in concert with the actions of others, social encounters along the transnational route across Mexico. It is through these impromptu performances that Central American migrants navigate the social terrain of the route and come to know one another. Even when they are dismissed as fantasy or lies, their narratives engage the social imaginary. Over time, new scripts diffuse along the route, circulating in gossip, advice, and entertainment as well as actions, thereby reinventing what it means to be a migrant and a man. In many cases gender might be conveyed unintentionally, exuded as a consequence of identity, but some migrants are keenly aware of the power of self-presentation; they know the value of the information that these performances radiate. Selective adherence to gender protocols and national cues provides an important resource to people moving across a violent and uncertain terrain. Improvisation on these social constructions is central to survival, because the most dangerous terrain for a foreigner to navigate is not the natural landscape of oceans and desert; it is the social landscape of enemies and potential betrayal. Over time, these improvisations become a font for cultural mobility, as well as human mobility.

In his study of the props migrants use to cross borders, Jason De León says that "one only needs to spend an hour talking with a group of recently deported migrants to hear a wide range of crossing techniques that range from 'rational' (e.g., drinking a lot of water) to preposterous (e.g., a person once told me he almost evaded Border Patrol in the dark by walking on all fours and pretending to be a wild animal)."[101] However, by taking such narratives at face value, scholars miss the idea of interview as performance. Rather than dismiss improbable stories as "preposterous," we must analyze what they say about the values, experience, and identity the storyteller wishes to express, and how these preposterous stories transform those values and experiences. Stories told in interviews *are* border crossing tactics, not just a retelling of tactics. Thus, a return to feminist methodological and ethical discussions about fieldwork performances and storytelling would be instructive for scholars of migrant journeys.

Migrants, whether inside or outside the interview setting, improvise on social boundaries, such as gender, nationality, class, and even research subject. These performances manipulate archetypes and scripts to impact their audience, sometimes with an effect unintended by the actors. However, in the context of grave danger and necessity, migrants often perform to facilitate the crossing of territorial boundaries. Thus, the performances themselves are acts with political effects. Similarly, methods for listening to and analyzing these performances are acts that potentially disrupt boundaries.[102] These methods disrupt social science boundaries, as the collective improvisation and reimagining of interview narratives trespass across the researcher/subject divide in an act of knowledge coproduction. Furthermore, the interview it-self becomes one scene among many that produces cultural mobility, desta-bilizing established identity categories. The interview scene itself, whether with journalists, academics, government interrogators, or human rights ad-vocates, is integral to the route.

In this ethnographic spirit, a study of impromptu performances compli-cates a narrative of gendered violence based solely on women's subjuga-tion and victimization. Examining their stories about the journey as *survival plays* highlights an important source of both mobility and social ambigu-ity along migration routes. Migrants manipulate self-presentation to cross Mexico, but in so doing, destabilize identities and the possibilities for the migrants who travel behind them. Along the migrant trail, these perfor-mances facilitate geographic mobility, and ultimately, cultural change. Perhaps surprisingly, the anonymity and vulnerability that characterize the migrant trail as a liminal space generate the potential for this process of territorial and cultural mobility.

This process and its political effects are complex, dynamic, and ongoing. Thus, we cannot yet foresee whether such performativity ultimately liber-ates migrants from gender categories or reinforces gender constraints. Indeed, migrants themselves may not even be aware of their performances or inter-ested in challenging the scripts that structure them. The likely outcome of such improvisations is mixed and ambiguous. Nor can we yet foresee whether such performativity ultimately liberates migrants from the confines of nationality or the borders of the nation-state. And again, migrants may not intend to be liberated from such confines. Nevertheless, imagined commu-nities that delineate between citizens and foreigners are also partially re-constructed in the route as migrants move through novel settings and interact with strangers. Passing blurs the social boundaries that states use to enforce territorial boundaries.

Ultimately, this social process is best made visible by *performing* ethnog-raphy. Thus, to make the methodological and theoretical underpinnings of my findings as clear as possible, and, following the tradition of feminist lit-erature, I described how I arrived at the insight of understanding migrant narratives as survival plays in the interview with Juan in his wheelchair. Without such attention to performances within interviews, scholars may too easily accept the false gender binaries and the imagined communities that structure migration narratives.

The interviews themselves are implicated in a struggle for survival. And in the very act of survival, migrants unwittingly rewrite the social scripts along migration routes. Indeed, even if Goliath defeats Central American David, even if the boy never sets foot in the United States, his roaming through Mexico contributes to a process of cultural exchange that changes national and gender profiles.

Chapter 5

THE STAGE

Mobile Images and Props

In December 2010, I visited the Catholic migrant shelter in Arriaga, Chiapas, and I revisited it in the aftermath of the revitalized *Plan Sur* in 2015. Before the reinvigorated *Plan Sur*, which targeted train yards and thereby tightened the migration control belts across southern Mexico established in 2001, Arriaga was an early resting place along the western migration route through southern Mexico, just before the first one-hundred-mile freight train ride to Ixtepec, Oaxaca.[1] In fact, the town's name had become synonymous with the beginning of the train route. The Central Americans I met in Arriaga had already crossed the Suchiate River at the Mexico-Guatemala border. To do so, they had paid the ferrymen to board the makeshift rafts that carry untaxed contraband commerce (ranging from toilet paper to cigarettes) and daily commuters in both directions. Like so many unauthorized activities along the routes through Mexico, this extensive "free trade" system is visible in daylight.[2] One only needs to look down from the official international bridge or across the banks of either side of the river to get a clear view of the ceaseless economic activity. It is not a secretive practice.

The migrants I interviewed in Arriaga had also already made a long trek along well-trodden paths through the wilderness around highway migration checkpoints. That the sole use of these trails is the evasion of migration enforcement is common knowledge, and they therefore attract many bandits and sexual predators. Some of the migrants resting in Arriaga had ridden the combi (passenger shuttle) networks. Drivers of these vans alternate between helping and harming the migrants, providing free information but often extorting exorbitant fees for transport. The majority of migrants in Arriaga had already made multiple attempts at crossing Mexico. Despite having already braved so many dangers, these migrants were still at the beginning of the long journey north, as they were only about 150 miles north of the Guatemala-Mexico border.[3] They had over 700 miles of this grueling travel to go.

José was the first man who agreed to an interview on an early December morning.[4] I choose to relay his story here because, unlike many others that I met in Arriaga, it was his first journey north. Thus, he could not draw on any previous personal experience to envision the road ahead. He was short and thin, and his age was not obvious by looking at him. He had a large bushy black mustache that seemed out of place on a youth. His brown eyes were large and round, ringed with equally round, tired circles in the otherwise youthful skin below them. He was from Nueva Santa Rosa, Guatemala. Three of his cousins had migrated to Los Angeles, but he had no communication with them. He was the oldest sibling in his house; the four others were still studying. Hurricane Agatha destroyed the properties his parents rented, devastating his poor family.[5] That was what ultimately pushed him to leave. He was traveling with four friends from the same community who had also suffered damage from the hurricane. Relying on word of mouth, the kindness of strangers, and God's protection, he and his companions had traveled quickly across Mexico's southernmost state of Chiapas. They had arrived safely at the migrant shelter where I found him.

Like many Central Americans I interviewed, he and his friends understood the dangers that would confront them during their journey. From anonymous rumors, stories recounted by friends, and the popular media, they had learned about the potential for raids by bandits, kidnappings for ransom that they could not afford to pay, demands for tributes paid to criminal territory bosses, robberies committed by other migrants, rapes endured by female migrants, abuses committed by Mexican officials, and deaths from exposure to the elements. But this man of humble origin demonstrated only a vague grasp of the particulars that lay before him; the social and physical geography of Mexico and the United States largely remained a mystery.

By examining how migrants like José navigate dangerous journeys across a shifting and unpredictable social, material, and political terrain, this chapter contributes to our understanding of how information works (or does not work) in a human security crisis. In so doing, the chapter builds on an ethnographic tradition in political science that seeks microfoundations for understanding a wide variety of violent situations, ranging from genocide to labor practices.[6] This analysis of migrant journeys reemphasizes the methodological importance of what Timothy Pachirat develops as "line-of-sight" ethnographic analyses for understanding violence, requiring that researchers immerse themselves in the physical context to literally *see* from new vantage points.[7]

Indeed, José's journey serves to remind us of the informational importance of the visual experience of these violent situations for people who seek to survive them. Line-of-sight ethnographic analysis of the route reveals how José's visual experience of the journey is a tactical resource for his own survival. Furthermore, over time the collective visual experience of the route shared by migrants becomes a strategic resource for activists who challenge state propaganda with such imagery. However, such alternative visualizations can be co-opted by the State and, like a beacon, draw unwanted attention from authorities and criminal predators alike.

With just a glance at the once bustling train yards, it is now clear that in the immediate aftermath of *Plan Sur*, Arriaga is no longer a staging ground for large numbers of Central American migrants in transit. Recent raids on local hotels, the train yards, and departing trains have forced many migrants to find alternative way stations. Migrants' adaptations to this new policing environment require improvisation on the material infrastructure of the route: a leveraging of old physical and informational resources to find new trails north. However, the visibility of migrants' survival strategies can both enhance the safety and simultaneously undermine the security of this vulnerable group. In other words, the paths people take and the people they can engage (whether humanitarian aid workers or for-profit smugglers) must be public enough to guide future migrants north, but publicity brings danger of criminal predation and policing. The capacity of violent criminals to exploit this visibility in order to prey on migrants highlights an important point:

visibility without effective political contestation, and ultimately protection, facilitates violent predation.

Under these conditions the visual experience of the journey itself plays an important role for migrants navigating a violent landscape; their step-by-step engagement with a social and material terrain matters. To arrive at this insight, I draw on Kevin Lynch's classic work on the geographical imagination to explain the role of public images along the route.[8] Public images, as defined by Lynch, are commonly shared mental pictures of a social landscape, rooted in a collective cultural experience and interaction within a physical terrain. This chapter describes how these public images are both tactical resources for navigating the journey and symbolic resources for negotiating the politics of migration. Using the examples of freight trains and shelters, this chapter explores how migrants encounter the material manifestations of these images in transit. While most observers emphasize their obvious benefits as a transport vessel or source of food and shelter, freight trains and shelters also have an informational role that is emphasized here. They have become relied-on public images that guide the journeys of the most vulnerable and poorest migrants along the route. Trains and shelters have become the most widely broadcast signposts for the clandestine route.

However, images of crowded trains have become emblematic of a humanitarian crisis and loss of control and are therefore used to justify further state control of migration.[9] This chapter acknowledges that criminal predators encounter these same materials, appropriating images to locate and identify their victims. For this reason, one should not equate migrants' visibility with their political recognition. The public diffusion of visual information about migration tactics potentially erodes the utility of that information for crossing a hostile terrain. In conclusion, I briefly reflect on the appropriation of these images by immigrant rights activists as political symbols.

By examining how migrants like José navigate dangerous journeys, this chapter highlights the lived experience of a shifting and unpredictable social terrain, and it traces the cumulative impact of these individually lived experiences on the material infrastructure of *el Camino*. Faced with a problem of extraordinary uncertainty, the poorest and most vulnerable migrants improvise on the resources at hand; they utilize the very physical terrain they must traverse and the material objects they encounter en route to charter their path forward. Some migrants tie themselves to boxcars with their belts to prevent potentially fatal falls when the siren of sleep overtakes them on their long journey by freight train. When immigration raids prohibit using the train as a vehicle for transport, migrants still make use of its tracks to guide them north. In so doing, they are remaking their region, transforming the North American geography.[10]

Over time, an informational infrastructure for sustained unauthorized migration emerges around popular routes, facilitating opportunities for human movement and cultural change. The artifacts, ranging from styles of clothing to messages scribbled on the walls of shelters, litter the transnational trail and become navigational clues for the next generation of migrants. Their passage becomes a beacon to others. Ultimately, each wave of migrants alters the possibilities for those that follow.

This material process limits, but also enriches, the performance metaphor explored in the previous chapter. Migrants' performances of social scripts define new relationships in transit. Nevertheless, all the world is not a stage. Migrants perform their roles on a *practiced terrain* that cannot be prefabricated to order and may change unexpectedly midperformance. A practiced terrain consists of the places and things shaped by sustained human movement. No stage manager can design the set and props for real world performances, and migrants' interaction with the physical world takes on an improvised character. The props and places migrants discover en route both inspire new skits and bind actors to resonant scripts. The material remnants of migration intentionally *and unintentionally* transmit information that can be interpreted and improvised on by both migrants and predators.

Mapping the Chapter

To make these points, this chapter takes several steps. First, I describe a visual ethnographic methodology, drawing on a series of mapmaking interviews in migrants' home community that augmented the semistructured and unstructured interviews and participant observation along migration routes, as discussed in previous chapters. I also briefly sketch the surprising content of these maps. In my analysis of the illustrations within maps, I extend the previous discussion of performing ethnography to the visual realm. Using the maps to arrive at a new understanding of the relationship between the material and symbolic dimensions of el Camino, I make a methodological argument in favor of visual approaches. The rest of the chapter elucidates novel findings generated by this approach.

Second, I explain the origins of public images along the route.[11] These public images are both tactical resources for navigating the journey and symbolic resources for negotiating the politics of migration. A transit political economy, a transnational imaginary, and the physical act of migration itself constitute this practiced terrain; these places and knowledge-based artifacts simultaneously emerge from and inform the practice of migration.

Third, I examine how public images become signposts that flag entry points to the underground. To do so, I explain the role of freight trains *as a compass* and migrant shelters *as an informational oasis* for the poorest, most vulnerable migrants. The practice of migration inscribes itself into the landscape of the route, and migrants learn to read it. Nevertheless, under conditions of uncertainty, the usefulness of information acquired from the physical terrain is fleeting. Therefore, throughout this chapter, I also discuss how criminal predators encounter these same materials, appropriating images to locate and identify their victims. The train route and migrant shelters represent both resources and danger for migrants.

The chapter concludes by reflecting on a final appropriation of these images as political symbols. I frame maps drawn by migrants and their political allies as a critical cartography, albeit one with limits. In an important sense, the maps are written performances of migrants' victimhood and agency, and these performances are meant to orient the viewer to their experience of an injustice. Thus, with fieldwork primarily conducted before *Plan Sur*, but updated with a targeted research trips afterward, this chapter explores the nexus between the material and symbolic dimensions of improvisations that tie together el Camino as a place.

Mapping the Migrating Imagination

I supplemented participant observation and ethnographic interviews with mapmaking workshops that were conducted in El Salvador from 2009 to 2010. Elisabeth J. Wood used mapmaking workshops in an ethnographic analysis of the collective memory of Salvadoran peasant resistance.[12] Building on a tradition of cognitive mapping,[13] I used similar mapmaking workshops to achieve a slightly different ethnographic goal. While I also examined the construction of social memory, I sought to understand the construction of the social imagination of the route. For that reason, in two Salvadoran home communities, I asked would-be migrants to imagine and draw maps of the route they expected to travel. Returned migrants were asked to remember and draw maps of the route they had taken. Twenty-two people completed the exercise.

The migrants' maps provide both the reason and means to rethink the nature of information under conditions of uncertainty, delving deeper into the relationship between the social imaginary and lived experience. Migrants transformed maps into artwork that conveys both their hopes and memories. Much more than representations of the natural terrain, these maps can be read as a political performance: a form of protest against immigration policies and violent crimes, viewed as injustices by migrants. The mapmakers interwove the normative aspects of the social imaginary into the material practices of migration. The migrant maps often depict borders, as do official maps, but they also (and sometimes exclusively) depict symbols informed by religion, common cultural motifs, and personal encounters to protest the suffering imposed by those borders.

A few maps took the form of collages, with only a loose relationship between distance and events. A few maps seemed like prototypes for board games, with a path weaving its way back and forth across various obstacles or safe places on the page. Other maps took the form of an itinerary or storyboard, with no reference to distance at all; they were simply the order of events. Some maps were a simple array of dots and lines on the page. One mapmaker drew a single manger scene and explained that her trip could be understood in the biblical story of Mary and Joseph searching for a home to have their baby (see Figure 5.1). The scene explains the injustice of the homelessness and mistreatment she and her family experienced during the journey through Tijuana.

Finally, some maps resembled conventional "maps" with a clear spatial orientation and geographical markers. Even in these maps, mapmakers drew elaborate symbols that represent values; for example, in one potent image, a mapmaker illustrated an upturned hand holding bread, symbolizing how God provides daily bread and how migrants follow His will by searching for it (see Figure 5.2).

This subset of more conventional maps illustrates national borders and landmarks as well as locations of personal challenges and home. Colors also play an important role in several of the maps. In one map, a color code

Figure 5.1. The Manger
A normative orientation to the route rather than a geographical orientation. By equating her
family's journey through Tijuana to a biblical scene of Mary, Joseph, and baby Jesus, the
mapmaker critiques U.S. border policing.

represents the different emotions experienced while traversing the terrain. The same person who drew the provocative daily bread image also drew black dollar signs in Mexico, as opposed to the green dollars at home and the United States, to illustrate the moral dirtiness of the activities to earn money there. In that illustration, day and night frame the route, because the lived experience is both good and bad, sad and exciting, and the two sides of that experience cannot be disentangled. In another example, the mapmaker, imagining the way forward, used only dark colors in order to represent how uncertain and ominous the journey seemed at its outset (see Figure 5.3).

The collection of maps offers a normative orientation to the journey, as opposed to a geographical orientation. As such, they reinterpret and represent migration experiences. This way of making sense of the journey reveals the social and political landscape of the route and not just its physical features. This method thereby reveals the "mental maps" that organize the perceived relationship between space and social belonging;[14] it shows where migrant maps self-

Figure 5.2. Daily Bread and Dirty Money
Journey of a young man who was later deported. Day and night frame the journey:
the good and bad of migration cannot be disentangled; the experience is one of both suffering
and hope. The U.S. border is larger than the Mexican-Guatemalan border in the illustration:
it was the point of no return for him. Green money in the United States is good money,
which can make his family's dreams come true; black money in Mexico represents the dirty
things he had to do to arrive. God offers daily bread, but migrants must earn
it through their efforts.

consciously converge and diverge from the official maps that cut space into discrete nation-states. Thus, they are a way of "seeing like a migrant."[15] Similarly, Amalia Campos-Delgado argues that migrant maps challenge the "carto-politics" of migration securitization; official depictions of the route abstract from lived experience, while migrant maps humanize journeys across terrain, imbuing them with meaning.[16] It is no coincidence that the themes and images conveyed in the maps echo popular media and political symbols, such as *la Bestia* (the Beast, as the train is known among migrants) and the Bible, harnessed by activists to delegitimize borders. These maps offer a normative orientation to the migration route and not just a geographical orientation.

Cartography, as a form of surveillance, augments the power of the State administrative apparatus.[17] As policing tools, state officials use maps in their

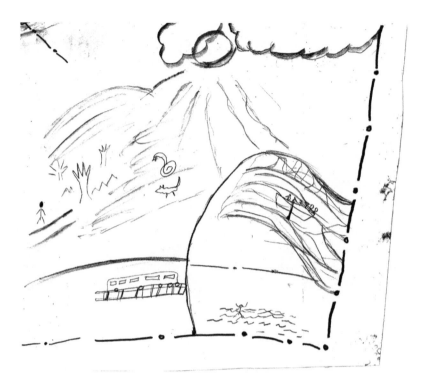

Figure 5.3. Noemi Does Not Want to Travel
The mountains convey Noemi's sense of uncertainty, her incapacity to predict
what might happen. This illustration echoes Karla's map, Figure 1.1, but Noemi chose
dark colors to convey her trepidation. At the time she made the map,
Noemi had no intention of leaving El Salvador.

daily planning and implementation of border control and immigration policies. As propaganda, maps nationalize territory and naturalize borders,
thereby reinforcing the legitimacy of state control over human movement.[18]
Finally, as bureaucratic artifacts, state maps justify expenditure and express
efficiency. Maps represent one form of political visualization, produced by
states to interact with illegal border crossers and project images of control
(or loss of control) to a public audience.[19]

In this sense, the migrant maps and the images they convey may be understood as a countermapping project.[20] Maps that illustrate the dangerous

route through Mexico, as opposed to myopically focusing on the borders, shift public vision from the periphery to the borderlands within. The form of the migrant maps, in particular, often privileges notions of place over an abstract space bounded by linear borders. Several migrants did not depict the journey as spatial, choosing instead to highlight the primacy of a universal morality and personal experience over territory. They thereby offer a non-territorial matrix to understand political authority and responsibility. Insofar that these images make claims to a higher moral authority of universal human rights and divine will, they overtly challenge the legitimacy of the state to exclude foreigners. Of course, alone the *legibility* of migration experience via countermapping does not automatically challenge national authority to exclude migrants from territory, and it must be embedded in a larger political narrative and struggle. Nevertheless, maps and public images provide signposts for politics, not only signposts for practice.

The diversity of form of the maps should, perhaps, not be surprising given that most would-be migrants and returned migrants with whom I spoke do not use written maps during their daily lives, and they did not plan to use a traditional map to navigate their journey north. Migrants rely on human guides, i.e., *coyotes*, to negotiate the spatial and social geography of the journey. Migrants who cannot afford guides rely on word of mouth from other migrants and more experienced travel companions, and they learn how to travel north by traveling and encountering new objects and terrain. Migrants converge en masse in freight train yards in southern Mexico as a site for both information and transportation.

To navigate their journeys in this way, migrants take visual cues from their surroundings.[21] Images of places, such as the trailhead, the river at the borders, the migrant shelter, and the train yard, provide focal points that orient migrants to the physical terrain. These four examples were common motifs in the maps drawn by migrants. In his classic work on the geographical imagination, Lynch explains that people navigate everyday by these "public images composed of key forms, in this case, paths, edges, nodes, landmarks."[22]

Sources of Public Images

When rendered memorable by their differentiation from other terrains of symbolic importance, landscape features such as train tracks or the rivers at borders guide people great distances. They also provide a basis for common knowledge of the location of migratory routes. The terrain of the route is thus hidden from official view, but easily found by searching for access points defined by public images.[23] Material cues, such as a trailhead that leads migrants north around a checkpoint, provide flags. Popular culture provides flags, too; the train has become part of the folklore in song, stories, and movies about the journey. As these symbols proliferate and become recognizable, they mark the existence of clandestine social spaces.

These "public images" emerge from the interplay between a transit political economy, transnational imaginary, and the material space traversed by generations of migrants.[24] The broad publicity of these images points to widespread social participation in unauthorized migration, including the complacency or collaboration of Mexican citizens and corrupt officials along the routes.[25] The images become visible to the general public, in part because migrants interact with citizens during their journey, conducting a variety of social and economic transactions that diffuse information. Once such images are public, they flag the location of the route and open informational entry points to the underground flow for newcomers—whether they be migrants or potential criminal predators.

Transit Political Economy

This socioeconomic interaction often transgresses the boundary between legal and illegal because transnational routes develop a spectrum of supporting informal economic and social activity that defies classification.[26] Unauthorized migration routes superimpose themselves on the infrastructure of the legal economy;[27] information leaks across these artificial boundaries between legal and illegal domains, linked by socioeconomic practice.[28] In Mexico, for example, the migrant smuggling industry is a much broader socioeconomic complex than illegal activity alone.[29]

On each journey, Central American migrants generally spend anywhere between several hundred to seven thousand dollars before they arrive at the U.S.-Mexico border, not only on bribes and smuggling services but also on a variety of travel incidentals and low-budget entertainment.[30] Smugglers and migrants purchase legal goods and services en route; e.g., prepaid phone cards, computer time at cyber cafes, room and board, fuel for vehicles, cigarettes, alcohol, Mexican and U.S. currency (often exchanged informally at disadvantageous rates for the migrants), international money transfer (e.g., Western Union, which charges fees), and clothing. Some male migrants, not immune to earthly temptations, may gamble or pay prostitutes picked up in bars. Purveyors of legal goods and services may employ unauthorized migrants as laborers. Vendors may knowingly provision smugglers for the journey or make extortion payments to criminal territory bosses.

One Salvadoran smuggler wryly explained the exorbitant price of a cup of coffee that Mexicans charge his Central American clients. He pointed out that even the laundresses in some Mexican towns were dependent on his human traffic.[31] He lamented that many people in these towns have no interest in going to school because they grow up in these businesses. He picked up a small saltshaker on the table between us to show me the size of a coffee that costs a dollar: "And the food they sell the migrants is bad. Expensive and ugly food. Five dollars a plate for next to nothing. . . . it's almost a fraud."[32] This Salvadoran smuggler estimated that perhaps as much 40 percent of the migrant remittances sent from the United States to El Salvador ultimately paved the route through Mexico and Guatemala for family members of immigrants, instead of fueling investment in his own country. Of course, despite the fact that he was profiting from the brokerage of these services for migrants, the smuggler's capacity to estimate the overall percentage of Salvadoran remittances spent in Mexico was limited; he simply could not know the number, and his estimate expresses a subjective sense of injustice at the usurious prices that Mexicans charge him.[33] Nevertheless, he correctly recognized that over time, small communities through which migrants pass reorient their economic expectations and prices to the flow of people. In this vein, he explained that Central American "migration has changed the culture, in particular, in Chiapas. Without [im]migration, Mexico would die. It is the commerce of the illegals that keeps it alive."

The relationship between border towns and the paths that crisscross the U.S.-Mexico frontier provides a stark example of the coevolution of transit political economies, the transnational imaginary, and material space. Jason De León explains that the so-called "trash" that litters the desert landscape is, in fact, the "distinct archaeological fingerprint" of migration practice.[34] He examines the artifacts discarded along the way. In particular, he argues that a collective folklore of migration is defined, in part, by images of these artifacts: dark clothes, cheap worn sneakers, and empty black water bottles, often decorated with religious symbols. These artifacts reveal a routinization of collective suffering and sacrifice by migrants.[35]

As U.S. border enforcement produced geographic bottlenecks in the routes north, key Mexican desert communities (such as Altar, Sonora, a community described by De León) became staging grounds for clandestine border crossings.[36] The convergence of the stream of people through these communities gave rise to a particular class of vendors that provision impoverished masses in transit. These daily economic routines make migration practice visible at the borders.

In fact, communities much farther south than the Sonoran Desert bear the imprint of unauthorized migration. Far from the border zone, in notorious towns such as Arriaga in Chiapas and Ixtepec in Oaxaca, or in neighborhoods in the immediate vicinity of the tracks in larger cities (such as Coatzacoalcos in Veracruz and Lechería in Mexico), transience became a pillar of the local economy. For example, a young Salvadoran man, struck by the extent of these operations, remembered his journey through Chiapas:

> The guide took us to a town in Mexico made by the illegal route. The town's whole existence is to provide for migrants. They cook for migrants, they house them for a fee and sell them what they need for the journey.[37]

Along the route, a multitude of small shops (selling inexpensive footwear, clothing, and other supplies for the journey), cheap hotels, smugglers' safe houses, brothels, bars, and restaurants have opened in private homes near the train tracks, testifying to a reorientation of economic activity by locals. Whenever the train stops in a populated area, women swarm in to sell home-cooked food and drinks to migrants. In these places, the desire to attract new customers motivates many purveyors of quasi-legal or unauthorized services to visibly and forthrightly market their availability; they approach complete strangers, rather than solely relying on word-of-mouth recruitment of clients. Debris of migrants' belongings litters the ground along the train tracks and trails across the length of Mexico—artifacts of a thriving transnational trade route. It is possible to follow this material infrastructure north with very little geographic information. Indeed, now that the train no longer serves as an efficient vehicle for transport due to raids by police and the exorbitant boarding fees charged by gang members for its use, migrants still follow the tracks where possible, using the physical remnants of the precrackdown route as a navigational tool.

From the Guatemala-Mexico border to the U.S.-Mexico border, an unsightly and pervasive moral economy of begging has also come to underwrite migrants' consumption of local goods and services.[38] While more fortunate migrants rely on remittances wired from the United States to pay for their travel expenses, anonymous begging also provides desperate Central American migrants the means to move toward work in Mexico and the United States. Along the route, shelter staff often ask them to refrain from begging, encouraging migrants to ask for day labor instead; the constant haranguing for handouts antagonizes locals and strains relations between the shelters and their surrounding neighborhoods. It is important for human rights activists and migrants to present themselves as workers, not vagrants, in order to claim moral authority and pressure authorities for recognition as people worthy of protection. Nevertheless, an uncommonly high number of people are obliged to beg while they travel the transnational route, and their visibility marks the pathways north. Migrants can navigate by following the ebb and flow of hopeful, but otherwise destitute, permanent wanderers.

Economic interdependence produces opportunities for migrants to camouflage their movement in the flow of legal goods and people, obscuring the official gaze.[39] However, at the level of social practice, clandestine interdependence also generates common knowledge about unauthorized activities between locals and migrants. Over time, sustained socioeconomic transactions give substance to the "public images" that guide migrants and their predators.

A Transnational Imaginary: Tactical and Symbolic Resources

Economic incentives for transactions with migrants structure information flows along the route, in concert with a transnational imaginary. Public images of migrant journeys also emerge from what Arjun Appadurai calls a "mediascape."[40] Some scenes depicted in the maps express a transnational imaginary shaped by printed publications, radio and television broadcasts, and artistic communications. From this perspective, the Bible has informed a transnational mediascape in the Americas since the arrival of the Spaniards over five hundred years ago. Both biblical and popular media representations of the route shape expectations and interpretations of migration experiences. Migrants encounter songs, movies, radio reports, and television news programs about the route before, during, and after their journey. Migrants post updates and images of the route on Facebook. As they travel, they contribute content of the migration mediascape.

Songs become a device that interprets migration possibilities for Central Americans. With rebellious narratives about heroes, martyrs, smugglers, outlaws, and migrants, Mexican *corridos* (traditional ballads that tell stories) and Caribbean hip-hop narrate the reasons for migration and recount the dangers migrants expect.[41] Whether penned by the traditional corridos band *Los Tigres del Norte* or younger hip-hop artists like *Calle 13*, these songs warn of deadly desert crossings, venomous animals, encounters with corrupt officials, and banditry. However, song also provides the means for migrants themselves to reimagine the journey, communicating within travel groups and across cyberspace. Song provides a structure for migrants to communicate. As people move, they discover and adapt new ways to express themselves. Migrants play songs on borrowed guitars in shelters. They raise their voices to praise God and ask for his protection along the route. They write lyrics or perform rap music that they upload to YouTube or Facebook, crowding around computers in shelters and cybercafes along the route to share their compositions. These amateur musicians perform their art to fortify themselves in the face of uncertain danger, project a positive self-image, and collectively reimagine their purpose in opposition to the State and other violent actors. In so doing, they transmit information about the route to those following in their footsteps.

The visual influence of movies may have an even greater impact on the geographical imagination. In El Salvador, a man contemplating whether he should undertake the journey asked me to sit and watch the classic film based on Los Tigres del Norte's song *Tres Veces Mojado* (Three Times a Wetback) (1989). By sharing the movie, he could more easily express his own trepidation about migration. It is an adventure story about a Salvadoran man crossing Mexico that ends with the death of a friend in the desert and his own capture by the U.S. Border Patrol. Alongside the more recent *Sin Nombre* (Nameless) (2009), *Tres Veces Mojado* is a cult classic.

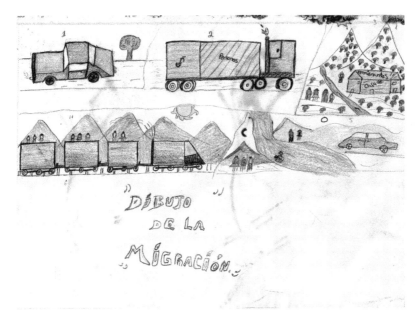

Figure 5.4. *Sin Nombre* as a Guide
The movie *Sin Nombre* inspired the images in this map, which is structured as a storyboard.
The mapmaker had immediate plans to leave his community, but many years later,
he still resides in El Salvador.

Several migrants discussed how *Sin Nombre* had impacted their expectations for the journey. A Honduran man en route to the United States explained how the movie informed his fear of the train. "I was thinking about this movie while crossing the river, and when I saw the tracks I thought, 'this is where things started to go wrong.'"[42] Similarly, at home in El Salvador, a different young man, still considering whether or not to embark on his journey, explained that *Sin Nombre* inspired some of the images that he drew in his map of the journey he planned to take (see Figure 5.4).

In a surreal turn of events, another migrant in El Salvador described a harrowing ordeal where kidnappers forced him to watch *Sin Nombre* while in captivity in Mexico. His kidnappers warned him that the route is dangerous, and they played the movie for him and his friends before they had escaped. The movie is the story of a young man who betrays his gang to save a Honduran immigrant girl on the way to the United States; he dies at the climax of the film, shot by his former friends, while she crosses the Rio Bravo.

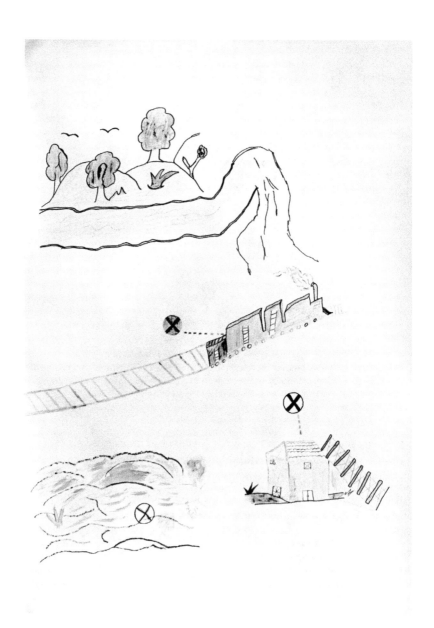

Figure 5.5. Living *Sin Nombre*
This journey ended in deportation home, rather than arrival in the United States.
The mapmaker had been kidnapped during his journey, and the kidnappers made him
watch the movie *Sin Nombre*, for unknown reasons.

Although the migrant has no idea why his kidnappers wanted him to see it or what message they had hoped to send, the film still had an emotional impact. His map (see Figure 5.5) not only echoes his own experience but also echoes the images from the movie. "The movie," he told me, "captures the reality." As bandits and migrants perform common knowledge scripts and roles along the route, experience itself also echoes the movie.

Like personal stories of migrants, none of these movies or songs has an unambiguous happy ending. Even in stories of redemption, like *Sin Nombre*, media depictions of the route share the theme of hardship, loss, and persecution. Whether fiction or nonfiction, migration stories of redemptive suffering and endurance abound. In her discourse analysis of all major Salvadoran newspapers from 1985 to 2004, Amparo Marroquín argues that a recurring theme of "exodus to the promised land" shapes the imaginary of the route, such that "the religious element present in the popular culture was reinforced by this journalistic treatment that views the migrant that passes this test [of the journey] as someone that has God as a helper in their crossing."[43] In the migrant maps and their accompanying narratives, popular tropes and religious iconography merge. While many migrants dismiss the television or newspaper reports as false or exaggerated, these popular religious allegories shape expectations and interpretations of experiences.[44] Powerful narratives of dangerous journeys also circulate in the Honduran press.[45] They generate popular images of places, both imbuing them with meanings and signaling where the route might be found.

It is worth noting that the mediascape is not entirely independent of the nation-state. In 1997, the U.S. Border Patrol launched its first media campaign to raise awareness of the dangers of illegal border crossing among potential migrants in Mexico. In 2004, the Border Safety Initiative of the U.S. Border Patrol launched "No Mas Cruces en la Frontera" (No More Crosses on the Border) through Elevación, a private advertising agency. Critics complain that these materials provide little transparency about their sponsorship.[46] The campaign first targeted potential Mexican migrants and was extended to Central America in 2010. It began with a focus on desert dangers, primarily targeted at male migrants, but has included warnings about human trafficking targeted at female migrants as well.

Given the small sample size, it is difficult to make generalizations based on categories of maps and mapmakers. Nonetheless, one theme is unmistakably evident across maps and their stories: religious imagery in the artwork reveals how migrants connect their experience to a larger normative critique of political and economic structures. The pervasiveness of Christianity is not surprising, of course. Jacqueline Maria Hagan documents the multiple ways that religion and faith influence Central American migratory journeys; migrants interact with the "sacred geography of Mexico."[47] First, organized religion provides sanctuary along the route with a system of shelters and social networks.[48] Second, everyday religious practices provide companionship in the face of hardship and a sense of consistency in periods of change.[49] Third, religious faith provides a lens through which migrants can make sense of the experience, and it provides a sense of belonging under conditions of uncertainty. Finally, Hagan notes that the journey transforms and often reaffirms faith.[50] Indeed, the maps of migrants reveal this sacred geography. Churches become public images that orient migrants to help when in need.

This orientation to the route is not simply passively received but continually reconstructed before, during, and after the journey. The Bible, popular music, movies, and news stories do not simply provide *information* about the route; they provide *inspiration* for migrants and activists imagining the route. As Amelia Frank-Vitale points out in her analysis of unauthorized migration as civil disobedience, priests and migrants politically interpret biblical passages, rather than simply parrot them;[51] for example, Padre José Alejandro Solalinde Guerra, a prominent human rights activist and founder of the migrant shelter in Ixtepec, Oaxaca, preaches the gospel from Matthew 25:35 as "I was hungry and you gave me food, I was thirsty and you gave me drink, I was a migrant and you housed me," when the usual translation is "I was a stranger and you welcomed me."[52] Migrants and other actors along the route actively reinterpret the Bible and other sources of information rather than take them as is. Whether drawn by a would-be migrant expecting the journey or a returned migrant remembering the journey, the maps are evidence of this conscious reimagining of the route. The symbols and public images that emerge from the transnational mediascape are continually reinterpreted as people move across terrain. Migrants simultaneously engage in tactical maneuvers to migrate safely and in a larger political contestation around the right to migrate safely.

Public Images: Signposts for the Underground

Before José left Guatemala, he consulted only two people. Neither one was a parent. His father had died eight years ago, and his mother lived far from him in Escuintla, a city on the western side of the country. He did not ask her. Nor did he talk to his cousins who had traveled the route before him. Instead, a female cousin who stayed behind in Guatemala warned him of the risks: assaults, kidnappings, murders, and the possibility of falling from the train. Her advice was simply to "be careful." A friend in the United States agreed to help, but his friend's advice was almost as vague: "Take care of yourself. Do not talk to unknown people. Do not sleep just anywhere. Do not walk in the mountains because of snakes and thieves." Of course, José had to do these things anyway, even though he had not planned to. He began the journey by asking God for protection, "because it is very complicated to get started with advice like that." Then he and his companions went in search of the train. When discovered en route, these public images indicate openings where further information about clandestine practice may surface. Two of these signposts have particular importance for José and the poorest migrants traveling north: trains and shelters.

The Freight Train: A Compass

The train is strictly for freight, not passengers. In the 1990s, the Mexican government suspended passenger service, leaving freight service as the only available train system except for a handful of short novelty lines for tourists and the Mexico City commuter system. At that time, the government granted concessions to a handful of private companies for the continuation of freight service. Migrants ride the freight trains like hobos. Until 2005, this route began in Tapachula, Chiapas, but that segment of the route suffered damage in Hurricane Stan and has been indefinitely suspended. Migrants lamented the closure of this southernmost segment, because crossing Chiapas now requires some combination of extensive hiking on dangerous trails and expensive passenger transport. Since 2014, the immigration crackdown of *Plan Sur* has made riding the train increasingly difficult; crossing Oaxaca also requires extensive hiking on dangerous trails. For migrants without financial resources for expensive smugglers or passenger transport, the journey to the interior of Mexico can take weeks on foot. This time spent on the route leaves them more vulnerable to criminal predation.

José left home with only a vague notion of geography.[53] However, he found the train yards in southern Mexico. He knew that the freight trains would carry him in the right direction. In that sense, the train yard served as an entry port to a clandestine terrain, where word of mouth and the physical space itself can lead a migrant to the U.S. border. The freight train was not just an inexpensive transport vehicle; its tracks and equipment were and remain a conduit for information.[54] For example, the colors and markings of the engines signal the destinations of the trains. If the train broke down or migrants had to flee into the wilderness to escape a migration raid, scattering and hiding among the bushes, they would regroup around the tracks as a focal point, using the steel rails to guide their long walk to the next shelter. Now, much of the hike through southern Mexico follows the old tracks, relying on the train tracks to locate the shelters. Simply put, the train is a compass.

It is not surprising that the train has come to serve as a focal point for migrants, particularly near the beginning of the route through Mexico. William Walters observes that vehicles play a pivotal role in the political drama of migration, as prominent settings for mobility and the contestation of borders.[55] In Lynch's words, the train has a high level of *imageability* that is:

> That quality in a physical object which gives it a high probability of evoking a strong image in any given observer. It is that shape, color, or arrangement which facilitates the making of vividly identified, powerfully structured, highly useful images of the environment.[56]

The source of the train's eminent imageability is twofold: material and symbolic. Beginning in the 1990s and intensifying with the first iteration of *Plan Sur* in 2001, the proliferation of highway migration checkpoints pushed an increasing number of migrants to the trains, generating a bottleneck for unauthorized traffic along the tracks.[57] The poorest migrants could not afford to pay smugglers or bribe corrupt officials who stop the bus.

The location and sporadic tempo of train service, combined with the increasing numbers of migrants converging on the train, created large crowds of migrants across southern Mexico. From Chiapas through Veracruz, trains run relatively infrequently and unpredictably, as a result of a schedule dictated by the weather, wear on the aging rail network, and the logistical needs of the patchwork of subsidiaries of the major railway companies. This unpredictability often produces a backlog of migrant hopefuls loitering around train yards.[58] The presence of these crowds illuminates the way forward, and sudden movements in the crowd signal either danger or the impending departure of a locomotive. In this southern zone, the tracks begin in Tenosique, Tabasco, in the east and Arriaga, Chiapas, in the west, merging in Veracruz and moving migrants to the outskirts of Mexico City before dividing into many alternative routes north. While such large crowds have become less common in the aftermath of the 2014–present crackdown, the social memory of the train as a conduit for this information lingers; migrants still converge on the tracks and train yards to search for information. The train-riding era has left a material and symbolic legacy for the time being, one that would likely be fully revived were such intense immigration policing to pause.

In contrast to those in the south, trains in the northern half of the country run faster, more frequently, and in more directions, thereby dispersing the crowds of migrants.[59] Because of this dispersion, the train began to lose its imageability in the north. As the journey progresses, this class of migrants relies increasingly on information transmitted by word of mouth or paid guides. If intense immigration policing persists along the southern section of the train route, it too will likely eventually take on these qualities.

The symbolism of *la Bestia*, as the train has become known colloquially, provokes strong emotions. In the past, the desert at the U.S.-Mexico border represented the most potent popular image of suffering during the journey. Today, the image of suffering is most commonly associated with the train, which dominates popular media and folklore in Central America. Legends about the terrible accidents and assaults that stalk its rails circulate widely. Images of people with severed limbs lost to train accidents are commonplace in the Central American press. Ironically, these harrowing stories orient Central Americans to the train, making the image of the locomotive and its relationship to migration recognizable, rather than scaring people away. Thus, as immigration policing and danger intensify along routes far from borders, the train has taken a central place in the social imagination of the route, thereby becoming a useful, albeit dangerous, arrow that points people north.

Shelters: Informational Oases

Catholic migrant shelters form an integral part of the "sacred geography" of the route.[60] They are the most common places that migrants turn to for help. In these places, migrants can learn about the latest security threats, receive updates about police movements, discover alternative routes north, find out about job opportunities, watch and mimic tactics employed by other migrants, ascertain their legal rights, and form new relationships with potential travel companions and smugglers. In contemplative moments, migrants receive spiritual support, and they listen to arguments by clergy and activists about their ethical obligations and rights.

The shelters, as spaces protected by their moral authority, political power, and physical barriers (sometimes including video monitoring systems, security guards, cement walls, etc.), usually offer sufficient physical security to facilitate conversations among strangers without an immediate fear of assault or apprehension by authorities. With some notable exceptions, people remain safe until they leave the sanctity of the shelter grounds. This modicum of security contributes to a relatively relaxed atmosphere when compared to the train yards at night and permits more information to surface. In this way, a migrant shelter becomes an oasis where information can surface along the route.

Nevertheless, nowhere along the route is the double-edged nature of information more apparent than at migrant shelters. The shelters are also an informational resource for a variety of other actors, some of them with nefarious intent. Spies (*rateros*) enter the shelters to retrieve information about migrants for kidnappers. More specifically, spies seek to identify those who receive money through Western Union, the phone numbers of relatives in the United States, the travel plans of migrants, and the presence of members of competing gangs. Recruiters for smugglers also enter the shelter, hoping to advertise their services to potential clients.

Shelter personnel are well aware of these problems. In January 2011, during a period of political activism in response to a mass kidnapping near Chahuites, Oaxaca, on December 16, 2010, criminals entered the shelter grounds in Ixtepec, Oaxaca. They did not disguise their intent to intimidate the staff, boasting of the intelligence they had gathered about the volunteers working there. These men allegedly found the shelter priest resting in his hammock and warned him: "Do you know why we do not kill you?

Because if we kill you, they are going to close the shelter and it is going to be more difficult to find the undocumented. However, with the shelter, you get them together for us."[61] Thus, these places become the site of a struggle over information, as migrants and criminals attempt to conceal their personal data and identities from one another. Indeed, the shelters provide a variety of services to migrants, but information is the single-most important resource *and* danger that migrants confront there. Like any other oasis, shelters draw predators.

How do shelters become informational oases? The activities within the shelters facilitate information flows, leaving a material trace that future migrants encounter as knowledge-based artifacts, which I describe in the section that follows. The shelters have fixed locations shaped by migration practice. Importantly, the shelters' security protocols can ensure safety for migrants to gather, but only at the expense of their informational value to migrants. In other words, attempts to enforce security protocols have the unintended consequence of spatially isolating migrants from potential predators and limiting their movement, thereby creating potential barriers to information flows. Finally, political contestation protects the space of the shelter. The preservation of the shelter as a space requires more than information flows visible at the level of clandestine practice; it requires public representation. Institutionalized religion projects moral authority and represents migrants in Mexican society to achieve public recognition, not just visibility. Nevertheless, the paradox of public images as beacons for predators as well as migrants continues to haunt these "safe spaces" along the route.

Firstly, shelter staff will sometimes organize information sessions for migrants to warn them of the dangers ahead. These briefings are sometimes part of the registration process. Staff may also give some carefully guarded advice to migrants they perceive as the most vulnerable to abuse, such as women traveling with small children. Therefore, shelter staff selects both the migrants and the circumstances under which they share that information carefully. When migrants successfully pass along the route, they relay the information back to the shelter staff by telephone.

Of course, most of the information passes without intent. People simply tell yarns to kill time. They also eavesdrop on gossip. The main source of entertainment for the poorest migrants is the conversation and reality drama that unfold in shelters. By participating in this drama, migrants come to understand the route and its inhabitants.

Migrants also use the shelters to communicate with family and friends in the United States and Central America via telephone or, where available, the internet. Some shelters offer free phone calls, while others provide public phones to be used with prepaid cards. In this manner, the shelters become a node for transnational informational (and financial) exchanges. Furthermore, family members of migrants from Central America often contact shelters in search of missing persons.

These attempts to access information at the shelter leave a material trace and that provides signposts for future migrants. The sad, yellowing posters of missing persons flapped in the breeze of a doorway in the shelter in Saltillo. The dirt yard in Ixtepec was littered with phone cards. On the walls of the now-defunct shelter in San Luis Potosi, migrants had lovingly inscribed the addresses of shelters in Mexico and the United States, as well as the contact information for the Denver day laborer center, El Centro Humanitario. They also left behind artwork, messages of encouragement, and their own names.

The semiotics of murals in shelters is unambiguous. The artwork created by migrants and activists challenges the legitimacy of immigration enforcement. These scenes empathize with the plight of migrants, compelled to follow a difficult path in Jesus's footsteps (see Figure 5.6). They often depict the promised cities of the north, shining and waiting for the deserving migrant who endures and completes the journey. The messages are decidedly cosmopolitan in their appeal to a larger understanding of the Americas and the globe. The messages show footsteps that trespass borders, the destruction of borders, or simply the removed borders altogether. The artwork depicts the suffering of the migrants through religious imagery with coffins or a cross. Finally, they may contain scenes that vilify immigration policing, placing state personnel in opposition to Jesus. In fact, such artwork is not limited to the walls of migrant shelters. The murals even co-opt the very spaces intended for immigration enforcement. Like the West German side of the Berlin Wall, the Mexican side of the U.S. border wall has become the medium for expressing frustration with government policies that separate transnational communities and put migrants in danger.[62]

However, the moral imperative and normative power conveyed by the murals and other activism within the shelter are insufficient to keep all covert predators away from the shelters. Kidnappers covet information about who is making phone calls to the United States. This information is used as an indicator for those victims who can pay handsome ransoms. They seek to

Figure 5.6. Mural in Shelter
This mural echoes themes that appear in migrant maps and other murals
along the route to the United States. Credit: Encarni Pindado.

identify these phone numbers for extortion rackets. Smugglers solicit potential clients and may also infiltrate the shelters posing as migrants. While they
rarely openly enter shelter grounds, bandits and corrupt police seeking bribes
often stalk the routes to and from these facilities.

Second, the locations of shelters are relatively fixed and shaped by sustained migration practice. The physical layout of the shelters differs dramatically from one to the next, depending on the unique history of the place.
Often the struggle over information and security drives physical changes to
the shelters, causing staff to erect large cement walls, gates, video surveillance,
and other precautions. Thus, the potential for violence against migrants
shapes the material contours of shelters. In turn, these material contours shape
the information available to migrants by segregating and isolating some populations and also changing patterns of movement within (as well as into/
from) the shelters.

The shelter layout inevitably adapts to new resources, threats, and needs
over time. Some shelters look like large converted homes. Others look like
secure compounds. Some sprout from congregational initiatives, growing as
wings to existing buildings owned by the Church. NGOs may make large
donations to shelters to enable specific projects, such as dealing with a press-
ing sanitation or security issue, depending on their own reading of priorities.

Skilled Central American masons or electricians occasionally take time from their journeys north to contribute, either by earning wages or volunteering. Migrants themselves have built many of these structures piecemeal over time, and the compounds often expand in a makeshift manner as financial resources, human capital, and construction materials become available. The rules and regulations of shelters are also often products of experience, changing and adapting as shelter staff confront new dilemmas and improvise on old ways of doing business. In the aftermath of the intensification of *Plan Sur* in 2014, some established shelters have seen the human flow turned away from them by police checkpoints that make migrants' arrival there difficult. At least one shelter has responded by setting up a satellite facility in a new location on the route. In this sense, the social and material structure of the shelters emerges from practice, an unintended collective residue of the actions of individual migrants.

In turn, the social and material structure of the shelter shapes migration practice. New shelters attract migrants, changing the course of the human flow. The regulation and physical layout of the place shapes the information available to migrants during their journey. There is a trade-off between physical security and the flow of information through the shelter. Physical security requires screening processes for selective entry of migrants deemed to be unthreatening to their potential travel companions, a schedule for entry and exit that promotes control, and segregation of sleeping areas by gender. The more isolated and selective the shelter becomes, the less opportunity for infiltration by criminal gangs.

However, the regulation of movement in and out of the shelter comes with a steep price for migrants: they become less capable of learning about and adapting to changes in the route. For example, shelters often segregate Mexicans and Central Americans to minimize opportunities for recruitment by smugglers and infiltration by kidnappers. This segregation by nationality also decreases the information available to migrants. It isolates them from the larger community. Within their grounds, shelters also often segregate sleeping areas by gender because sexual assault is so common. However, the segregation of men and women decreases the information available to the female minority by cutting them off from gossip at night. Indeed, in an extreme case, men and women are locked behind bars in separate wings of the facility at a regulated hour. Shelters often deny entry to repeat customers, who come under suspicion as smugglers or spies. However, in so doing, the shelter excludes the most experienced migrants from sharing their stories with others. In the most regulated shelters, migrants cannot leave to go to the train when they receive information about its immediate departure. They cannot leave to make travel arrangements and reenter to wait. Finally, and most importantly, migrants may choose not to enter the shelter for fear of missing vital information about the movement of the trains:

> Because of the irregular schedule of the trains, there is a need to sleep in the vias and that is where the danger of the attacks comes from.[63]

At night, the train yards, or vías (along the train tracks), are extraordinarily dangerous places, and it is a measure of the high value of this information to migrants that they would risk sleeping there to receive it. Thus, the regulation of movement in and out of the shelter is an important security consideration. Movement must be monitored to prevent kidnappings out of the shelter and to prevent the smuggling of guns and drugs into the shelters. This is required in order to maintain the safety of the shelter, and that safety is key for the survival of an informational oasis. However, too much regulation also undermines the informational utility of the place. These security regulations undermine the flow of information through the shelter and ultimately erode the human security of migrants.

Finally, institutionalized religion facilitates the shelter's visibility under these quasi-legal conditions, deterring intervention by federal Mexican authorities and deterring the most flagrant assaults by organized criminal gangs. In the 1980s, Catholic shelters mostly clustered in the northern border zone, the most dangerous place for migrants at that time.[64] At first, these shelters provided a respite for weary Mexican travelers. As the refugee flow from Central America accelerated, the shelters became the front line for human rights activism on behalf of Central Americans fleeing political violence. During the 1990s, when U.S. Border Patrol effectively closed the migration corridor through Tijuana-San Diego and deportations intensified, some shelters in the northern border zone began to cater to Mexicans deported back across the border. These Mexican migrants sometimes returned penniless and became stranded in frontier towns far from their homes. Mexican and Central American activists and humanitarian workers, like the sister sanctuary movement in the United States, drew inspiration from liberation theology and their broader Christian faith.[65]

In the 2000s, awareness of the horrors of the journey from Central America spread, and the number of migrant shelters along the route multiplied despite the fact that they were not exactly legal. In 2008, the Mexican Supreme Court decriminalized humanitarian aid to migrants; it had not previously been clearly distinguished from smuggling under Article 77 of the Population Law. While humanitarian workers and activists still report some harassment from police, this ruling facilitated the expansion and further institutionalization of the shelter system.

By 2012, there were approximately fifty-four shelters from Guatemala to the U.S. border. Any estimate of their presence is complicated by the fact that new shelters periodically open and others close. Many of them, however, congregate in the most visible corridors of the route, serving the poorest and most vulnerable migrants who travel along the train tracks or linger at the borders. Catholic faith has inspired both clergy and laypeople to organize most of these shelters; they serve migrants from any religion. Most of them are loosely networked through the Church but are not funded by it. While the relationship with the surrounding community may be friendly or hostile, the shelters become a hub of local economic activity. For this reason, Wendy Vogt conceptualizes them as depots along the unauthorized route; i.e., places of constant coming and going through which migrants are "transformed into commodities where they were traded, bought, sold and distributed."[66] As such, the shelter is a hub in the clandestine political economy, but protected as a space by the moral authority of the Church.

Outside of shelters, there are also informal encampments built by migrants. During exceptional moments, the Mexican federal government has provided temporary migrant camps; the most recent example was in the summer of 2012, during a major backlog of migrants in Veracruz caused by the cessation of train service following a derailment.[67] However, these informal encampments and ad hoc camps lack the moral and political power of the migrant shelter system. The moral authority of the Catholic Church in Mexico creates a political space for particularly open informational oases. In an often-cited poll conducted by Consulta Mitofsky, Mexicans have consistently ranked universities and the Catholic Church as the least corrupt institutions in Mexican society.[68] Most Mexicans are Catholic, and even criminals fear for their immortal soul. Thus, accusations that priests participate in smuggling do not generally persuade the public and therefore protect priests against criminal charges for trafficking. The institutional and normative power of the Catholic Church enhances the power of individual priests to maintain these facilities despite threats from both governments and criminals.

Shelters that project information of the route to transnational human rights networks provoke additional security guarantees from politicians, and they may receive material resources for surveillance, guards, and cement walls. Thus, shelters play a vital role in political contestation for migrants' rights. They provide an access point to the underground for the general public. A multinational cadre of journalists, human rights investigators, researchers, and activists arrive at the shelters daily to take testimonies from the migrants that congregate there. For this reason, the shelters are not only a platform for migration. Shelters also become a platform for the projection of information necessary for national and international political activism.

Conclusion: Toward a Politics of Migrant Navigation

José had made a kindly impression on me. After meeting him, I hoped against the odds that I might hear from him again. It was an unlikely prospect, but I did encounter six migrants at multiple locations during my research. Before I left Mexico, I also received rumors about the whereabouts and activities of various migrants indefinitely moving along the route. After my return to the United States, I maintained contact with some Salvadoran families that span the United States and El Salvador. A handful of tech-savvy migrants also found me after their arrival in the United States. So, it was possible that I would see or hear from the Guatemalan again. Alas, years passed and I never received any communication from him or the vast majority of the people I met en route.

Dynamic conditions and the obscurities of anonymity along the route complicate the view of an ethnographer as much as that of migrants. Put simply, the route as I knew it during fieldwork had changed even before my own act had come to a close. Thus, I could not predict the likelihood of José's success or failure, and I still wonder about his fate. Whatever ultimately happened to him, the possibility of violence haunted his journey. The testimonials of kidnapping victims remind us that the information provided by the material infrastructure of the route cuts two ways. Ironically, migrants read the artifacts of sustained migration to orient their journey, but these same artifacts can betray their location. The utility of information about the route is fleeting and unpredictable. If migrants can learn by moving along this terrain, so can the authorities and criminals that hunt them. Oases draw predators. The combination of the routes' "hidden but known" qualities produces a geographic vulnerability to criminal violence:[69] a predictable place to prey on people in the shallows of the law.

Thus, the practiced terrain of the route provides both a resource and a danger for migrants. As information condenses in material form around the transit political economy and landscape of the route, it becomes visible to a variety of strategic actors. The micropolitics of migrant navigation has two dimensions. First, at a tactical level, visibility of the route cuts two ways, producing vulnerability and informational resources for migrants. Second, at a political level, visibility provides a first step to public recognition and demands for rights. This too, however, cuts both ways, as the State may also manipulate images of migration to justify the deepening and extension of its control efforts. In summary, public images function at both tactical and political levels, marking sites of the underground economy for participants and providing the symbols that represent that activity to the larger political audience. The tactical and political worlds become one social reality along the route.

Of course, it is no coincidence that activists appropriate these same public images to locate migrant victims of crime and gather their testimonies. Nor is it a coincidence that academics and journalists travel to migrant shelters or board freight trains to understand human security. Indeed, this chapter suggests that such "line-of-sight" methods, such as participant observation and ethnographic immersion, are necessary to understand the full range of survival resources available to people in violent situations.

The fact that tactical and political worlds become one social reality should both encourage and caution researchers engaged with these human security dilemmas. On the one hand, political visibility is essential strategically for activists and the larger population of migrants in transit across Mexico, and research can enhance this agenda. On the other hand, tactical invisibility is essential for migrants traversing a dangerous terrain, and research that renders routes across this terrain visible potentially exposes migrants to predators, whether those predators are criminals or the State.

The same signposts that guide migrants also guide activism and research around clandestine migration, and informational tensions also haunt activism and research around vulnerable clandestine populations. In particular, the imagery of the train as *la Bestia* offers a clear illustration of the desperation and sacrifice of the hundreds of thousands of Central Americans who attempt the journey each year and, as such, has become a rallying cry against the abuse of migrants in transit. Walters suggests that "vehicles can be mobilized in counter-narratives where they are means to articulate a politics of hope and injustice as well [as risk and suffering]."[70] Indeed, activists periodically board the train as an act of protest. Human rights activists reproduce such public images to raise awareness of the plight of migrants and heighten a sense of humanitarian crisis; they explicitly seek to make "invisible victims" visible. As explained by Christine Kovic and Francisco Arguelles, "The coexistence of visibility and invisibility of blinding and being a blind spot applies to Central American transmigrants and other marginalized groups. To make someone invisible is an act of violence. . . . Yet members of marginalized groups are also hypervisible; that is, in being defined as outsiders, they stand out and are perceived as being out of place."[71] The images promoted by activists attempt to challenge both the invisibility of migrants to the protections of the law and the visibility of migrants as *other*.

With these goals in mind, visualizations of the route enabled by participant observation and mapmaking offer a path forward for understanding and advocating on behalf of vulnerable populations caught in violent situations. However, it is a path that presents an informational paradox and an ethical dilemma that must be carefully navigated. These images overtly question the legitimacy of the State to exclude foreigners. For this reason, such images can also signal to state agencies where it can best neutralize clandestine routes to project control. Visual information, whether in the tactical environment confronted by migrants during individual journeys or the strategic environment confronted by activists during political contestation, has a dual life as both potential resource and danger.

ACT 3

Climax

Chapter 6

A Tragedy

Conclusions and Implications

In the migrant shelter in Arriaga, Chiapas, a way station where many Central Americans started the train route north, I sat next to a middle-aged man with a faded tattoo above his eyebrow.[1] He said that "el norte" was blowing hard, and with that way of talking about the wind, I knew immediately that he was Salvadoran. He was in Los Angeles for a while. But, he explained, he is now a man without welcome into any society. It does not matter where he goes. He is always unwanted. He cannot go back to El Salvador, and he cannot go to Los Angeles. Why? I asked, even though I already knew the answer. He thought for moment about how to respond. He took his baseball cap off and licked his chapped lips—"You see, I got involved in things that were not good. I knew they were sins, but I got involved anyway. Drugs, and . . . ," his voice trailed off.

This man no longer feels that people identify him as belonging to a Salvadoran, Mexican, or American community. His odyssey is not taking him home, nor will it transport him to a better life, but his presence and the presence of scores of other wanderers is transforming the route. They are a growing underclass of transnational homeless men. Their transience generates social ambiguity that complicates the fragile relationship between nationality, territory, and citizenship, revealing the makeshift nature of identity. Thus, they transform the route by facilitating the cultural exchanges that blur social boundaries between migrants and citizens. Passing within the migration corridor blurs the defining traits of nations and renders citizenship boundaries difficult to enforce. Their passing reshapes both the social and material landscape, giving rise to an infrastructure of transit that provides information to both future migrants and those that would prey on them. As the State attempts to impede the movement of people and deport unwanted foreigners, a permanent social transience comes to characterize the stage where migrants, citizens, and state officials encounter one another. Once we travel the route, tracing the footsteps of these migrants through ethnographic method, we see a transnational social process that transforms foreigners and citizens alike.

This concluding chapter highlights the ambiguities produced by this transnational social process. First, I explore the illusive boundaries of transit, emphasizing how the beginning and end of these migration journeys cannot be clearly determined. Second, I draw parallels to transit corridors leading to Europe, showing how the analysis of migrant improvisations in the Americas resonates across regions within a tightening global border regime. Third, I point to how a focus on routes, as opposed to borders, reveals contradictions of liberalism. In other words, I call on scholars to build on *border studies* to develop *route studies*, expanding the insights from borderlands research and bringing those insights into dialogue with politics that unfold far from geographic margins of the nation-state. Analysis of the route shows how the State, via its internal migration policing, actually weakens citizenship for all. Fourth, building on this analysis, I reflect on a methodological and analytical direction for future research. Ultimately, improvised transnationalism does not necessarily undermine the nation-state but instead complicates borders with deleterious consequences for migrants and citizens alike. Our destination as a global society in transit remains unclear. In final thoughts, I discuss the implications of this uncertainty for sovereignty and the State.

A Story of Impossible Return: Blurring the Boundaries
Between Transit, Home, and Destination

Buffeted by unexpected calamities, migrants sometimes become permanent wanderers. Frequent encounters with English speakers, who were acculturated to the United States after residing there for many years, also underscore the illusory nature of boundaries between home, transit, and destination in lived experience. Indefinite journeys, which migrants sometimes undertake without real hope of settling in the United States, complicate the very idea of destination.[2] Somewhere along the way, home, abroad, and in-between become confused. On my last night of fieldwork in the shelter in Ixtepec, Oaxaca, as I was preparing to travel the long road north through the migrant shelters, I met a black Honduran woman, Cindy, who reinforced this impression for me.[3] As I listened to her impeccable English, I was struck by the irony that we were both trying to go home; the juxtaposition of our divergent paths homeward to the United States provided a moment of inspiration that brought many similar stories into focus.

Cindy's gently graying hair had been styled into a crew cut and a baggy shirt concealed her breasts. If not for her voice, I would have assumed she was a thickly built man; with my knowledge of the importance of gender performances en route, I wondered if this so-called masculine style had been assumed as a safety precaution to avoid sexual harassment during the journey or if she always dressed this way, but I did not feel comfortable asking directly. In that moment, both of us longing for home, we were too busy reminiscing to interrupt our shared nostalgia for the United States with seemingly invasive questions. Whatever her gender orientation, Cindy had the kind of smile that always seemed to be winking at you, and I liked her immediately. She had lived in the United States most of her life. As a young girl, she had tired of her dependence on her younger sister's translation from Spanish to express herself in public. For this reason, she had forced herself to learn English well enough to rival any native speaker. When we met that night in the migrant shelter, her mother, sister, and whole family were still in the United States. Cindy alone had lost her legal residency and had been deported to Honduras after "a few" drunk-driving incidents. She told me all this with a smile.

Of course, Cindy's family did not understand the violence unfolding along the route, and she was not going to tell them: "They would worry so much. They know nothing about this." Her mother did not know that Cindy had been robbed and abandoned. Cindy had paid a hundred quetzals, about thirteen dollars, to cross the Guatemala-Mexico border with a woman in a taxi without inspection. This low-budget female coyote took her to Puerto Madero, Chiapas, and introduced her to people with a boat. Cindy paid them to take her to Puerto Escondido, Oaxaca. About ten other people rode on a small boat with her. They were from all over Latin America, with even a few people from Brazil. The boat encountered a storm and big surf, before the captain dropped them on a beach that he proclaimed to be Puerto Escondido. The migrants disembarked the little boat in the rain, but found themselves stranded on a desert island. Cindy laughed incredulously while telling the story, "Can you believe that? I was left on a desert island in Mexico! I would have never guessed. I was on an island in the ocean! There weren't even trees. It was just sand." For Cindy, who had taken her membership in U.S. society for granted until her loss of legal status, this utterly implausible adventure belonged to the plot of a farfetched television sitcom, not real life, and certainly not *her* life.

The island where the smugglers abandoned the migrants was small, and the migrants easily walked its circumference. Luckily, it was raining and they were able to collect rainwater to drink. But she had no food for several days. Finally, some fishermen rescued them; "You should have *seen* the looks on their faces." The fishermen informed the migrants that they were still only a few miles north of the border: "We didn't even make it out of Chiapas! And they had collected three thousand pesos [approximately $240 dollars] from each of us. That's a lot of money. I think they drop people on that island."

The loss of her spending cash had been difficult. Cindy had her U.S. credit card with her, but it did not help. She had been shocked to discover that "These tiny little towns don't have ATMs! There aren't banks!" As she shouted this, I hushed her and hastily explained the danger of boasting about owning a credit card or bank account.[4] Ever more alarmed by her apparent unfamiliarity with the ways of the road and her obvious foreignness in rural Latin America, I asked her how she managed to find the shelter. Cindy explained that some other migrants told her about the shelter in Arriaga, Chiapas, and she followed them there, where she learned about the train.

The experience of the train had been no less surreal than the desert island. She saw people clambering to the top of the boxcars, and she saw one of them fall. There was a big group of Guatemalans with a smuggler, "and they scurried up there like monkeys. There weren't even ladders all the way to the top." She could not fathom how they did it. The tops of the cars were slippery, and she was too scared to climb up. Instead, she found a place wedged below, between two boxcars. She had just a tiny ledge, and she had to hold on for dear life. She tried to tie herself to the train with a belt. She was shaken the whole time by the vibrations of the train. At this point in the conversation, she demonstrated how she sat, with her hands up, holding onto some bars overhead. She even fell asleep that way, because she was so tired: "It was twelve hours in that position!" Another migrant would shout at her, "Don't fall asleep! You'll fall!" And she would wake up.

From Ixtepec, where I met her, Cindy wanted to go to Tijuana, Baja California, on the U.S. border. From there, she expected that she would try to enter with her (now obsolete) green card. She had heard a rumor that it would take six months for her green card loss to be recorded into the U.S. Border Patrol's computer. I doubted whether her passport and green card were likely to survive the journey, and I warned her that it sounded like a fool's errand. Because she seemed so unschooled in Central American and Mexican street life, I encouraged her to consult the shelter priest about safety precautions. However, it was clear that Cindy did not necessarily think her plan would work, and I had the impression that she was still searching for a better idea. What else was she going to do? Nobody in her family knew about contemporary dangers or maintained contacts with smugglers. They had all lived legally in the United States for so long that their information about the journey had expired. She had devised this idea on her own. She would try to pass as a legal resident. In an important sense, Cindy was impersonating her past self.

Remembering Cindy as I write this concluding chapter, I can easily imagine that her odyssey took her to many other unexpected places on a winding and uncertain path, though I am unsure whether she ever returned home. The most desperate migrants become transnational vagabonds across Central America, Mexico, and the United States. In transit, they sometimes become uncertain about the distinction between home and passage; their destination may not be clear to themselves. And because of harsh socioeconomic realities in their birthplace, they become vagabonds long before they ever embark on the migrant road. Across Central America, nation-states have not provided the basic physical stability that, in an important sense, defines home. Whether they make the journey or not, many Central Americans are, in an important sense, strangers to community life. Under long-term conditions of scarcity and insecurity, envy and rumor have taken root, expelling people onto the routes without communal resources. A cycle of poverty, insecurity, and lack of upward mobility make Central Americans outcasts in their own societies.[5] For this reason, the Catholic Church has openly expounded a conditional right to migrate, a right based in the fact of Central American governments' failure to provide a homeland.[6]

The pioneers of Central American migration, like Cindy, who had first gone to the United States decades ago, were unwillingly torn from their birthplace by violence and economic turmoil. Deportees travel the unauthorized routes in desperation. Citizenship may officially mark them as Salvadoran, Honduran, or Guatemalan, but their families, jobs, and lifestyle reveals a de facto membership in a transnational society of the Americas. Permanent transience produced by the conditions of the migration corridor, from home to back again, creates a mismatch between their place of legal domicile (Central America), their physical location (in transit through Mexico), and the place where they feel they belong, or at least, where they feel they might have the opportunity to build a home (the United States). Because of harsh legal realities and mass deportations in their adopted countries, they may be forced to lead vagabond lives long after they have arrived in the United States.

Following deportation from the United States back to Central America, some migrants accumulate days, months, and even years stranded in perpetual transit through Mexico. These people become embedded in relationships and practices along the route from Central America through Mexico and the United States. Their fluid stories complicate the demarcation of distinct spaces of home, transit, and destination. They improvise new directions. A broader social transformation mirrors this personal transformation, as the improvisations of migrants reinvent cultural scripts and reorient the economy in societies of transit. Sustained human movement sweeps citizens and foreigners, and settlers and migrants, into its domain. It spawns new practices and relationships, diversifying the social space of the route, generating new associations, and thereby creating new challenges for the states that would seek to impede these flows.

Beyond the Borders of the Americas

The journey I took while writing this book followed migrants from El Salvador through Mexico and into the United States, and the argument and evidence focuses on this North American migration corridor. Nevertheless, the story told here resonates around the globe, from Mexican migrant shelters that provide a platform for crossing the Arizona desert to makeshift camps in Calais, France, that provide a platform for crossing the English Channel. Transit corridors through the Mediterranean basin and the eastern edges of Europe have suffered from a sudden visibility. Intensified migration policing of these corridors at Europe's periphery—in North Africa, the Mediterranean, and Turkey—has dramatically reordered this migration practice.[7] And these migration routes increasingly reorder the geopolitics of Europe and its neighbors.[8]

Recent scholarship on migrant journeys to Europe has also emphasized ephemeral social interactions as migration resources, thereby suggesting that my argument is not unique to the Americas. That scholarship indicates that increased policing has "fragmented journeys" and forced migrants to use social networks in new ways.[9] Indeed, the journey to Europe has become so fragmented that scholars have begun to challenge the very notion of transit as a discrete experience.[10] Work with African migrants in transit suggests the importance of *weak ties* to cope with a new and more harrowing migration experience.[11] Weak ties are interpersonal relationships with relatively low levels of emotional intensity, trust, and obligations.[12] By providing recognizable scripts and roles for strangers to assume, the performance of gender or nationality can establish new ties along the migration route. In other words, performances of established social scripts help strangers navigate first encounters to achieve some collective understanding of their relationship. For Afghan migrants interviewed in Turkey, the capacity to craft a narrative about their own journey becomes a resource for mobility en route.[13] For migrants arriving by boat in Malta and Cyprus, encounters with fisherman and officials at sea must be negotiated with knowledge of legal and social scripts. In that context, migrants can sometimes leverage the laws of rescue and expected social roles to manipulate officials' reactions and thereby achieve a safe landfall in the desired port of entry.[14] Even when the expectation of durable reciprocity from these encounters is zero, improvisation on social scripts en route provides a migration resource. Migrants improvise on social scripts on both sides of the Atlantic, and this migration resource has become increasingly important under intensified border policing and violence along migration routes to all destinations in the Global North.

Globally, academics have begun to document the relationship between intensified policing and physical dangers (not limited to violence) to migrants at the borders of the European continent.[15] Médecins sans Frontières (MSF) documented a rise in sub-Saharan migrant injury from criminal violence along routes through Morocco to Europe and included a special report on sexual violence suffered by these migrants.[16] Michael Collyer links this criminal violence to a de facto bilateralism in the European-Moroccan relationship that led to a "spatial reconfiguration of migration control": augmented patrols within Moroccan territory as well as at the borders.[17] As a result, transit spaces became increasingly violent places.[18] Analyzing the deaths of migrants in the Mediterranean and their relation to sovereign power, Maurizio Albahari argues that this violence constitutes a "crime of peace" rather than accidental or incidental fatalities.[19]

Borders and Routes: Revealing Contradictions of Liberalism

When we shift the focus from borders to transnational migration routes and the migrant deaths and suffering along them, the contradictions of liberal governance come into sharp contrast. James F. Hollifield identifies a "liberal paradox" in contemporary immigration policies, when sovereign borders clash with liberal ideals of global socioeconomic integration and universal rights.[20] Indeed, liberal governance of globalization takes on a Janus-faced character in practice, welcoming free trade and capital flows while impeding human mobility. The coupling of mass deportations and neoliberal economic policy gives rise to a transnational *securityscape* that connects, but also segregates, the American continent.[21] Within this transnational securityscape, a cultural mobility emerges and challenges the real-world distinctions between citizen/foreigner and settler/transient on which liberal justifications for sovereign borders rest. In other words, migration produces hybridity, giving rise to new and unpredictable cultural recombinations that subvert imagined communities. This ambiguity destabilizes the dichotomies that organize the liberal conceptual map.

The liberal conceptual map organizes itself around binaries, such as free/unfree, open/closed, citizen/foreigner, and settler/transient. These binaries define political subjects and the boundaries of liberal community. However, as this book has shown, the practice of controlling migration, as applied by street-level bureaucrats such as migration agents, further destabilizes notions of the liberal political subject. Liberal subjects may be ordered by gender neutral and ethnically neutral categories of citizen/foreigner and settler/transient. Nevertheless, illiberal categories, such as race, resurface as state instruments in the day-to-day practice of border enforcement, revealing the fiction of universal rights bearing citizens.[22] Such enforcement ultimately harms the very people the state security apparatus claims to protect. Along a transnational route embedded in the transit society, migrants and citizens, and settlers and transients, suffer together.

As national distinctions become illusive, the restriction of territorial access to foreigners without the infringement on citizen rights becomes impossible. The cultural markers and materials associated with nationality become diffused, corrupted, and co-opted. Internal policing of sustained human migration applies arbitrary cultural markers to a brown and gray social reality. Consequently, race and gender, stereotypes of cultural difference used to profile suspected migrants and smugglers, reemerge within the liberal polity. These illiberal categories thereby come to constitute citizenship in practice, and illegality becomes racialized.[23] Whatever the merits of external border enforcement might be, the boundaries between foreigners and citizens, and settlers and migrants, cannot be impartially upheld along transnational routes through the interior of the nation-state.

Now that the state security apparatus recognizes the transnational clandestine routes that run through it and vigorously attempts to control them, the contradictions inherent in the dual fiction of liberal societies with closed borders have surfaced in the extreme form and frequency of violence, both legal and criminal, along the routes. The eruption of these contradictions, in the deaths and violence suffered by migrants, as well as the harassment of citizens by officials along routes, represents a challenge for the delicate bargain between nation-states and individuals. When traditional migrant destination states, such as the United States and European countries, promote *internal* policing to their neighbors, they are exporting an illiberal politics. A cycle of forced return, perpetual movement, and desperation conspire to produce a permanent underclass of transnational homeless people—outcasts by law and made vulnerable by exclusion from it, but regionally integrated along a transnational routes on both sides of the Atlantic.

Indeed, in the global context of intensified migration enforcement and violence within transit states, the impact of these borders is not restricted to the territorial margins of nation-states.[24] The new migration enforcement strategy targets the arteries of the migration system as it crisscrosses the heartlands of nation-states, not just their frontiers: federal governments confer border enforcement authority on local and state police; encourage information sharing and cooperation between law enforcement agencies for these tasks; require identity verifications for employment and services; conduct immigration and drug raids within their territory; establish internal inspection checkpoints (many miles away from the border along major highways and at major domestic transit hubs: bus stops, train stations, etc.); extend roving areas where border control agents may function; and increase criminal penalties for both smugglers and migrants.[25] Legal residents face deportation for nonviolent crimes. Etienne Balibar eloquently summarizes these changes:

> Sometimes noisily and sometimes sneakily, borders have changed place. Whereas traditionally, and in conformity with both their juridical definition and 'cartographical' representation as incorporated in national memory, they should be at the edge of the territory, marking the point where it ends, it seems that borders and the institutional practices corresponding to them have been transported into the middle of political space. They can no longer function as simple edges, external limits of democracy that the mass of citizens can see as a barrier protecting their rights and lives without ever really interfering with them.[26]

Of course, the edges of citizenship have never really been defined in practice.[27] Despite the essentialist rhetoric of fixity necessary to construct the "imagined community," nation-states have always been porous entities born from common "pilgrimages."[28] "Societal security," defined by Ole Waever as "the sustainability within acceptable conditions for evolution of traditional patterns of language, culture, association and religious national identity and custom,"[29] has always been an appendage to that process of national mythmaking, never a reality. Long before "globalization" became a buzzword, state survival depended on the capacity to harness transnational trade, capital, and migratory (and, as Stephen Greenblatt shows us, cultural) flows to their advantage.[30] Even smuggling of ostensibly illegal goods has been manipulated by states for power and resources across history.[31] Cultural and social changes have always accompanied both licit and illicit flows. As explained by Greenblatt's manifesto for the study of cultural mobility, "the reality, for most of the past and come again for the present, is more about nomads than natives."[32] As migration-policing regimes become increasingly repressive in both the Americas and the Mediterranean, the practices of human mobility and survival, with their accompanying social ambiguities, forcefully demonstrate that borders do not enclose or protect the coherent national identities that justify exclusion in a liberal polity.[33]

A story of an informer illustrates this ambiguity and the uncertain ends that some migrants find along a trail that no longer clearly leads them north. In December 2010 in Ixtepec, Oaxaca, where the routes north bottleneck in the Isthmus of Tehuantepec, a mass kidnapping, the murder of a *marero*, and threats against the life of the shelter priest provoked one such conflicted soul to turn informer against his own street gang. When a competing group within his own gang allegedly collaborated with the Zetas, the informer told human rights activists and police.[34] Sometimes his loyalties seemed to lie with the priest and the abused Central Americans along the route. I personally enjoyed his company, and he was well liked among the shelter staff, even while they doubted his capacity to stay out of trouble for long. Killing time with small talk in the dusty yard of the shelter, the informer would shake his head and lament the exploitation of his fellow migrants.[35] On occasion, he would announce his commitment to protect them by any means necessary, savoring the idea of being a sort of *social bandit* riding the rails to bring justice.[36] At other times, he would commit crimes against his fellow migrants or work as a recruiter for smugglers.[37] A cynic might view his testimony to authorities as pure power politics rather than a crisis of conscience.[38] He had murdered people, after all. The informer vied for control of the Arriaga-Ixtepec smuggling corridor with challengers from both inside and outside the ranks of his own gang, and he might have expected the police to clear away his competition for him.

Thus, while the tattoo on the side of his face marked him as a member of the MS-13, his identity was more complicated. By his own admission, he was neither Mexican nor Central American anymore. As an unaccompanied child, he had left Honduras behind, beginning an indefinite odyssey along the train tracks.[39] He improvised a living with the materials at hand and had performed many roles in his time.

When I met him, he had been hiding in the Catholic shelter with a girlfriend, taking refuge from his own gang. He left that shelter for the last time when people began to gossip and warn that someone was coming to get him, whether he remained under the protection of the shelter priest or not. The informer had many enemies, before and after his betrayal, and his ultimate disappearance from the route triggered many rumors. Some people (myself among them) wanted to believe that he had faked his own death and gone into hiding, maybe in Mexico City.[40] However, the general consensus among migrants and shelter staff was that he had died. Some migrants passing through the shelter heard the rumor that his own gang killed him. Others whispered in hushed tones that it was the Zetas who killed him and then dissolved his body in acid.[41] A mutual friend told me different stories on various occasions. When I pressed him on the inconsistencies, he responded with mild exasperation that all the stories were probably true.[42]

In this case, the acceptance of inconsistencies is not evasive; it is instructive about the nature of truth, violence, and uncertainty along the migratory route. Given the complex and fluid relationships along the route, there will never be a final answer about the violence—who did it and why. There is no expectation that a court of law can arrive at the truth, and there is no expectation among migrants that only one uncontestable truth about violence exists. Indeed, when I asked a legal advocate for migrants about the possibility of justice in the courts, she laughed, "Justice ... ha ha ... that's a big word. Go ask the priest about that." In an uncertain context that implicates authorities in violence, this attitude is simply realistic, not jaded. Within an ambiguous and uncertain social structure, multiple plausible alternative versions of a violent event can coexist, long after formal arrests have been made and the official investigation comes to a close. As Ellen Moodie explains in her analysis of the sociopolitical role of crime narratives in the aftermath of the Salvadoran peace accords:

> What is important is that people imagined a common shape of their world. What is important that the stories had patterns—and that they were seen (or rather, heard) as possible. ... They created convictions, social facts, structures of feelings, senses of reality that had effects. They had consequences in and on the world. Consciousness cannot be false in that sense.[43]

The coexistence of multiple unofficial versions (and the lack of credibility of official versions) of criminal events says something important about the actors and alliances that perpetrate that violence. The relationships among these actors are extraordinarily flexible. Along the route, people betray their loyalties, transgress agreements, and rebuild relationships. People may not be able to distinguish between kidnappers, authorities, smugglers, and migrants, because individuals switch roles without warning. The uncertainty produced by such ambiguities has a profound impact on how migrants and smugglers navigate the route.

Faced with this uncertainty, migrants and smugglers redouble their improvisations on identities, transforming the social roles available to them and discovering new paths forward. They subvert expectations for their social performances and migration practice to their advantage. In so doing, they shape a new society in their wake. Of course, migrants are not the only people who participate in this transformative process. A larger social conversion unfolds, as transnational routes become transmission belts for newly improvised practices and roles.[44] As a result of the possibility for surprising personal and social transformations, the route becomes an increasingly ambiguous place. Possibilities for concealment and betrayal complicate trust and render the behavior of travel companions unpredictable. Local communities both trade with and prey on the transients in their midst, producing uncertain loyalties among migrants and citizens alike. Under the constant barrage of new faces and intensifying violence along the route, the social roles and relationships that underpin both settlement and migration become untethered.

A Final Tragedy

Migrants and citizens transcend national categories and complicate territorial control, but the State has its revenge. People suffer and sometimes die during unauthorized migration. As Rocío Magañas explains, nation-states use migrants' deaths as a stage to project their authority.[45] She argues that the Mexican state's management of death converts its failure to protect lives into a perverse expression of its agency. In other words, the efficient management of this bureaucratic process demonstrates state capacity.[46] The State "performs" its sovereignty in the behind-the-scenes negotiation of which bodies belong to what country, as well as in the front stage act of returning them to their proper burial place. The theatrical and political value of these acts has not been lost on government officials, who honor the dead. For example, following the massacre of seventy-two migrants in Tamaulipas, flag-draped coffins of migrants returned to El Salvador in an official ceremony.[47]

For this reason, we must remember that unauthorized migration is never a fully autonomous activity, and the micropolitics of migrant death illustrate how people also become unwilling props in a macabre theatre of the State. This became clear to me as I stared, transfixed, by the digital photograph of the dead man displayed on the computer in the office of the migrant shelter.[48] I saw a young man with a tattoo around his neck and the initials ES tattooed in Old English across his chest. His face was swollen purple with dried blood filling his mouth, and he had a large open wound over his eye. His legs twisted oddly. He had been thrown from a train two days prior. On his body, they found the artifacts of a transnational life: an identification card and recording of a birth in Usulutan, El Salvador, in 1988, alongside a Six Flags 2010 season "Play Pass" issued in California less than seven months before his demise. Tattoos branded him as a gang member, but something was wrong with the official documents. One of the migrants in the shelter, peering over the shoulder of the office manager at the photos, claimed to have seen the boy in the photo on the identification cards alive and well on the tracks.

The body had now become a prop in other people's performances. His death sent a message: to fear the gangs and to obey their rules. And now his corpse played a part in a farcical death of another mysterious young man known along the route only by a nickname, not the words inscribed on his identification cards. But the dead man, who lay there on the side of the train tracks, played these parts unknowingly.

Later that day, two men arrived, one of them wearing a black vest with the yellow letters AEI (the initials of a Mexican law enforcement agency that investigates homicides) scrolled across the back. Whispers erupted among the migrants as they watched the office door close behind the police, and the speculative drama unfolding around the body hit a crescendo. Rumors circulated. At one point, someone claimed to know that the dead man was, in fact, Panamanian. But this theory was quickly dismissed; Panamanians do not usually run with the street kids that live along the tracks in Southern Mexico.[49] The Mexican police had to identify the body to repatriate it through the appropriate consulate, and they asked the shelter for help. The shelter manager questioned the migrants known to have friends in the gangs, which included most anybody who spent significant time living in the shelter. Several of the dead man's friends could identify the victim only by his nickname and reputation, not his family names.

Ultimately, a tattoo of a Salvadoran flag on his arm helped to lead to his burial in El Salvador, rather than an anonymous grave in Mexico.[50] Together, shelter staff, migrants, Mexican police, and Salvadoran consular officials came to a consensus about the national identity of the body, each performing a crucial role in its identification.[51] They redefined their relationships with one another, in this instance collaborating to know the transnational route and the dangers that lurk along it. In accepting a conclusion, they renegotiated and reconfirmed the symbols and material that delineate nationality.

This process continues in Mexico on a larger scale as forensic teams investigate mass graves of people presumed to be migrants and attempt to identify the proper consulates to carry home the bodies. In August 2010, Mexican authorities discovered a mass grave of more than seventy-two migrants from El Salvador, Guatemala, Honduras, Brazil, and Ecuador, but the nationality of at least twelve of those migrants could not be identified. That highly publicized massacre marked only the first discovery of a mass grave of migrants; more mass exhumations and repatriations of foreign nationals have followed.[52] The bodies are props in the opening scene of an unfolding drama between competing drug gangs and smugglers, and the discovery of mass graves becomes the set for the next act in which national governments claim those bodies as citizens.[53] The Mexican government must identify each body with a nationality for shipment to country of citizenship.

Indeed, the process of returning the dead mirrors, however imperfectly, the process of identifying and deporting living migrants.[54] To do so, forensic anthropologists search for the informal cultural tells that can help identify nationality, ranging from tattoos to the prayer cards of local saints to national currency.[55] They improvise on the objects intended for other purposes, things that are carried as an expression of faith, serve as personal mementos, or facilitate economic exchange; they must transform these artifacts into evidence supporting a performance of national sovereignty: repatriation. Such objects become contested sites that redefine the State and citizens, and even what it means to be human.[56]

A desire to provide closure to the families of the dead motivates anthropologists and human rights advocates, but in the process, they must learn to read nationality when it has been unintentionally obscured by transnational lifestyles or intentionally disguised to mislead police.[57] Human rights advocates must convince families to collaborate with government bureaucrats and scientists to assign nationality and receive an institutional response. As they establish the nationality of the deceased, the participants in this drama establish new cooperative roles for actors along the route. In other words, human rights activists and migrant families must briefly overcome the contentious scripts that usually attend their relationship with the State. The State attempts to reassert its sovereignty, claiming the authority and capacity to categorize the dead, but it must collaborate with social actors to do so.[58] Even when migrants fail in their quest to arrive safely in the United States, their drama changes the theater of the State; the State becomes tasked with repatriating the dead rather than protecting the living.[59] Or alternatively, in the absence of effective advocacy for migrant families, the State allows unidentified bodies to rot or succumb to exposure, in what Jason De León labels *necroviolence:* a form of state discipline imposed by sacrilegious or offensive treatment of corpses.[60] Such violence leaves a wake of ambiguity, loss, and profound suffering, mixed with desperate hope, for the families of migrants.[61] Either way, however, deceased migrants impact the politics of sovereignty.

Sovereignty, defined most simply as the authority and capacity to control territory, is the central organizing concept of the study of international relations (IR). From scholarship on migration that bridges IR and anthropology, we know that in the Americas and the Mediterranean, the humanitarian crisis of the routes evidenced by these deaths is "a crisis of sovereignty that is repeatedly instigated, first and foremost, by diverse manifestations of the autonomous subjectivity of human mobility itself."[62] Under international law, states do not have the authority to control refugee flows with the heavy-handed tactics they currently employ: denying asylum seekers the right to due process, illegally repatriating refugees to dangerous situations against the principle of non-refoulment, and routinely deporting victims of human rights abuses such as trafficking. Furthermore, the capacity of destination states to prevent such flows relies on the outsourcing of enforcement to transit states along the periphery, undermining the notion of an autonomous State with the capacity to defend its own territory. Scenes of border crossings expose the sovereign stagecraft of policymakers.

For this reason, a burgeoning ethnographic literature examines migrant agency to challenge mainstream concepts of sovereignty, security, and citizenship.[63] Contributing to this literature, I have also focused on how human mobility becomes enacted by migrants, both despite and because of the State. However, the final tragedy reminds us that the State performs with a diversity of audiences, improvising its own scripts and relationships, and shaping the human drama that unfolds along the route.[64] Dead bodies of migrants, left to rot in the desert, become props to demonstrate the risks of the journey to potential trespassers.[65] Repatriated bodies, whether dead or alive, rewrite the role of the State, assigning new purpose.[66] Encounters with migration police become "a border spectacle" of exclusion for audiences both foreign and domestic.[67] Walls at borders become a "theatrical object" that performs sovereignty, while paradoxically materially demonstrating state weaknesses.[68] The State even improvises on the language of humanitarianism to justify further securitization of the border, leveraging scenes of suffering migrants and scripts of "rescue" to justify further interdiction efforts.[69]

Finally, the State exploits its capacity to demarcate "on-stage" and "off-stage" practices, benefiting from clandestinity every bit as much as underground actors do. Through the transnationalization and thickening of border policing, human rights violations are offshored, pushed outside of the domestic public view.[70] The State draws curtains around migrant detention facilities, limiting their transparency and accountability to migrant advocates.[71] In his analysis of the production of illegality on the fringes of Europe, Ruben Andersson notes that Frontex employs "a communications strategy that aimed to strike a balance between visibility and invisibility—promoting Frontex just enough while letting it work in the shadows, leaving both glory and blame to the host state."[72] Similarly self-aware of the politics of information projection, the U.S. Border Patrol hires public relations firms to manage its image for constituents and potential recruits at home, while relaying the dangers of border crossings to audiences abroad. Perhaps less self-aware, academics and journalists also become unwitting actors, collaborating with the State by conveying images of risk to the public or re-creating melodramas with oversimplified victims and villains.[73]

Indeed, recent scholarship that builds on feminist approaches to security highlight the performative, contested, and improvised nature of borders themselves.[74] This research suggests that an analytical focus on the performativity of everyday state practice, as well as migration practice, potentially unsettles sovereignty by spotlighting the ongoing nature of state making.[75] By exposing the everyday stagecraft at the center of border politics, the dialogue between anthropology and IR becomes a political act. To conduct further research in this vein, ethnographers must trespass difficult logistical boundaries, gaining access to the State as a field site, which is one explanation of why ethnography has made small inroads into IR.[76] In the sort of nights that keep researchers awake, puzzling over the politics of their own role in the theater of borders, I have often felt wary about the relative ease with which I could interview a vulnerable, clandestine population, migrants whose very survival depends on being undocumented and illegible to the State. It is much more difficult to witness the inner workings of the State itself; the entry points to the State are more closely guarded than the entry points to the underground. Based on my own fieldwork experiences, the ethics and logistics of listening to people experiencing confinements at home (trapped by state repression or criminal violence, for example) can sometimes be more challenging than listening to people still moving through the clandestine corridors.[77] Transnational mobility, and its accompanying possibilities for anonymity and distance, produces unexpected opportunity for voice, even for a vulnerable population of migrants. Immobility, which by definition denies such possibilities, implies unique ethical and safety challenges for ethnographers and their research participants. Continued reflection on the boundaries that researchers trespass and reinforce, whether wittingly or unwittingly, in their fieldwork performances can help us understand the ongoing construction of the nation-state and its limits. Power and politics makes such access and the task of "ethnography of the State" an inherently difficult, but ever more important, next step for this research on the route.[78]

Moving forward in this way, scholars must continue to be attentive to the lived experience of im/mobility—and by that I mean the various ways migrants must forfeit their agency at key points during the journey to facilitate mobility.[79] For example, migrants may allow a smuggler to lock them in a hidden compartment, file an asylum claim through a slow and tedious bureaucratic process in a detention facility, or wait at a migrant shelter for resources to continue their journey.[80] In those examples, migrants experience moments of what Martha Balaguera calls "confinement in motion," which demonstrate how the State structures a carceral politics along the route, limiting possibility.[81] Binary notions of mobility and immobility, settlement and transit, and citizen and outsider fail to capture this reality or its implications for state sovereignty.

In fact, a state-structured vulnerability haunts people of the transnational corridor, whether or not they ever leave home. For example, a man who had voluntarily returned to El Salvador from the United States, leaving most of his family in the adopted homeland, echoed a common sentiment among the people left behind: "To be a migrant is to be exploited . . . migrants are migrants, whether they move or not." With these words, he expressed both a profound sense of alienation in his country of origin and a resignation to his family's transnational destiny. The experience of undocumented migration and international displacement is neither a rupture nor a transition from citizen to outsider. Instead Central American migrants' lived experience of illegality simply perpetuates the lack of membership in their so-called homeland; even the people who never leave Central America are, in an important sense, transients trapped in their own polity.[82]

This final act reinforces the point that the nation-state and its boundaries have a lingering impact on the world, but sovereignty remains incomplete and continually redefined in relation to the trespassing it portends to protect against.[83] The human and cultural movement within the transnational corridor troubles the imagined boundaries between settlement/transit and citizen/foreigner. As people leverage national, racial, and class stereotypes and material artifacts to move across territory, transnational migration flows demonstrate tremendous resilience. However, the resilience of this practice comes with a terrible human cost, illustrated in this example by the mass graves that mar the landscape of Mexico. The State thwarts many transnational dreams, imposing immobility and suffering on would-be migrants. Thus, a methodology that *performs* ethnography exposes the theatrical nature of this sovereignty, and migrants' own *survival plays* spotlight the backstage villainy of the State, but with no curtain call on the tragedy of borders in the near future.

ACKNOWLEDGMENTS

This book is an artifact of a long ethnographic journey, an odyssey that I began many years before I realized I had embarked on anything of the sort. For this reason, I have accumulated many debts, and I cannot possibly do justice to them all. I will start, however, by thanking my father, J. Kraig Brigden, and my mother, Katie Kelly. From my childhood in southern California in the 1980s, I remember the queues of migrant men waiting at street corners, hoping to catch a day of labor, and my parents' righteous anger at the failure of our society to guarantee these workers' rights and well-being. My father in particular raised me on stories of the Great Depression that echoed the images of inequality before my eyes. Without a doubt, the work presented here draws on this social imaginary and ethics.

To my father, I also owe the somewhat dubious gift I have for stubbornness, rebelliousness, and learning from the rough hand of experience. He unwittingly bred an ethnographer. As a child, I once threatened to run away to join the temporary settlements of migrants living in cardboard boxes in the canyons outside San Diego. These camps sometimes sprouted up within sight of the homes that employed Spanish-speaking housekeepers and gardeners. I had forgotten some of those scenes until I found myself sleeping on a cardboard box in a crowded cement room with Central American migrants en route to the United States. Only then did it occur to me that perhaps this research is, in some way, a long-forgotten promise kept.

When as a teenager, I joined the Army; I traveled the world only to find that Tijuana seemed to be following me wherever I went. Around military bases and border towns, the same local economy thrived: saloons, brothels, cheap clothing, and tacky souvenirs, all animated by gray and black markets of every sort. The experience engendered a respect for the everyday practice of the global economy and a sense of the larger political system in which unauthorized transactions take place. During my time in the military, my father and I often talked philosophically about these observations and traded stories of our misadventures. I thank him for letting his daughter teach him about the world, which in turn is the most valuable lesson he has given me. I wish he had lived long enough to read this book.

My intellectual debts accumulated rapidly during my return to college after my enlistment. I thank the wonderful counselors and professors at Colorado Mountain College, a community college in the Rockies, for encouraging me and informing me about the possibilities in higher education. Jon Van Goethem taught me English and shaped my prose into something much more coherent and clear. Lupita Benítez taught me Spanish, which became invaluable for conducting this research. Laurie Marano from the TRiO Student Support Services program played a special role, propelling me on the journey that culminated in this book. In these times when government-funded programs that support low-income and disabled college students, like TRiO, face dramatic budget cuts, it is worth noting that such resources made my transition from military to civilian, from high-school dropout to doctorate, and from aspiring student to published author possible. This book would not likely have been written without such an important public resource.

At the University of Denver, my teacher, mentor, and friend George DeMartino showed me the value of intellectual courage. Friends like Tangi Lancaster, Claudia Minoiu, Kerry West, and Suzette Holiday made it possible for me to continue my studies despite a surprise pregnancy before finishing my undergraduate degree. If it takes a village to raise a child, it takes a particularly kind and generous village to write a book while raising a child.

In my doctoral program at Cornell University, I had the great fortune to be mentored by Peter J. Katzenstein, who has a well-earned, epic reputation. At a personal level, I cannot express the gratitude I feel for his brilliance, guidance, patience, trust, and support throughout my training as a social scientist. More generally, Peter has opened intellectual space in the discipline of political science and continues to defend creativity and real-world relevance in academia. Richard Bensel has also played a profound and generous role in my intellectual development and the research that informed this book. Long conversations with Richard, both in person and via email, have provided much inspiration for the work presented here. I hope some of his genius has rubbed off along the way. Kenneth Roberts has offered many perceptive comments and excellent fieldwork advice. In particular, his rich understanding of the Latin American social and political reality has been invaluable to the project. Christopher Way has always been a great advisor and teacher. His sharp intellect and natural enthusiasm for the process of discovery have prevented me from making many grave errors along the way. Michael Jones-Correa has provided insightful commentary on this work.

Of course, my debts during graduate school were not limited to the Cornell faculty. Over the years, both during and after graduation, my student cohort has been a font for creative conversations, instructive tips for navigating research, and emotional support (and sometimes even emergency childcare). Since that beginning, Jennifer Erickson, Maria Sperandei, Jen Hadden, Phil Ayoub, Danielle Cohen, Daniel Kinderman, Andrew Yeo, Kristin McKie, Sinja Graf, Pinar Kemerli, Desmond Jagmohan, and Alison McQueen have kept me sane. Alice Michtom, a dear friend from those Cornell days, has passed away, but I still imagine conversations with her when playing with ideas or coping with the stress of research. The brilliant Lucia A. Seybert was a source of intellectual and emotional inspiration, and the epitome of grace and genius rolled into one. As I completed this manuscript, I watched her struggle against cancer with unparalleled dignity and courage. I'm sorry she did not live to see its completion.

Several people have graciously read early ideas or drafts of chapters in development, providing key feedback: Alexandia Innes, Alison Mountz, Joe Wiltberger, Maria Lorena Cook, Susan Bibler Coutin, Ronald Herring, Jared McCormick, Paul Roge, Shoshana Perry, Guarav Kampani, Don Leonard, Lisa Björkman, Steve Samford, Burke Hendrix, Angelica Duran Martínez, Paola Eisner, Kristian Berg Harpviken, Celeste Montoya, Kristen Hill

Maher, Nukhet Sandal, Jan Kubik, Katrina Burgess, Susan Ellison, Thea Riofrancos, Patrick James, John Mollenkopf, Alejandro Olayo-Méndez, Gabriella Sánchez, Roxani Krystalli, Aysen Üstubici, Lindsay Goss, Neepa Acharya, Amalia Campos-Delgado, Noora Lori, Margaret Walton-Roberts, Cristina Dragomir, Lindsey Carte, Carmen Fernández, Priscilla Solano, Santiago Martínez Junco, and Geoffrey MacDonald. Conversations with Sonja Wolf have also been extraordinarily helpful for understanding both El Salvador and Mexico. I would like it on the record that, in addition to being a wonderful intellectual collaborator, Cetta Mainwaring is the best dancer in the study of international relations. I am grateful to contributors to an online symposium of my work, who pushed me to explore the larger implications of my argument for the concept of sovereignty: Stephan Scheel, Nora El Qadim, and Philippe M. Frowd.

During fieldwork, I depended on the kindness and intelligence of several key colleagues and gatekeepers. Kay Andrade Eekhoff made my smooth transition to fieldwork possible. I thank her for sharing her extensive knowledge of Salvadoran migration and also, for keeping a watchful eye over my family's safety. I often turned to her as a voice of reason when tempted to take unnecessary risks, and she kept me on a sane, healthy path. A very special thanks to Sister Barbara Dundon of the Sisters of the Sacred Hearts of Jesus and Mary for her wisdom and guidance during my time in El Salvador. The convent became a home away from home. The sight of its Coca-Cola fridge on a hot day is a very happy memory. Journalist Óscar Martínez kindly gave me logistical advice about fieldwork along the train route, helping me balance research with the safety of my family.

In Mexico, Padre Jose Alejandro Solalinde Guerra of the Hermanos en el Camino shelter in Ixtepec, Oaxaca, granted extraordinary access and inspiration for understanding the route. Conversations with the late Alberto Donis Rodriguez also provided much insight. Activist Ireneo Mujica, whom I accompanied for several noteworthy adventures, has become a lifelong friend and continues to shape my understanding of the migration corridor with updates from afar. My time at the shelter was the experience of a lifetime, and I encourage curious readers to go there themselves. Ali Baker, Anne Schaufele, Elizabeth Kennedy, Natalia del Cid, Catalina del Cid, and Wendy Vogt have all become my very special research sisters along the route. Amelia Frank-Vitale became my twin sister, attached at the keyboard, if not the hip. I hope the sisterhood of the route continues to collaborate in the future. To

Janice Gallagher, I owe a personal debt for a fateful day of babysitting in Puerto Escondido. She knows what I'm talking about. Many friends made fieldwork enjoyable for my family: Tere and Julio, Eliza and Manuel, Isabel, Jeanie and Rob, Jerianne, Heidi and Paolo, and Gilles, along with the imported beer selection at Mopelia.

A special thanks goes to the anonymous mapmakers. These people imagined and remembered their journeys and took time to draw their experiences for me, sometimes over the course of many hours and even days. During the informed consent procedure governed by Cornell University Institutional Review Board, I promised anonymity to all participants. Therefore, I cannot thank them by name here, but I deeply appreciate their artwork and willingness to share their lives with me. I also could not include every map in this book, but I am grateful for all of them. Another special thanks to the ever talented Encarni Pindado and Nico Jankowski for permission to use their photographs of the mural in the shelter and the people on the train, and thanks to Rodolfo Casillas for his kind support and permission to use his map of the route.

This book underwent dramatic revision during my postdoctoral year at the Watson Institute for International Studies at Brown University, where I was fortunate to have Peter Andreas providing feedback on the manuscript. At Brown, Jose Itzigsohn and Richard Snyder also provided helpful feedback. And of course, I am in both intellectual and personal debt to my friend, colleague, and perennial dance partner Giovanni Mantilla, who has both helped me through the process of writing and guided me through my midlife crisis. The final stages of the manuscript underwent revision while on a research fellowship at the Princeton Institute for International and Regional Studies, where I had the great fortune to be office mates with David Cortez, and I relied on long conversations with María Inclán, Gyoonho Kong, and Pablo Domínguez Galbraith to stay motivated in my work. Special thanks to Carly Johnstone, my favorite rebel girl, for the adulting lessons and for making me feel less lonely while away from home.

At my home institution, Marquette University, I have a brilliant, generous community of colleagues who support me. Barry McCormick and Michael McCarthy have both read and provided detailed comments on chapters. Rich Friman was also supportive. As my department chair, Lowell Barrington has repeatedly gone to bat for me with the university administration to make sure that I had the resources necessary to complete the project in a timely manner. My Marquette colleague Jessica Rich deserves a special thanks. Whether I was hearing her laughter through my office wall in Milwaukee, binge-eating mangos late night in San Juan, dragging my teenager on a "death march" through the streets of Lima, furiously Facebook messaging about my latest crisis from opposite sides of the globe, or having serious intellectual debates and exchanging papers for commentary, Jessica has been a source of inspiration and fortitude for my writing.

Several institutions deserve thanks. I received fieldwork funding from the National Science Foundation's Dissertation Research Improvement Grant, the Bucerius Scholarship Program in Migration Studies "Settling into Motion" from the ZEIT-Stiftung, the Social Science Research Council's International Dissertation Research Fellowship, the Fulbright-Garcia Robles Scholarship, the Institute for the Social Sciences and the Einaudi Center for International Studies at Cornell University, and the Center for Transnational Justice at Marquette University.

At Cornell University Press, I never doubted that my manuscript was in the best hands—those of the skilled, witty, and patient Roger Haydon. Two reviewers have greatly improved the manuscript with constructive criticism and brilliant suggestions. One remains anonymous, and the other is David Spener, whose work has provided a strong analytical foundation for my own thoughts about smuggling since the beginning of the project.

Family members have long tolerated my eccentricities and frequently bailed me out of trouble. My Aunt Sally and Uncle Dick Brigden took me in during a crucial period of my life, and my Aunt Anne Fisher nursed me back to health after the spinal injury that precipitated my military discharge. For nearly two decades, my in-laws John and Rosemary Martin have played a central role in my education and career. Their love, support, and example have been a beacon to me, and I am so fortunate to have them as the grandparents of my children.

Throughout this journey, my husband and children have made this work happen. My partner John Martin has followed me from Germany to Colorado to New York to El Salvador to Mexico to Rhode Island to Wisconsin, and he has tolerated my tendency to suddenly trot around the globe and leave him in new, strange places with children to tend. I love you, John. In the process, our son James Kraig Martin has adapted to a migratory life with grace and dignity. James was my little "research assistant" for much of this work. I love you, and I'm unspeakably proud of you, James. I discovered I was pregnant with our daughter Etta Rose Brigden in a migrant shelter in Saltillo, en route to the United States. When she was born, I was almost too busy explaining my research to the anesthesiologist to notice that my cesarean had ended. Beginning with that moment, the first five years of her life have been overshadowed by her mother's anxious obsession with this manuscript, and to her, I would like to apologize and ask forgiveness. I love you, and I'm sorry for missing so much time with you, Etta. And thank you for bringing me home.

Finally, I thank the many Central American men and women who taught me during this project. To them I hope to keep my unspoken promises, made while I listened in silence to stories of injustices suffered. While I am sure there is, in this book, much with which many individual participants in interviews would disagree, I hope that I have successfully conveyed their dignity.

Portions of the manuscript were published as:

Noelle K. Brigden. 2016. "Improvised Transnationalism: Clandestine Migration at the Border of Anthropology and International Relations." *International Studies Quarterly* 60 (2): 343–354, doi: 10.1093/isq/sqw010.

Noelle K. Brigden. 2017. "Gender Mobility: Survival Plays and Performing Central American Migration in Passage." *Mobilities* 13 (1): 112–125, https://www.tandfonline.com/doi/abs/10.1080/17450101.2017.1292056.

Noelle K. Brigden. 2017. "On Metaphors, Motion and Methods: A Response." In "Symposium: Walking with Migrants: Ethnography as Method in International Relations," Meera Sabaratnam et al., Harvard Dataverse, V1, doi:10.7910/DVN/WUK8AN.

Noelle K. Brigden. 2018. "A Visible Geography of Invisible Journeys: Central American Migration and the Politics of Survival." *International Journal of Migration and Border Studies* 4(1/2): 71–88.

Notes

1. The Opening Scene: A Journey Begins

1. All names are pseudonyms.

2. Special travel packages for pregnant women, infants, disabled people, or other vulnerable people can run much higher in price.

3. Andreas 2000.

4. This motif recurs in the map of another would-be migrant, whom I will call Noemi.

5. On the difference between risk and uncertainty, see Blyth 2006, Giddens 1999, Keynes 1948, and Knight 1921.

6. For sophisticated work on how migration practice and smuggling is socially embedded in migrant sending communities, see, for example, Gaytan et al. 2007; Kyle 2000; Kyle and Scarcelli 2009; Singer and Massey 1998; Spener 2001, 2004, 2009.

7. See Mainwaring and Brigden 2016 for a critique of this oversight. Important early exceptions include a growing literature on transit migration, primarily examining from the European context. See for example: Collyer 2010; Collyer, Düvell, and de Haas 2012; Düvell 2012; BenEzer and Zetter 2015; Khosravi 2011. Outside academia,

readers can find ample journalism exploring migrant journeys on both sides of the Atlantic. See, for example, Kenyon 2009, Martínez 2015, Moorehead 2005, Nazario 2006.

8. Ibid. For an excellent unpacking of the journey that interviews migrants en route but focuses primarily on the U.S.-Mexico divide, see De León 2015.

9. Greenblatt 2005, 165.

10. Ibid.

11. Brigden 2014.

12. Mainwaring 2016, p.3.

13. See, for example, Hobson and Seabrooke 2007, Hopf 2013.

14. Salter 2008.

15. Anzaldua 2007, 25.

16. Andreas 2003; Rosas 2012; Salter 2004; Sassen 1996. On both sides of the Atlantic, border control is no longer isolated at the geographic periphery of destination countries, but instead executed through international cooperation and surveillance and a shifting of control and asylum responsibilities to neighboring countries, rather than traditional destinations (Brigden and Mainwaring 2016). Borders themselves have become "mobile," internally and externally (Mountz 2010).

17. Rosas 2012.

18. Ibid.

19. Rosas 2012: 101.

20. Galemba 2017, Mountz 2010, Rosas 2012.

21. For extensive journalistic accounts of the dangerous journey from Central America to Mexico, see Martínez 2010, Martinez 2013, and Nazario 2006.

22. See, for example, Frelick 1991.

23. Amnesty International 2010, CDHDF 2011, Vogt 2013.

24. CNDH 2009, 2011.

25. More corpses were later discovered at this same site.

26. Rosas 2012.

27. Bonello 2016, de León 2015, Kristof 2016.

28. Cornelius 2001, de León 2015, Eschbach et al. 1999.

29. Casillas 2007, Isaacson, Meyer, and Morales 2014, Martínez 2011, Rosas 2012.

30. Casillas 2007, Chávez-Suárez 2013, Galemba 2017.

31. Bonello 2016; ICG 2016; Isaacson, Meyer, and Morales 2014.

32. Wilkinson 2010.

33. Ibid.

34. Quoted in Archibald 2010.

35. O'Donnell 2004, 41.

36. Galemba 2017; Rosas 2012, 106.

37. The historical process of making sedentary state subjects was (and is) coercive. For this reason, James Scott (2009) understands ungovernable borderlands of early states as zones of relative freedom, necessary for the maintenance of nascent state orders. However, unlike the borderlands described by Scott, the contemporary borderlands are not a utopian, stateless space.

38. Archibald 2013, Miroff 2012.

39. While migrants engage in illegal entry, I use the term "criminal" as shorthand for violent or exploitive criminals, rather than those people engaged in a class of "victimless" crimes.

40. In her study of migrant disillusionment in receiving communities on Long Island, Sarah Mahler (1995, 75–81) described the often-painful personal transformation that the journey entails.

41. Primo Levi (1988, 36–49) understood this transformative space as a "gray zone" where victims and bystanders unintentionally or intentionally commit violence while attempting to survive, blurring the boundary between master and slave, perpetrator and victim. Survival often requires subtle forms of collaboration with victimizers.

42. Likewise, genocidal violence is a dynamic process with the power to transform identities and complicate categories of "perpetrator," "victim," "bystander," and "rescuer" as people occupy multiple positions or change their positions in response to a shifting context over time (Fujii 2009, 8–11).

43. Some accounts of "globalization from below" offer reason for optimism concerning the potential of solidarity of peoples in communities that transcend the nation-state (Keck and Sikkink 1998, Soysal 1995). The experience of violence and injustice can encourage solidarity, political participation, and collective resistance to oppression (Wood 2003). A shared migrant identity, for example, can facilitate collective resistance to violence among Central Americans in transit through Mexico (Frank-Vitale 2011). The journey can also create allies of strangers in a time of need and generate a sense of community en route. However, escalating violence has recently unleashed a seemingly contradictory tendency toward both social fragmentation and displays of solidarity (Vogt 2012, 17). In fact, the potential for complex responses that transcend the dichotomy between disloyalty and solidarity increase the unpredictability of individual reactions to violence.

44. Coutin 2005.

45. For a paired comparison of two Salvadoran migrant communities that arrives at this point, see Brigden 2014.

46. Kamal Sadiq (2009) also draws our attention to "blurred citizenship" and the limited capacity of the state to distinguish between citizens and migrants, thereby complicating governance. In subsequent chapters, I will explore how his approach to identity differs dramatically from my own, with consequences for our understanding of policy.

47. See, for example, Keohane and Nye 1977, Ruggie 1993.

48. Castells 1996, Sassen 2006.

49. Appadurai 1996.

50. Andreas 2009.

51. See, for example, Kahler 2009, Keohane and Nye 1998.

52. Adamson and Demetriou 2007, Itzigsohn 2000.

53. See, for example, Doty 2006, Berman 2003.

54. Müller 2008.

55. Heyman 1999, Schneider and Schneider 2008.

56. Andreas 2009, Magañas 2011.

57. Mahler 1999, 72.

58. Conley 2007, 1–2.

59. Mainwaring and Brigden 2016.

60. See also De León 2015.

61. Andreas 2009, De León 2015, Magañas 2011.

2. The Plot: Migration Stories Take Shape

1. Interview in El Salvador, April 11, 2010.

2. Interview in El Salvador, April 18, 2010.

3. Over fifty Catholic shelters provide the poorest migrants a place of respite during their journey north through Mexico.

4. Coutin 2016, 56–57.

5. Ibid.

6. Adler and Pouliot 2011, 7.

7. Brigden and Andreas 2018; Jones 2012, 687.

8. The empirical chapters that follow build on this discussion, elaborating on the method in even greater depth and demonstrating its utility for uncovering inductive insights.

9. Interview in El Salvador, March 1, 2010.

10. The baby's sunken facial features and distorted size suggested the possibility of impending death to me, but I do not know what happened to her ultimately. She may have survived.

11. Clifford Geertz (1973, 5–6) famously calls this "thick description." For a discussion of the value of immersive experience for understanding power in political science, see Schatz 2009.

12. This is not to say that surveys have no place in migration research.

13. Pieke 1995.

14. Yanow 2009, 292.

15. Tilly 2006.

16. Summarizing these interdisciplinary standards, Richardson (2000) argues that ethnography should be a well-written, self-conscious, and systematic work that resonates with the reader as credible and valuable depiction of the "real" social world under study.

17. Tilly 2006.

18. For a well-founded warning about how such research can devolve into academic voyeurism, see De León 2015.

19. Marcus 1995.

20. For a lengthier discussion of the methodological challenges and advantages of extended field sites, see the appendix in Andersson (2014).

21. I wrote notes during interviews and whenever I could in the course of each day. I then transcribed these handwritten notes on the computer each night. I did not record interviews. Instead, all quotes have been reconstructed from shorthand. The vast majority of interviews and informal conversations were in Spanish, but I also con-

ducted a handful of interviews in English, in some cases alternating between the two languages. In all cases, the preference of the participant determined which language was used.

22. I discuss these workshops in greater depth in Chapter 5.

23. I conducted this follow-up fieldwork to develop a sense of recent changes in migration practice, but I did not conduct interviews at that time.

24. Interview in El Salvador, April 18, 2010.

25. See, for example, Coutin 2005; Galemba 2012; Heyman and Smart 1999; Nordstrom 2007; Abraham and van Schendel 2005; Watts 2008.

26. Coutin 2005.

27. Jourde 2009, 201.

28. Aradau and Huysmans 2013, Squire 2011.

29. Spener 2009, 95.

30. De León 2015.

31. See De León's (2015, 160) description of Altar and Sasabe's markets for travel technology and accessories, for example.

32. For a compatible definition of the social imaginary, see Taylor 2004, 23. On the "gaps" in the social imaginary that migrants can exploit, see Coutin 2016.

33. Cohen 2004, 5.

34. Bourdieu (1977) would refer to this as a habitus.

35. Abraham and van Schendel 2005, 22.

36. Frank-Vitale 2017.

37. Greif 2006, 134.

38. De León 2015.

39. Ibid.

40. See also Andersson 2014, 136, on this point on the routes leading from Africa to Europe.

41. De León 2015, Heller and Pezzani 2017.

42. Interview, El Salvador, April 9, 2010.

43. Andreas 1995, 75.

44. Andreas 1996, 58; Andreas 2003, 96.

45. Tagliacozzo 2005, 5.

46. Coutin 2005, 198.

47. Such sites also become sites of struggle over resources. For example, frequent tensions emerge among migrants as well as between shelter staff within the shelter over the distribution of food and other goods. However, my focus here is on the central role played by a struggle over information, which may provide potential access to or control of other resources.

48. Surowieki 2004.

49. Bikhchandani, Hirschleifer, and Welch 1998, 994.

50. Adler 2008, 196.

51. Ibid.

52. E.g., Frank-Vitale 2011.

53. Goffman 1959.

54. Appadurai 1996, 33.

55. Bourdieu 1986.

56. Zilberg 2004, 2011.

57. See the story of the undocumented Mexican in Chapter 4.

58. Galemba 2017.

59. Galemba 2017, Lakhani 2016. Border residents nevertheless eagerly rely on racial stereotypes to distance themselves from Salvadoran and Honduran immigrants, who under conditions of border securitization are increasingly understood as potential threats to the Mexican-born community (Galemba 2017, 10–11).

60. This class of wanderers seems to be almost all male.

61. Spener 2010.

62. Hayek 1976, 30.

63. Appadurai 1996.

64. As previously discussed, the social imagination represents the boundaries of the thinkable within a collective. See Taylor 2004, 23.

65. Greenblatt 2005, 165.

66. Curtis 1997, xviii; Yanow 2001.

67. Scott 1998.

68. Interview in El Salvador, January 5, 2010.

69. Bourdieu 1980, 57; Butler 1990; de Certeau 1984, 81–82.

70. Goffman 1959, 249.

71. Goffman 1959, 75–76.

72. Arjun Appadurai (1996) calls this the "mediascape."

73. Here I paraphrase Curtis's (1997, xx) discussion of the development of improvisational jazz genre in the self-consciously migratory society of the Americas.

74. Tagliacozzo 2005, 5–18. Tagliacozzo is talking about Southeast Asia, but the insights about features conducive for smuggling transfer across time and place.

75. For sophisticated works on how migration practice and smuggling is socially embedded, see Gaytan et al. 2007; Kyle 2000; Kyle and Scarcelli 2009; Singer and Massey 1998; Spener 2001, 2004, 2009.

76. Social capital is the primary benefit of reciprocal relationships. Bourdieu (1986) explains that "the reproduction of social capital presupposes an unceasing effort of sociability, a continuous series of exchanges in which recognition is endlessly affirmed and reaffirmed."

77. Mainwaring 2016, 3.

78. On the development of a landscape of squatter communities and slums to accommodate the unplanned life that takes place within planned cities, see Scott 1998, 103–146. See also Spener (2010) for a similar description of ingenuity of life at the margins and "rasquachismo." Rasquachismo is an improvised use of materials for artistic purposes, associated with Chicano aesthetics.

79. Coutin 2005, Hess 2010, Menjívar 2000.

80. Ted Conover (1987) traveled these seasonal circuits with Mexican farmworkers in the 1980s.

81. Drawing from his fieldwork in the late 1990s and early 2000s, Spener (2009, 68) writes that migrants often faced even greater difficulties crossing the wilderness of southern Texas than they encountered at the border.

82. If I had ever heard from Roberto in the United States, I would have done my best to help him find a job, but our paths have not crossed again.

3. The Cast of Characters: Actors and Their Relationships En Route

1. Quote from *As You Like It,* act 2, scene 7, in which Shakespeare describes our changing role over the course of a lifetime: "All the world is a stage, And all the men and women merely players; They have their exits and their entrances, And one man in his time plays many parts, His acts being seven ages. . . ."

2. Interviews in El Salvador, December 30, 2010, January 6, 2010, January 24, 2010.

3. Hamilton and Chinchilla 1991; García 2006.

4. Amparo Marroquín (2012) notes that in the early period of Central American migration, "It was not only the houses of the migrants that stood out in the local urban infrastructure, but those of the coyotes as well." One community member of a small town in El Salvador explained to me that these days, the migrants who leave do not build the big houses, but the coyotes collect land from defaults on loans. Since the economic recession of 2006 in particular, migrants have had a difficult time paying off the debts they accrue during the journey. If I want to identify the human smugglers, he told me, I should look at who owns more and more property in town. Indeed, when a new migrant does build a large home in the present era, he or she may be accused of various illegal activities in local gossip (Pedersen 2012).

5. Spener 2009, 88.

6. On the duplicitousness and dangers of coyotes operating from this period to present, see Coutin 2007, 104.

7. Spener 2009.

8. Classified ads in newspapers in El Salvador still occasionally advertise smuggling services in thinly veiled code. Online advertisements also occasionally surface.

9. Interview with a police officer, El Salvador, March 4, 2010.

10. In one memorable story from 1975, a woman was abandoned by her guide in a hotel in San Salvador, but she tracked down her smuggler and demanded that he fulfill his responsibility (interview with a returned migrant, El Salvador, July 1, 2010). She and her travel group did not know his name or other identifying information. So, they grabbed a taxicab and drove around the capital city until they located his car. They knocked on various doors in that neighborhood until they found him. They warned him that now that they knew where he lived, he had to comply with the terms of their contract. He did.

11. Coutin 2007, 83; Marroquín 2008, 36–40.

12. See, for example, the career of Narciso "Chicho" Ramirez for just one example of a well-respected coyote who became a local mayor.

13. Marroquín 2012, Spener 2009.

14. De León 2015; Dunn 1996; Rosas 2016, 123.

15. Ibid.

16. García 2006, 56.

17. Ibid.

18. Ibid.

19. Casillas 2007, 7.

20. De León 2015.

21. Conover 1989, 224.

22. This description of the border is strikingly similar to the no-man's-land between Tijuana and San Diego described by Ruben Martínez (2001, 196).

23. E.g., ACLU 2012.

24. Falcón 2008; Spener 2009, 132–133; Heyman 2017.

25. Interview with returned migrant, El Salvador, January 19, 2010.

26. Interviews with returned migrants, El Salvador, April 17, 2010, February 19, 2010.

27. Given how endemic abuse and corruption are at the hands of Mexican authorities, this relative evaluation should not be read as a vote of confidence in or a high standard of professionalism on the part of U.S. authorities. Indeed, Heyman (2017) outlines persistent problems of corruption, excessive force, and abuse that coincide with U.S. Border Patrol and ICE hiring surges, and he provides recommendations for improving immigration policing practice.

28. Interview with Salvadoran migrant, Ixtepec, March 2, 2011. For a discussion of how this criminal predation by Mexican authorities is turned against Mexicans (as well as Central Americans) and informed by the larger context of neoliberalism, see Rosas (2012, 57–59).

29. In Cecilia Menjívar's (2000, 63) study of migrants of this era, 33 percent of Salvadoran respondents had traveled by airplane for some segment of the route. Air travel rarely happens today with tighter security in airports, but for enough money, officials can sometimes be paid off for clandestine domestic Mexican air travel.

30. O'Dogherty 1989; Menjívar 2000, 63.

31. Coutin 2007, Frelick 1991, Mahler 1995, Menjívar 2000.

32. In Menjívar's (2000, 63) survey of Salvadorans living in San Francisco in the early 1990s, the majority of whom had traveled in the 1980s, 33 percent of her respondents had been assaulted once and 34 percent of her respondents had been assaulted multiple times. Thus, most people had been assaulted at least once during the journey.

33. Andreas 2009; Interview with a migration official, February 9, 2010.

34. Interview, ibid.

35. In practice, despite the U.S. government's legal obligations to ensure that people with credible fear are not forcefully repatriated to dangerous situations, Salvadoran asylum seekers faced (and still face) an uphill battle to receive recognition and protection, and Marcos was lucky to be released. For a summary of some of the obstacles to this protection, see Coutin 2007, 51–52.

36. Coutin 2007, 51–52; García 2006, 111–112.

37. Menjívar 2000.

38. E.g., Interview with a Salvadoran migrant, February 8, 2010.

39. Rosas 2016.

40. Ibid.

41. U.S. DHS 2003, 2011.

42. Interviews, July 18, 2010. During fieldwork in Central America and Mexico, I met several people who claimed that they preferred English to Spanish. Some of them prob-

ably enjoyed showing off their English language skills but remained fluent in Spanish. Others felt like non-native Spanish speakers after living away from their country of birth for many years. Alberto preferred to speak English.

43. Rosas 2012.

44. Cruz 2010, 396.

45. Cruz 2010.

46. Valdez 2011, 24.

47. Ibid.

48. Valdez 2011, 25; Wolf 2011, 48.

49. Zilberg 2004, 2011.

50. Interview with a Salvadoran police officer, May 1, 2011.

51. Wolf 2017, 10; Zilberg 2004, 2011.

52. Cruz 2010, 385; Interview with a Salvadoran police officer, May 1, 2011.

53. Papachristos 2005, 53.

54. Cruz 2010; Papachristos 2005, 53.

55. Cruz 2010, 393–394.

56. Wolf 2017, 13

57. Papachristos 2005, 51.

58. Interview with a Honduran migrant, Ixtepec, March 29, 2011.

59. Fieldnotes, November 5, 2010.

60. Fieldnotes, March 3, 2011.

61. According to Brenneman (2012), conversion sometimes provides a legitimate path to retirement, granted permission from the gang to forego active participation.

62. Wolf 2017, 11.

63. Brenneman 2012, 34.

64. Cruz 2010; Hume 2007.

65. Wolf 2017, 50–54.

66. Interview with an activist, Ixtepec, November 6, 2010.

67. Interview with shelter staff, Ixtepec, April 1, 2011.

68. Correa-Cabrera 2017, 6.

69. Ibid., 89.

70. For an analysis of the pros and cons for alliances between Central American street gangs and Mexican cartels, see Steven Dudley (2012). He points out that if the Zetas did, in fact, ally with the MS-13, it represented a de-professionalization of the cartel.

71. Fieldnotes, Saltillo, July 17, 2010.

72. Friman 2004, 98.

73. Fieldnotes, Ixtepec, May 13, 2011.

74. Interview, San Salvador, April 28, 2010.

75. Private communication, July 29, 2013.

76. Dunn 1996, 173.

77. Ibid., 174.

78. Spener 2009, 116.

79. *INS v. St. Cyr.*

80. Bustillo 2013.

81. García 2006.

82. Frelick 1991, 221–222.

83. Carlsen 2008; Castillo 2003; Casillas 2007; Sassen 1996.

84. Casillas 2007, 16.

85. Ibid., 18.

86. Ibid., 10.

87. Ibid., 19.

88. Interview with an activist, San Salvador, November 24, 2009.

89. Andreas 2003, 79.

90. E.g., Nazario 2006.

91. Interview, El Salvador, March 1, 2010. Brigden and Mainwaring (2016) analyze the interplay between immobility and agency in Gabriel and Jorge's stories, using different pseudonyms.

92. Interview, El Salvador, April 11, 2010.

93. E.g., Interview with returned migrants, El Salvador, April 15, 2010.

94. Ramos 2005.

95. Ibid.

96. Interview with police officer, El Salvador, March 4, 2010.

97. Brigden 2015.

98. David Spener (2009) comes to the same conclusion after fieldwork among Mexican migrants.

99. Interview, Ixtepec, December 3, 2010.

100. Wilkinson 2012.

101. After forensic analysis, the death count for that mass grave rose to 193 (Dudley 2012). However, I use the number originally reported in the media, because today the victims collectively are known across Latin America simply as "the 72."

102. CDHDF 2011, 7.

103. Najar 2012.

104. Interview with shelter staff, January 20, 2011.

105. Castillo 2010; For the most complete history and analysis of the Zetas to date, see Correa-Cabrera 2017.

106. Otero and Aviles 2003.

107. Medellin 2004.

108. El Universal 2003; Logan 2009.

109. Thompson 2005.

110. Interview with an activist, Tenosique, June 2, 2010. Correa-Cabrera (2017, 63–67) argues that a franchise is not the correct business analogy for the Zetas cartel, which usually maintains more control over outsourced practices and might also be a subsidiary model, though she also notes that the "Zeta brand" has been a careful business strategy.

111. Fieldnotes, Saltillo, July 17, 2010.

112. Logan 2009.

113. Meyer 2007, 4. On their carefully crafted self-marketing through social media as well as traditional communications, see Correa-Cabrera (2017, 67–69).

114. Martinez 2011.

115. Dudley 2012. Only one migrant in my interviews believed that he had been kidnapped by the Gulf cartel.

116. Najar 2012.

117. Correa-Cabrera 2017, 51–55.

118. Corchado 2009.

119. Quoted by Althaus 2013.

120. Interview, Ixtepec, April 1, 2011.

121. Interview, Lecheria, July 13, 2010.

122. Fieldnotes, Saltillo, July 17, 2010.

123. Interview, Ixtepec, March 29, 2011.

124. E.g., Interview with Salvadoran migrant, Ixtepec, March 30, 2011.

125. Dudley 2012; Ramsey 2011.

126. Fox 2013.

127. Ibid.

128. For example, on March 7, 2013, the Mexican Navy freed 105 Central Americans held in Nuevo Laredo, Tamaulipas, but they did not capture a single kidnapper at the scene of the crime (Cawley 2013). In this case, there is no certain evidence that a leak provided information to the kidnapping gang. However, I speculate that the frequency with which these gangs escape before the authorities arrive indicates that they receive some insider tips. Most observers arrive at the same conclusion.

129. Amnesty International 2010; CNDH 2011.

130. Interview, Ixtepec, June 28, 2011.

131. Interview, Ixtepec, June 29, 2011.

132. Fieldnotes, September 5, 2010.

133. Cervantes 2011.

134. Pachico 2012; Pachico and Dudley 2012.

135. Interview, Arriaga, December 1, 2010.

136. Later in the interview, the woman explained that her travel companion was not her husband after all. After a pause, she said, "He is not my husband. My husband died long ago. It's just that this man helped me. My coyote abandoned me in his town, and his family let me into their house and he offered to take me north. He was kind and helped me." In Central America, it is fairly common for monogamous sexual partners to pronounce themselves husband and wife for a time.

137. Interview, Saltillo, July 18, ,2011.

138. Dudley 2012.

139. See Cervantes (2011) for a brief description of each of the major crime groups and their leadership and characteristics, as described by Mexican government reports.

140. Interview, El Salvador, July 5, 2010.

141. Fieldnotes, July 20, 2011.

142. Interview with a Salvadoran migrant, July 16, 2011.

143. Roberts et al. 2010.

144. Brigden and Mainwaring 2016.

145. Avila 2011.

146. Fieldnotes, January 11, 2011.

147. Rape, a special case of endemic violence along the route, is beyond the scope of this chapter. I will discuss it in greater depth in Chapter 5.

148. Spener 2009.

149. E.g., Interview with a returned migrant, El Salvador, April 15, 2010.

150. Sheridan 2009, 66.

151. Amnesty International 2010, 29.

152. After watching the accused man visit the shelter multiple times, I interviewed him and he did not admit to any involvement with the gang. I did not push the matter, but the allegations against him seem plausible, because he spent a great deal of time along the route on the tracks in the company of others with ties to the street gangs.

4. The Performance: Migrant Scripts and Roles

1. The eruption of laughter may be a symptom of a destabilization of identity (Butler 1990, 138–139).

2. Interview, Ixtepec, December 13, 2010.

3. Goffman 1959, 15.

4. Ibid., 4.

5. A trustworthy smuggler or experienced friend can be a cultural guide to these scripts, but such cues are incomplete, because migrants must expect an interactive and unpredictable audience. Lacking the benefit of a Mexican childhood, Central American migrants may practice the correct accent, memorize local facts, or prepare the appropriate disguise. However, many performances emerge in earnest, as people unconsciously adapt internalized scripts. Furthermore, since no one knows exactly whom they might encounter or under what circumstances along the way, these interactions must be staged and realized in the same moment. Not everyone has the dramatic talent, confidence, and attention to detail to play the part; migrants may miss the signals about how to travel or fail to improvise upon them, repeating stale performances rather than slightly revising them to avoid detection. Nevertheless, survival depends on the unpredictable context in which migrants perform, as much at it depends on the talents of individuals. Even though performances can be viewed as a survival resource for migrants, a flare for such daily dramas does not determine who arrives at their intended destination.

6. Greenblatt 2005, 165.

7. Brubaker 2004, 11.

8. Schlossberg 2001, 1–2.

9. E.g., Gibson-Graham 2008, Miles and Crush 1993, Pratt 2000, Rose 1997.

10. Pratt 2000, 650.

11. Butler (1990, 272) defines a script as one that "survives the particular actors who make use of it, but which requires individual actors in order to be actualized and reproduced as reality once again."

12. The performance of regional identities sometimes become primary, and can even render the performance of nationality believable, by offering subtle nuances on an otherwise generic national script. At other times, regional scripts and national scripts do

not coincide, as with indigenous identities of Chiapas or the coastal communities of Oaxaca of African descent that are rendered invisible by Mexican national discourse grounded in mestizaje. Indeed, foreigners are not the only ones who may need to "pass" in a society that neglects multiple communities that constitute the nation.

13. Ginsberg 1996, Schlossberg 2001.

14. García 2014.

15. Anderson 2006, Hobsbawm 1992.

16. My understanding of identity differs from Sadiq (2009, 184), who implies that an authentic ethnic identity provides a proxy for loyalty. In contrast, my approach does not speak to loyalties or the elusive boundary between good faith and bad faith performances.

17. Migdal 2004, 4.

18. Sassen 2006, 296; see also Sadiq 2009, 74.

19. Martínez 2010, Nazario 2006, Vogt 2013.

20. The regional history of population movements, particularly the seasonal migration of Guatemalans to Southern Mexico, dates at least to the 1960s, and a porous Guatemala-Mexico border had been tolerated until the refugee crisis of the 1980s and 1990s (García 2006, 45; Hamilton and Chinchilla 1991).

21. Frelick 1991.

22. Ibid.; García 2006, 56.

23. Hamilton and Chinchilla 1991, 98.

24. García 2006, 45.

25. For descriptions of the journey during that time period, see Coutin (2007), Mahler (1995), and Menjívar (2000).

26. Archibald 2013, Tuckman 2013.

27. Interview with a Honduran migrant, Ixtepec, March 4, 2011.

28. Interview, El Salvador, February 9, 2010.

29. De León 2012, 477–495; Gilroy 1991; Heyman 2009; Sadiq 2009.

30. E.g., Interview with a returned migrant, El Salvador, June 2, 2010.

31. Interview with a smuggler, El Salvador, July 5, 2010.

32. However, a smuggler attributed the increased vulnerability of Hondurans to their relative lack of resources to pay high-end service providers, like himself, rather than attributing this increased vulnerability to their race and racism (Interview, El Salvador, July 5, 2009).

33. Ruiz 2001.

34. Furthermore, shelter workers describe migrants from far-flung countries, such as Cuba, as "like gold" for kidnappers, who assume that such long-distance journeys require more resources (Interview, Ixtepec, May 31, 2010). Migrants repeat these rumors among themselves. Selvin, whose interview is recounted later, claimed that he had personally witnessed Mexican immigration authorities giving apprehended Indian and Brazilian migrants to kidnappers, who receive much larger ransoms for them than for Central Americans (Interview, Coatzacoalcos, June 1, 2011). His account, while believable, constitutes nothing more than rumor, because I could not verify the veracity of his claims. Shelter workers and humanitarian activists have documented similar corruption (Interview, Saltillo, July 17, 2011). True or not, these rumors are nonetheless

important, because they alter migrants' perceptions of the dangers and thereby incentivize complex passing performances.

35. De León 2012.
36. Vogt 2012.
37. Interview, Ixtepec, March 2, 2011.
38. Interview with a Guatemalan migrant, Ixtepec, March 4, 2011.
39. Papachristos 2005.
40. Zilberg 2011, 196–199.
41. Rosas 2012, 80.
42. Zilberg 2011, 198.
43. De León 2012, 487.
44. Interview, Ixtepec, 2/3/11.
45. Hagan 2008.
46. Interview, Ixtepec, March 4, 2011. During follow-up research along the route in December 2014/January 2015 and May 2015, it became clear that due to the diffusion of communication technology in the region, this cultural tell has expired. I observed many migrants traveling with cell phones, and the shelter in Ixtepec now offers some Wi-Fi service. Cultural tells come and go. Nevertheless, the suspicion cast on well-connected, "known" travelers remains.
47. Interview, Ixtepec, March 4, 2011.
48. Interview, Ixtepec, November 4, 2010.
49. E.g., Interview with a humanitarian activist, Ixtepec, December 14, 2010.
50. Exceptions to the rules may be made under extenuating circumstances, i.e., for migrants who are awaiting asylum claims, who are denouncing human rights abuses they suffered en route, or who are volunteering a needed craft of skill at the shelter. Exceptions may also be made for women and children that may put them in a privileged position to serve as "connectors" along the route, producing advantages from the wide acknowledgment of their hypervulnerability to violence.
51. E.g., Fieldnotes, Ixtepec, October 20, 2010.
52. E.g., Fieldnotes, Ixtepec, November 6, 2010.
53. E.g., Interview with a Honduran migrant, Ixtepec, December 3, 2010.
54. Interview, Coatzacoalcos, June 1, 2011.
55. Ibid.
56. E.g., Interview, Ixtepec, December 2, 2010.
57. E.g., Interview with a Honduran migrant, Ixtepec, March 5, 2011.
58. E.g., Interview with a Honduran migrant, Coatzacoalcos, June 1, 2011.
59. E.g., Interview with a Guatemalan migrant, Ixtepec, April 15, 2010.
60. Fieldnotes, January 31, 2010.
61. Butler 1990, 140.
62. Shelley 2010.
63. Interview, Lechería, July 14, 2011.
64. Castro Soto *et al.* 2010.
65. Shewly 2016
66. Vogt 2013.
67. Donato 2006.

68. E.g., Boehm 2008, McIlwaine 2010.

69. Hondagneu-Sotelo 1994, Menjívar 2002.

70. Dreby 2009, 43; McEvoy et al. 2012.

71. Arguelles and Rivero 1993, 269.

72. Castro Soto et al. 2010, 43; Hume 2008, 67–68; Mahler 1999; Menjívar 2008, 197.

73. Interview with a Honduran migrant, Ixtepec, March 29, 2011.

74. Interview, El Salvador, January 27, 2010.

75. Diaz and Kuhner 2007. U.S. officials have also committed abuses (Arguelles and Rivero 1993, 265; Falcón 2008; Solomon 2005).

76. E.g., Frank-Vitale 2011; Vogt 2012, 212–214.

77. Interview, El Salvador, April 9, 2010.

78. González-López 2007, 240.

79. These performances of sexual morality have parallels in encounters with U.S. immigration authorities. Until 1990, LGBT migrants had to "pass" as straight to gain legal entry to the United States or face exclusion as "sexual deviants" (Lubhéid 2005).

80. Arguelles and Rivera 1993, 268; Nazario 2006, 78.

81. Interview, El Salvador, January 19, 2010.

82. Vogt 2016.

83. Interview, Tenosique, June 2, 2011.

84. Goffman 1959. Menjívar (2000, 71) also discusses how women leverage pity during the journey.

85. Siegel and de Blank 2010, 436–437.

86. Sanchez 2016.

87. Hlavka 2016, 18.

88. Hume 2008, 65–66.

89. Interview, Ixtepec, March 31, 2011.

90. Brenneman 2012.

91. Gutmann 1996.

92. Arguelles and Rivero 1993, Lubhéid 2005.

93. Cantú et al. 2005.

94. E.g., Stephen 2002.

95. Cantú et al. 2005.

96. Gutmann 1996, 234.

97. Interview, Ixtepec, February 3, 2011, February 4, 2011.

98. E.g., Stacey 1988.

99. Green 1995, 112–113.

100. Denzin 2003, Miles and Crush 1993, Mountz 2007.

101. De León 2012, 492.

102. Aradau and Huysmans 2013, 17.

5. The Stage: Mobile Images and Props

1. See also Kovic and Arguelles 2010, 87.

2. Galemba 2012.

3. Kovic and Arguelles 2010, 87.

4. Interview, December 2, 2010.

5. A volcanic eruption followed by Tropical Storm Agatha in May 2010 hit the municipality of Nueva Santa Rosa, Santa Rosa, very hard. This dual disaster displaced thousands of people and resulted in the loss of many homes.

6. See, for example, Autessere 2010; Fujii 2009, Pachirat 2013 Wood 2003.

7. Pachirat 2013.

8. Lynch 1960.

9. Brigden and Mainwaring 2016, 427.

10. As explained by Peter J. Katzenstein (2005, 2), "regions have both material and symbolic dimensions, and we can trace them in patterns of behavioral interdependence and political practice." In this chapter, I trace microlevel interdependence and practice among Central American migrants and individuals in the societies through which they pass. Migration practice, shaped by American imperium in Latin America, has both material and symbolic dimensions that complicate borders.

11. Lynch 1960.

12. Wood 2003.

13. See for example, Fenster 2009, Lynch 1960, Powell 2010, Seyer-Ochi 2006.

14. Migdal 2004.

15. Kyle and Siracusa 2005.

16. Campos-Delgado 2017.

17. Harley 1989, 12.

18. Black 1997, Harley 1989.

19. Mainwaring and Brigden 2016, 248; Van Schendel 2005, 42.

20. In a similar vein, Campos-Delgado (2017) also frames migrant maps as a counter-mapping project.

21. These visual cues can also be important to migrants unexpectedly separated from their high-end smugglers.

22. Lynch 1960, 7–8.

23. In this vein, Susan Bibler Coutin (2005, 198) defines clandestine as "hidden but known."

24. Similarly, Lynch (1960, 7) argues that public images "might be expected to appear in the interaction of a single physical reality, a common culture, and a basic physiological nature."

25. Casillas 2007, 40.

26. Andreas 1995, Galemba 2008, Nordstrom 2007.

27. Casillas 2007.

28. Unauthorized routes also become superimposed on the infrastructure of other unauthorized routes, at least insofar that drug runners permit the migrants to trespass. For example, street gangs often guard drug shipments for the cartels, and the unauthorized cargo is hidden in compartments under where migrants sit on the train (interview with a Salvadoran official, April 28, 2011). At other times, the cartels exterminate the gangs as a nuisance. Cartels also attempt to deter migrants from following drug routes, by kidnapping or killing them, because migration calls the attention of authorities.

29. Spener 2009.

30. The multiplier effect of migrant traffic has a profound impact on economic life along the route. During fieldwork, I unsuccessfully attempted to run a survey at a shelter to document migrant expenditures in a transit community and then estimate a multiplier effect for the town's economic activity. Within a few days of data collection, I abandoned the effort for two reasons. First, questions about income and expenditure are extraordinarily sensitive and truthful answers require an intimate rapport. People do not want to share this information because they do not want to admit to having access to funds (which makes them vulnerable to robbery or kidnapping) nor do they want to admit to buying alcohol, drugs, or contraband (which makes them vulnerable to expulsion from the shelter). Therefore, I could only gather such information via observation and ethnographic interviews with key informants, methods that violate conventional survey methodology. Second, even honest migrants with scarce resources seemed incapable of accurately accounting for their purchases; the exercise required a level of organizational skill and effort that exceeded the capacity of very tired, hungry, and anxious individuals. Frankly, they had more important things to worry about than my survey. Therefore, while I can describe the economic, social, and cultural impact of migrants on transit towns, I cannot provide numerical estimates of that impact beyond the most general impressions of my ethnographic experience.

31. Interview, El Salvador, July 5, 2010.

32. In a lament echoed by human rights activists and migrants along the route, a friar at a migrant shelter in Tenosique, Tobasco, explained that "it is a mined countryside. And when there aren't assaults, there are other abuses. The locals charge prices of fifty pesos for a Coca-Cola. They threaten to call the *migra* if anyone complains about the prices" (interview, June 2, 2011). Such petty extortion drives up prices for migrants along the route. On a panel at an event in Juchitan, Oaxaca (April 12, 2011), a Mexican human rights official explained: "They leave due to necessity. They deserve dignified treatment. The CNDH is an ally of the good father, good son, good husband. . . . And the abuses that I am talking about include the people who charge twenty pesos, rather than eight, for glass of water or sixteen rather than eight for a soda, knowing the person is a migrant. The taxi driver who charges too much and says if you don't pay me, I'll tell migration."

33. People in the United States as well as Latin America often use percentages to express emotion, rather than objective estimates of fact. For example, one Salvadoran man (interview, October 7, 2009) who had returned from the United States, estimated that today, unlike when he traveled, "the route is 60 percent death and 40 percent surviv[al]." At one point, he argued that only 10 percent survive (interview, November 13, 2009), and then he estimated the odds of survival as zero. I interviewed him several times and this percentage changed, perhaps depending on his mood, each time I asked him about it.

34. De León 2012, 478.

35. Ibid.

36. Ibid.

37. Interview, El Salvador, February 19, 2010.

38. The institutionalization of this transit political economy, including the kidnapping industry that victimizes migrants for ransoms, has also been facilitated by transnational

financial flows, e.g., money sent via Western Union and Elektra to migrants from U.S.-based relatives, as unexpected situations arise along the route through Mexico (Casillas 2007, 42). For a description of the relationship between informal transit political economy and Western Union, see Vogt (2012, 198–200; 2013).

39. Andreas 1996, 58; 2003, 96.

40. Appadurai 1996, 9.

41. Martel and Marroquín 2007; Sheridan 2009, 148–151.

42. Interview, Ixtepec, March 5, 2011.

43. Marroquín 2008, 36–38.

44. Ibid., 39.

45. Sladková 2007

46. Ceresole 2009, LeBron 2009, Marosi 2005, Surdin 2009. An official website (now defunct—http://www.nomascruces.org) highlights stories of suffering and death. For the company hired by the U.S. Border Patrol, see http://www.elevation-us.com/home/.

47. Hagan 2008, 163–168.

48. Ibid.

49. Ibid.

50. Ibid.

51. Frank-Vitale 2011, 120.

52. Ibid.

53. For example, he mistakenly identified his hometown as located in the northern part of Guatemala. Nueva Santa Rosa is located approximately seventy miles south of Guatemala City.

54. According to migrants and human rights activists, the price of riding the freight train has been increasing since 2011, as the street gangs are again attempting to extend and deepen their control of the train route. Their capacity to extort boarding fees, in particular along the eastern route through Tenosique, has increased. Migrants and smugglers who cannot pay may be thrown from the train. The price of riding the train remains high, despite the police raids that frequently disrupt train journeys.

55. Walters 2015.

56. Lynch 1960, 9.

57. Casillas 2007.

58. The most dramatic of these backlogs in recent history occurred in Veracruz in June and July 2012 when hundreds (or thousands, depending on whose estimate one uses) of migrants became stranded without resources after a derailment suspended freight train service (Barranco 2012).

59. Private security on most trains can be bribed for passage, but some migrants know better than to try to board the most freshly painted engines that connect Saltillo with auto dealers in the United States; the security on that line is too effective for migrants to ride in the open.

60. Hagan 2008.

61. Quoted in Ruiz Parra 2011; the translation of the quote is mine. Vogt (2012, 270) repeats a very similar quote from a shelter priest whose life was spared because a street gang did not want the shelter to close. Vogt also describes the ironic symbiosis between migrant shelters and the gangs who prey on migrants. Her purpose in describing

this contradiction is to examine how structural violence undermines solidarity and leads to the corruption of safe spaces by violent actors.

62. Sheridan 2009, 111–137.

63. Interview with a Guatemalan migrant, Ixtepec, May 14, 2011.

64. Hagan 2008.

65. García 2006, Hagan 2008.

66. Vogt 2012, 39.

67. Barranco 2012.

68. Archibald 2012.

69. Coutin 2005, 197; 2007, 105.

70. Walters 2015.

71. Kovic and Arguelles 2010, 94.

6. A Tragedy: Conclusions and Implications

1. Interview, Arriaga, December 2, 2010.

2. Coutin 2005.

3. Interview, June 30, 2010.

4. During my fieldwork, I generally assumed that migrants knew the dangers and the route better than I did, and as a result, I did not directly answer many questions about the safety of the route. As a shelter volunteer, I would sometimes provide information that I could obtain online about migrants' legal rights. More than once, I printed out information about asylum, and on another occasion, provided a map of the train route. I often provided contact information for the Catholic priest and encouraged vulnerable people to speak to him directly. However, in this case and a few others, I felt there was an ethical imperative to intervene with some limited safety advice in the context of the interview. I recognized that any advice could be expired by the time I gave it, and I provided this disclaimer.

5. Juan Gonzalez (2011) persuasively argues that these political, social, and economic conditions that push migrants from Latin America are themselves a product of U.S. foreign policy in the region—a "harvest of empire."

6. Hagan 2008.

7. For a cross-regional comparison of the lived experience of im/mobilities produced by this policing environment, see Brigden and Mainwaring 2016.

8. Greenhill 2016, Mainwaring 2014.

9. Collyer 2007, 2010.

10. Mainwaring and Brigden 2016, Ustubici 2016.

11. Collyer 2005.

12. Granovetter 1973, 1361.

13. Kaytaz 2016.

14. Mainwaring 2016.

15. Albahari 2015, Carling 2007, Spijkerboer 2007, Grant 2011. For a review of the burgeoning literature on transit migration and the "new" geography of migration in the European context, see Collyer, Düvell, and de Haas 2010.

16. MSF 2005, 2010a, 2010b.

17. Collyer 2007, 671–673. At this time, there is a richer interdisciplinary literature on transit migration into Europe than is available in the United States. Interestingly, Sabine Hess (2010) traces this interest in "transit migration" and migratory routes into Europe to studies commissioned by the International Organization for Migration (IOM) on Turkey in the context of EU-expansion debates.

18. Collyer 2007, Hess 2010.

19. Albahari 2015.

20. Hollifield 2004, 885.

21. Zilberg 2011.

22. Balibar 2004Rosas 2012.

23. Rosas 2012.

24. Mainwaring and Brigden 2016, Rosas 2012.

25. Balibar (2004, 111) explains a similar transition in Europe: "[T]here is another aspect that has been forced on our attention by the problems relative to the treatment of asylum seekers and the modalities of control of so-called clandestine immigrants in Western Europe, which pose serious problems for the protection and institution of human rights: the system of identify verifications (generally occurring with the territory) allowing a triage of travelers admitted to and rejected from a given national territory. For the mass of humans today, these are the most decisive borders, but they are no longer lines."

26. Balibar 2004, 109.

27. Bosniak 2006, 4.

28. Anderson 2006, 53–58; Greenblatt 2010a, 1–23.

29. Waever 1993, 23.

30. Greenblatt 2010a. In this vein, Rey Koslowslki (2002) argues that human migration has long played a vital role in world politics, shaping the fate of states and the reach of empire since premodern civilization.

31. Hibou 2004, 352.

32. Greenblatt 2010a, 6.

33. De Genova 2107, 20.

34. Fieldnotes, May 13, 2011.

35. Fieldnotes, January 14, 2011.

36. On social banditry, see Hobsbwam 1959, 13–29.

37. Fieldnotes, March 28, 2011.

38. E.g., Interview with a government official, April 28, 2011.

39. Fieldnotes, January 14, 2011, May 30, 2011.

40. Fieldnotes, May 30, 2011.

41. Fieldnotes, May 13, 2011.

42. Fieldnotes, May 12, 2011.

43. Moodie 2010, 14.

44. Bentley 1993, 22–23.

45. Magañas 2011.

46. Ibid.

47. Brigden and Vogt 2015.

48. Interview, Ixtepec, November 4, 2010.

49. In all my interviews, I only encountered one Panamanian (Arriaga, December 2, 2010).

50. Interview, Ixtepec, November 5, 2010.

51. Interview, Ixtepec, November 6, 2010.

52. Reineke 2013.

53. When bodies are left to decay at the border or in mass graves without identification, De León (2015, 69) labels this necroviolence: a form of state discipline imposed by sacrilegious or offensive treatment of corpses.

54. Felix 2011, Magañas 2011.

55. Reineke 2013.

56. Squire 2014, Sundberg 2008.

57. Reineke 2013.

58. Felix 2011.

59. Magañas 2011.

60. De León 2015, 69.

61. Ibid., 274.

62. De Genova 2017, 13.

63. Innes 2014, 2015; Nyers and Rygiel 2012; Mainwaring 2016.

64. Thanks to El Qadam (2017), Frowd (2017), and Scheel (2017) for pushing me to answer these questions.

65. De León 2015.

66. Magañas 2011.

67. De Genova 2002, 2013, 2017.

68. Brown 2014.

69. Brigden and Mainwaring 2016, Andersson 2017

70. Mountz 2013, Mountz and Lloyd 2014.

71. Ibid.

72. Andersson 2014, 75.

73. Ibid.

74. Hiemstra 2014; Mainwaring 2016; Mainwaring and Silverman 2017; Mountz 2010, 2013; Mountz and Lloyd 2014; Salter 2008; Squire 2011.

75. See also Scheel 2017.

76. Lie 2013.

77. For a thoughtful discussion of these methodological, logistical, and ethical challenges, see Maillet, Mountz, and Williams (2017).

78. Mountz 2007, 2010.

79. Brigden and Mainwaring 2016. Thanks also to Frowd (2017) for pushing me to explain my position on immobility, as well as mobility.

80. Brigden and Mainwaring 2016.

81. Balaguera, forthcoming.

82. On the forced mobility along the route, see Frank-Vitale 2017.

83. See also Rosas 2012.

References

Abraham, Itty, and Willem van Schendel. 2005. "Introduction: The Making of Illicitness." In *Illicit Flows and Criminal Things: States, Borders, and the Other Side of Globalization*, edited by Willem van Schendel and Itty Abraham, 1–37. Bloomington: Indiana University Press.

Adamson, Fiona, and Madeleine Demetriou. 2007. "Remapping the Boundaries of State and National Identity: Incorporating Diasporas into IR Theorizing." *European Journal of International Relations* 13 (4): 489–526.

Adler, Emmanuel. 2008. "The Spread of Security Communities: Communities of Practice, Self-Restraint, and NATO's Post-Cold War Transformation." *European Journal of International Relations* 14 (2): 195–230.

Adler, Emmanuel, and Vincent Pouliot. 2011. "International Practices: Introduction and Framework." In *International Practices*, edited by Emmanuel Adler and Vincent Pouliot. Cambridge: Cambridge University Press.

Albahari, Maurizio. 2015. *Crimes of Peace: Mediterranean Migrations at the World's Deadliest Border*. Philadelphia: University of Pennsylvania Press.

Althaus, Dudley. 2013. "What Follows Zeta Leader's Take Down in Mexico." *InSight Crime*, July 13, http://www.insightcrime.org/news-analysis/what-follows-zetas-leaders-takedown-in-mexico (accessed July 27, 2013).

American Civil Liberties Union (ACLU). 2012. "Human Rights Violations on the United States-Mexico Border." Statement Submitted to the U.N. High Commissioner for Human Rights Side Event, 67th Session of the United Nations General Assembly, October 25, http://www.aclu.org/files/assets/121024_aclu_written_statement_ochcr_side _event_10_25_12_final_0.pdf (accessed July 19, 2013).

Amnesty International. 2010. *Invisible Victims: Migrants on the Move in Mexico.* London: Amnesty International Publications.

Anderson, Benedict. 2006. *Imagined Communities: Reflections on the Origins and Spread of Nationalism.* London: Verso.

Andersson, Ruben. 2014. *Illegality, Inc: Clandestine Migration and the Business of Bordering Europe.* Oakland: University of California Press.

——. 2017. "Rescued and Caught: The Humanitarian-Security Nexus at Europe's Frontiers." In *The Borders of "Europe": Autonomy of Migration, Tactics of Bordering*, edited by Nicholas De Genova, 64–94. Durham: Duke University Press.

Andreas, Peter. 1995. "Free Market Reform and Drug Market Prohibition: U.S. Policies at Cross-Purposes in Latin America." *Third World Quarterly* 16 (1): 75–87.

——. 1996. "U.S.-Mexico: Open Market, Closed Border." *Foreign Policy* 103: 51–69.

——. 2003. "Redrawing the Line: Borders and Security in the Twenty-first Century." *International Security* 28 (2): 78–111.

——. 2009. *Border Games: Policing the U.S-Mexico Divide.* Ithaca: Cornell University Press.

Anzaldua, Gloria. 2007. *Borderlands/La Frontera: The New Mestiza,* 25th Anniversary, 4th ed. San Francisco: Aunt Lute Books.

Appadurai, Arjun. 1996. *Modernity at Large: Cultural Dimensions of Globalization.* Minneapolis: University of Minnesota Press.

Aradau, Claudia, and Jeff Huysmans. 2013. "Critical Methods in International Relations: The Politics of Techniques, Devices and Acts." *European Journal of International Relations* 20 (3): 1–24, doi: 10.1177/1354066112474479.

Archibald, Randal C. 2010. "Victims of Massacre in Mexico Said to Be Migrants." *New York Times,* August 26.

2012. "Adding to Unease of a Drug War Alliance." *New York Times,* May 30.

——. 2013. "Central Americans Flow into Mexico, Bound for U.S." *New York Times,* April 26.

Arguelles, Lourdes, and Anne M. Rivero. 1993. "Gender/Sexual Orientation Violence and Transnational Migration: Conversations with Some Latinas We Think We Know." *Urban Anthropology and Studies of Cultural Systems and World Economic Development* 22 (3/4): 259–275.

Autessere, Séverine. 2010. *The Trouble with the Congo: Local Violence and the Failure of International Peacebuilding.* Cambridge: Cambridge University Press.

Avila, Edgar. 2011. "50 migrantes viajaban entre carga de naranjas." *El Universal,* February 10.

Balaguera, Martha. Forthcoming. "Trans-migration: Agency and Confinement at the Limits of Sovereignty." *Signs.*

Balibar, Etienne. 2004. *We, the People of Europe? Reflections on Transnational Citizenship*, trans. J. Swenson. Princeton: Princeton University Press.

Barranco, Rodrigo. 2012. "Derailment, crowd 'Migrantes, 'encallados' en Veracruz." *El Universal,* July 10, http://www.eluniversal.com.mx/estados/86747.html (accessed July 19, 2013).

BenEzer, Gadi, and Roger Zetter. 2015. "Searching for Directions: Conceptual and Methodological Challenges in Researching Refugee Journeys." *Journal of Refugee Studies* 28 (3): 297–318.

Bentley, Jerry. 1993. *Old World Encounters: Cross-cultural Contacts and Exchanges in Pre-Modern Times.* New York: Oxford University Press.

Berman, Jacqueline 2003. "(Un)Popular Strangers and Crises (Un)bounded: Discourses of Sex-Trafficking, the European Political Community and the Panicked State of the Modern State." *European Journal of International Relations* 9 (1): 37–86.

Bikhchandani, Suchil, David Hirshleifer, and Ivo Welch. 1998. "Learning from the Behavior of Others: Conformity, Fads, Informational Cascades." *Journal of Economic Perspectives* 12 (3): 151–170.

Black, Jeremy. 1997. *Maps and Politics.* Chicago: University of Chicago Press.

Blyth, Mark. 2006. "Great Punctuations: Prediction, Randomness, and the Evolution of Comparative Political Science." *American Political Science Review* 110 (4): 493–498.

Boehm, Deborah. 2008. "Now I Am a Man and a Woman! Gendered Moves and a Transnational Mexican Community." *Latin American Perspectives* 35 (1): 16–30.

Bonello, Deborah. 2016. "Criminal Groups Benefit from Mexico's Crackdown on Migrants," *InSight Crime,* July 28, http://www.insightcrime.org/news-analysis/criminal-groups-and-corrupt-officials-beneficiaries-of-mexico-migrant-policy (accessed April 2, 2017).

Bosniak, Linda. 2006. *The Citizen and the Alien: Dilemmas of Contemporary Membership.* Princeton: Princeton University Press.

Bosworth, Mary. 2014. *Inside Immigration Detention.* Oxford: Oxford University Press.

Bourdieu, Pierre. 1977. *Outline of a Theory of Practice,* trans. R. Nice. Cambridge: Cambridge University Press.

——. 1980. *The Logic of Practice,* trans. R. Nice. Stanford: Stanford University Press.

——. 1986. "The Forms of Capital." In *Handbook of Theory Research for the Sociology of Education,* edited by J.E. Richardson, 241–258. Westport, CT: Greenwood Press.

Brenneman, Robert. 2012. *Homies and Hermanos: God and Gangs in Central America.* Oxford: Oxford University Press.

Brigden, Noelle K. 2013. "Like a War: The New Central American Refugee Crisis" *NACLA* 45 (4): 7–11.

——. "Transnational Journeys and the Limits of Hometown Resources: Salvadoran Migration in Uncertain Times." *Migration Studies* 3 (2): 1–19.

Brigden, Noelle, and Peter Andreas. 2018. "Border Collision: Power Dynamics of Enforcement and Evasion Across the U.S.-Mexico Line." In *Power in Uncertainty: Exploring the Unexpected in World Politics,* edited by Peter J. Katzenstein and Lucia Seybert. Cambridge: Cambridge University Press.

Brigden, Noelle, and Cetta Mainwaring. 2016. "Matryoshka Journeys: Im/mobility During Migration." *Geopolitics* 21 (2): 407–434, doi: 10.1080/14650045.2015.1122592.

Brigden, Noelle, and Wendy A. Vogt. 2015. "Homeland Heroes: Migrants and Soldiers in the Neoliberal Era." *Antipode* 47 (2): 303–322.

Brown, Wendy. 2014. *Walled States, Waning Sovereignty*. New York: Zone Books.

Brubaker, Rogers. 2004. *Ethnicity Without Groups*. Cambridge, MA: Harvard University Press.

Bustillo, Miguel. 2013. "Near the U.S.-Mexico Border: A Grim New Reality." *Wall Street Journal,* April 13, http://online.wsj.com/article/SB1000142412788732382030457841256 1295471882.html (accessed July 27, 2013).

Butler, Judith. 1990. *Gender Trouble: Feminism and the Subversion of Identity*. New York: Routledge.

Campos-Delgado, Amalia. 2017. "Counter-mapping Migration: Irregular Migrants' Stories through Cognitive Mapping." Unpublished manuscript.

Cantú, L. Jr., with E. Luibhéid and A.M. Stern. 2005. "Well-Founded Fear: Political Asylum and the Boundaries of Sexual Identity in the U.S.-Mexico Borderlands." *Queer Migrations: Sexuality, U.S. Citizenship, and Border Crossings*, edited by E. Luibhéid and L. Cantú Jr. Minneapolis: University of Minnesota Press.

Carling, Jorgen. 2007. "Migration Control and Migrant Fatalities at the Spanish-African Borders." *International Migration Review* 41 (2): 316–434.

Carlsen. Laura. 2008. "Armoring NAFTA: The Battleground for Mexico's Future." *North American Congress on Latin America* (September/October), https://nacla.org /news/armoring-nafta-battleground-mexico%E2%80%99s-future (accessed July 27, 2013.).

Carter, Anthony T. 1988. "Does Culture Matter? The Case of Demographic Transition." *Historical Methods* 21 (4): 164–169.

Casillas, Rodolfo R. 2007. *Una Vida Discreta, Fugaz y Anónima: Los Centroamericanos Transmigrantes en Mexico*. Mexico City: Comisión Nacional de los Derechos Humanos.

Castells, Manuel. 1996. *The Rise of Network Society*. Oxford: Blackwell Publishers.

Castillo García, Gustavo. 2010. "Capacita el narco a mas sicarios; el Ejercito destruye Campamentos." La Jornada, September 4, 5.

Castillo, Manuel Ángel. 2003. "The Mexico Guatemala Border: New Controls on Transborder Migration in View of Recent Integration Schemes?" *Frontera Norte* 15 (29).

Castro Soto et al. 2010. *Mujeres transmigrantes*. Mexico City: INDESOL.

Cawley, Marguerite. 2013. "Mexico Rescues 104 Kidnapped Migrants near Texas Border." *InSight Crime,* March 12, http://www.insightcrime.org/news-briefs/mexico-rescues -104-kidnapped-migrants-at-texas-border (accessed July 27, 2013).

Ceresole, Carlos. 2009. "US Uses Songs to Deter Immigrants." *BBC Mundo*, February 15, http://news.bbc.co.uk/2/hi/americas/7879206.stm (accessed August 4, 2011).

Cervantes, Jesusa. 2011. "Solucion viable: unificacion pactada." *Proceso,* February 11, 6–10.

Chávez-Suárez, __Xiomara. 2013."Immigration Policy Responses to Transmigrants in Mexico." *Cornell Policy Review* 3 (2): 39–58.

CDHDF. 2011. *Migrantes y mexicanos asesinados y desaparecidos en San Fernando, Tamaulipas, Mexico. Solicitud de Medidas Cautelares*, July 13, 3.

CNDH. 2009. *Informe Especial Sobre los Casos de Secuestro en contra de Migrantes*, June 15.

CNDH. 2011. *Informe Especial Sobre Secuestro de Migrantes en Mexico*, February 22.

Cohen, Jeffrey H. 2004. *The Culture of Migration in Southern Mexico*. Austin: University of Texas Press.

Collyer, Michael. 2005. "When do social networks fail to explain migration? Accounting for the movement of Algerian asylum seekers to the UK." *Journal of Ethnic and Migration Studies* 31 (4): 699–718.

———. 2007. "In-Between Places: Trans-Saharan Transit Migrants in Morocco and the Fragmented Journey to Europe." *Antipode* 39 (4): 668–690.

———. 2010. 'Stranded Migrants and the Fragmented Journey' *Journal of Refugee Studies* 23 (3): 273–293.

Collyer, Michael, Franck Düvell, and Hein de Haas. 2012. "Critical Approaches to Transit Migration." *Population, Space and Place* 18 (4): 407–414.

Conley, Tom. 2007. *Cartographic Cinema*. Minneapolis: University of Minnesota Press.

Conover, Ted. 1987. *Coyotes: A Journey Across Borders with America's Illegal Aliens*. New York: Vintage Books.

Corchado, Alfredo. 2009. "Mexico's Zetas gang buys businesses along border in move to increase legitimacy." *Dallas Morning News*, December 6.

Cornelius, Wayne. 2001. "Death at the Border: Efficacy and Unintended Consequences of U.S. Immigration Control Policy." *Population and Development Review* 27 (4): 664–685.

Correa-Cabrera, Guadalupe. 2017. *Los Zetas Inc: Criminal Corporations, Energy and Civil War in Mexico*. Austin: University of Texas Press.

Coutin, Susan Bibler. 2005. "Being en Route." *American Anthropologist* 107 (2): 195–206.

———. 2007. *Nations of Emigrants: Shifting Boundaries of Citizenship in El Salvador and the United States*. Ithaca: Cornell University Press.

Coutin, Susan Bibler. 2016. *Exiled Home: Salvadoran Transnational Youth in the Aftermath of Violence*. Durham: Duke University Press.

Cruz, José Miguel. 2010. "Central American maras: from youth street gangs to transnational protection rackets." *Global Crime* 11 (4): 379–398.

Curtis, David Ames, ed. 1997. *The Castoriadis Reader*. Oxford: John Wiley and Sons.

de Certeau, Michel. 1984. *The Practice of Everyday Life*. Berkley: University of California Press.

De Genova, Nicholas P. 2002. "Migrant Illegality and Deportability in Everyday Life." *Annual Review of Anthropology* 31 (1): 419–447.

———. 2013. "Spectacles of Migrant 'Illegality': The Scene of Exclusion and the Obscene of Inclusion." *Ethnic and Racial Studies* 36 (7): 1180–1198.

———. 2017. "Introduction: The Borders of Europe and the European Question." In *The Borders of Europe: Autonomy of Migration, Tactics of Bordering*, edited by Nicholas De Genova, 1–35. Durham: Duke University Press.

De León, Jason. 2012. "Better to Be Hot than Caught: Excavating the Conflicting Roles of Migrant Material Culture." *American Anthropologist* 114 (3): 477–495.

———. 2015. *The Land of Open Graves: Living and Dying on the Migrant Trail*. Berkeley: University of California Berkeley Press.

Denzin, N. 2003. *Performance Ethnography: Critical Pedagogy and the Politics of Culture*. Thousand Oaks: Sage.

Diaz, Gabriela, and Gretchen Kuhner. 2007. "Women Migrants in Transit and Detention in Mexico." *Migration Information Source*, March 1, https://www.migrationpolicy .org/article/women-migrants-transit-and-detention-mexico (accessed March 30, 2013).

Donato, Katharine M. 2006. "A Glass Half Full? Gender in Migration Studies." *International Migration Review* 40 (1): 3–26.

Doty, Roxanne L. 2006. "Immigration and National Identity: Constructing the Nation." *Review of International Studies* 22 (3): 235–255.

Dreby, Joanna. 2009. "Gender and Transnational Gossip." *Qualitative Sociology* 32 (1): 33–52.

Dudley, Steven. 2012. "Reports of Zetas-MS-13 Alliance in Guatemala Unfounded." *InSight Crime*, April 17, http://www.insightcrime.org/investigations/reports-of-zetas -ms-13-alliance-in-guatemala-unfounded (accessed July 17, 2013).

Dunn, Timothy J. 1996. *The Militarization of the U.S. Mexico Border 1978–1992: Low Intensity Conflict Doctrine Comes Home*. Austin: CMAS Books.

Düvell, Franck. 2012. 'Transit Migration: A Blurred and Politicised Concept.' *Population, Space and Place* 18 (4): 407–481.

El Qadim, Nora. 2017. "Can IR Be Anthropological?" In *Walking with Migrants: Ethnography as Method in IR*, Meera Sabaratnam et al. An International Studies Quarterly Online Symposium.

El Universal. 2003. "Adjudican asesinatos a grupo 'Los Zetas.'" June 13, http://www2 .eluniversal.com.mx/pls/impreso/noticia.html?id_nota=49654&tabla=estados (accessed February 20, 2011).

Eschbach, Karl et al. 1999. "Death at the Border." *International Migration Review* 33 (2): 430–454.

Falcón, S.M. 2008. "Rape as a Weapon of War: Militarized Rape at the U.S.-Mexico Border." In *Women and Migration in the U.S.-Mexico Borderlands: A Reader,* edited by D.A. Segura and P. Zavella, 203–223. Durham: Duke University Press.

Felix, Adrian. 2011. "Posthumous Transnationalism: Postmortem Repatriation from the United States to Mexico." *Latin American Research Review* 46 (3): 157–179.

Fenster, Tovi. 2009. "Cognitive Temporal Mapping: The Three Steps Method in Urban Planning." *Planning Theory & Practice* 10 (4): 479–498.

Fox, Edward. 2013. "Figures Show Corruption Rife in Mexico's Migration Agency." *InSight Crime*, January 9, http://www.insightcrime.org/news-briefs/figures-corruption -rife-under-calderon-mexico-migration-agency (accessed July 27, 2013).

Frank-Vitale, Amelia. 2011. "Guerreros en el Camino: Central American Migration Through Mexico and Undocumented Migration as a New Form of Civil Disobedience." Master's thesis, American University, Washington, DC.

———. 2017. "Stuck in Motion: Migrants, Victims, and Smugglers in Central American Transit Migration." Paper presented at Latin American Studies Association Annual Meeting, Lima, Peru.

Frelick, Bill. 1991. "Running the Gauntlet: The Central American Journey in Mexico." *International Journal of Refugee Law* 3 (7): 208–242.

Friman, Richard. 2004."Forging the Vacancy Chain: Law Enforcement Efforts and Mobility in Criminal Economies" *Crime, Law and Social Change* 41: 53–77.

Frowd, Philippe M. 2017. "The Underbelly of Transnationalism." In *Walking with Migrants: Ethnography as Method in IR*, Meera Sabaratnam et al. An International Studies Quarterly Online Symposium.

Fujii, Lee Ann. 2009. *Killing Neighbors: Webs of Violence in Rwanda*. Ithaca: Cornell University Press.

Galemba, Rebecca. 2008. "Informal and Illicit Entrepreneurs: Fighting for a Place in the Neoliberal Economic Order." *Anthropology of Work Review* 29 (2): 19–25.

——. "Corn is food, not contraband: the right to 'free trade' at the Mexico-Guatemala border." *American Ethnologist* 39 (4): 716–734.

——. 2017. "'He Used to be a *Pollero*': the securitisation of migration and the smuggler/migrant nexus at the Mexico-Guatemala border." *Journal of Ethnic and Migration Studies* 44 (5): 870–886, doi: 10.1080/136918X.2017.1327803.

García, Angela S. 2014. "Hidden in Plain Sight: How Unauthorised Migrants Strategically Assimilate in Restrictive Localities in California." *Journal of Ethnic and Migration Studies* 40 (12): 1895–1914.

García, María Cristina. 2006. *Seeking Refuge: Central American Migration to Mexico, the United States and Canada*. Berkeley: University of California Press.

Gaytan, Seidy et al. 2007. "The Contemporary Migration Process." In *Impacts of Border Enforcement on Mexican Migration: The View from Sending Communities*, edited by Wayne A. Cornelius and Jessa M. Lewis, 33–52. La Jolla: Center for Comparative Immigration Studies.

Geertz, Clifford. 1973. *The Interpretation of Cultures*. New York: Basic Books.

Gibson-Graham, J.K. 2008. "Diverse economies: performative practices for 'other worlds.'" *Progress in Human Geography* 32 (5): 613–632.

Giddens, Anthony. 1999. "Risk and Responsibility." *The Modern Law Review* 62 (1): 1–10.

Gilroy, Janet A. 1991. "Deciding Who Gets In: Decision Making by Immigration Inspectors." *Law & Society Review* 25 (3): 571–600.

Ginsburg, E. 1996 "Introduction: The Politics of Passing." In *Passing and the Fictions of Identity*, edited by E.K. Ginsberg. Durham: Duke University Press.

Goffman, Erving. 1959. *The Presentation of Self in Everyday Life*. Garden City: Doubleday.

González-López, Gloria. 2007. "Nunca he dejado tener terror: Sexual Violence in the Lives of Mexican Immigrant Women." In *Women and Migration in the U.S.-Mexico Borderlands*, edited by Denise A. Segura and Patricia Zavella, 224–246. Durham: Duke University Press.

Gonzalez, Juan. 2011. *Harvest of Empire: A History of Latinos in America*. New York: Penguin Books.

Granovetter, Mark S. 1973. "The Strength of Weak Ties." *American Journal of Sociology* 78 (6): 1360–1380.

Grant, Stefanie. 2011. "Recording and Identifying European Frontier Deaths." *European Journal of Migration and Law* 13 (2): 135–156.

Green, Linda. 1995. "Living in a State of Fear" In *Fieldwork Under Fire: Contemporary Studies of Violence and Survival*, edited by Carolyn Nordstrom and A.C.G.M. Robben, 105–128. Berkeley: University of California Press.

Greenblatt, Stephen. 2005a. "Culture." In *The Greenblatt Reader,* edited by Michael Payne, 11–17. Oxford: Blackwell.

———. 2005b. "The Improvisation of Power." In *The Greenblatt Reader,* edited by Michael Payne, 161–196. Oxford: Blackwell.

———. 2010a. "Cultural Mobility: an introduction." In *Cultural Mobility: A Manifesto,* edited by Stephen Greenblatt et al., 1–23. Cambridge: Cambridge University Press.

———. 2010b. "Theatrical mobility." In *Cultural Mobility: A Manifesto,* edited by Stephen Greenblatt et al., 75–95. Cambridge: Cambridge University Press.

Greenhill, Kelly. 2016. "Open Arms Behind Barred Doors: Fear, Hypocrisy and Policy Schizophrenia in the European Migration Crisis." *European Law Journal* 22 (3): 317–332.

Greif, Avner. 2006. *Institutions and the Path to the Modern Economy: Lessons from Medieval Trade.* Cambridge: Cambridge University Press.

Griffiths, Melanie. 2014. "Out of Time: The Temporal Uncertainties of Refused Asylum Seekers and Immigration Detainees." *Journal of Ethnic and Migration Studies* 40 (12): 1991–2009.

Gutmann, Matthew C. 1996. *The Meanings of Macho: Being a Man in Mexico City.* Berkley: University of California Press.

Hagan, Jacqueline Maria. 2008. *Migration Miracle: Faith, Hope and Meaning on the Undocumented Journey.* Cambridge: Harvard University Press.

Hamilton, Nora, and Norma Stoltz Chinchilla. 1991. "Central American Migration: A Framework for Analysis." *Latin American Research Review* 46 (1): 75–110.

Harley, J.B. 1989. "Deconstructing the Map." *Cartographica* 26 (2): 1–20.

Hayek, Friedrich A. von. 1976. *Law, Legislation and Liberty,* vol. 2. Chicago: University of Chicago Press.

Heller, Charles, and Lorenzo Pezzani. 2017. "Liquid Traces: Investigating the Deaths of Migrants at the EU's Maritime Frontier." In *The Borders of Europe: Autonomy of Migration, Tactics of Bordering,* edited by Nicholas De Genova, 95–119. Durham: Duke University Press.

Hess, Sabine. 2010. "De-naturalising Transit Migration: Theory and Methods of an Ethnographic Regime Analysis." *Population, Space and Place* 18 (4): 428–440.

Heyman, Josiah McC. 1999. "State Escalation of Force: A Vietnam/US-Mexico Border Analogy." In *States and Illegal Practices,* edited by Josiah Heyman, 285–314. Oxford: Berg Publishers..

———. 2009. "Trust, Privilege, and Discretion in the Governance of US Borderlands with Mexico." *Canadian Journal of Law and Society* 24 (3): 367–390.

———. 2017. *Why Caution Is Needed Before Hiring Additional Border Patrol Agents and ICE Officers.* Washington, DC: American Immigration Council.

Heyman, Josiah McC., and Alan Smart. 1999. *States and Illegal Practices.* Oxford: Berg Publishers.

Hibou, Béatrice. 2004. "Conclusion." In *Boundaries and Belonging: States and Societies in the Struggle to Shape Identities and Local Practices,* edited by Joel S. Migdal. Cambridge: Cambridge University Press.

Hiemstra, Nancy. 2014. "Performing Homeland Security within the US Immigration Detention System." *Environment and Planning D: Society and Space* 32 (4): 571–88.

——. 2017. "Periscoping as a Feminist Methodological Approach for Researching Seemingly Hidden." *The Professional Geographer* 69 (2): 329–36.

Hlavka, H. 2016. "Speaking of Stigma and the Silence of Shame: Young Men and Sexual Victimization." *Men and Masculinities* 20 (4): 482–505.

Hobsbawm, Eric J. 1992. *Nations and Nationalism since 1780.* Cambridge: Cambridge University Press.

Hobson, John M., and Leonard Seabrooke, eds. 2007. *Everyday Politics of the World Economy.* New York: Cambridge University Press.

Hollifield, James F. 2004. "The Emerging Migration State." *International Migration Review* 38 (3): 885–912.

Hondagneu-Sotelo, Pierrette. 1994. *Gendered Transitions: Mexican Experiences of Immigration.* Berkeley: University of California Press.

Hopf, Ted. 2010. "The logic of habit in International Relations." *European Journal of International Relations* 16 (4): 539–561.

——. 2013. "Common-sense Constructivism and Hegemony in World Politics." *International Organization* 67 (2): 317–354.

Hume, Mo. 2007. "Mano Dura: El Salvador Responds to Gangs." *Development in Practice* 17 (6): 739–751.

——. 2008. "The myths of violence: gender, conflict, and community in El Salvador." *Latin American Perspectives* 35 (5): 59–76.

Immigration and Naturalization Service v. Enrico St. Cyr, 533 U.S. 289. 2001.

Innes, Alexandria J. 2014. "Performing Security Absent the State: Encounters with a Failed Asylum Seeker in the UK." *Security Dialogue* 45 (6): 565–581.

——. 2015. *Migration, Citizenship and the Challenge for Security: An Ethnographic Approach.* Routledge.

International Crisis Group (ICG). 2016. "Easy Prey: Criminal Violence and Central American Migration." Report No. 57, July 28, https://www.crisisgroup.org/latin-america-caribbean/central-america/easy-prey-criminal-violence-and-central-american-migration (accessed December 4, 2016).

Isaacson, Adam, Maureen Meyer, and Gabriela Morales. 2014. "Mexico's Other Border: Security, Migration, and the Humanitarian Crisis at the Line with Central America." August, Washington Office for Latin America, http://www.wola.org/sites/default/files/Mexico's%20Other%20Border%20PDF.pdf (accessed April 8, 2018).

Itzigsohn, José 2000. "Immigration and the Boundaries of Citizenship: The Institutions of Immigrant's Political Transnationalism," *International Migration Review* 34 (4): 1126–1153.

Jones, Reece. 2012. "Spaces of Refusal: Rethinking Sovereign Power and Resistance at the Border." *Annals of the Association of American Geographers* 102 (3): 685–699.

Jourde, Cedric. 2009. "The Ethnographic Sensibility: Overlooked Authoritarian Dynamics and Islamic Ambivalences in West Africa." In *Political Ethnography: What Immersion Contributes to the Study of Power,* edited by Edward Schatz, 201–216. Chicago: University of Chicago Press.

Kahler, Miles, ed. 2009. *Networks Politics: Agency, Power, and Governance*. Ithaca: Cornell University Press.

Katzenstein, Peter J. 2005. *A World of Regions: Asia and Europe in the American Imperium*. Ithaca: Cornell University Press.

Kaytaz, Esra Stephanie. 2016. "Afghan Journeys to Turkey: Narratives of Immobility, Travel and Transformation." *Geopolitics* 21 (2): 284–302.

Keck, Margaret E., and Kathryn Sikkink. 1998. *Activists Beyond Borders: Advocacy Networks in International Politics*. Ithaca: Cornell University Press

Kenyon, Paul. 2009. *I am Justice: Journey Out of Africa*. London: Preface Publishing.

Keohane, Robert O., and Joseph S. Nye Jr. 1977. *Power and Interdependence: World Politics in Transition*. Boston: Little, Brown.

Keohane, Robert O. and Joseph S. Nye Jr.. 1998. "Power and Interdependence in the Information Age." *Foreign Affairs*, http://www.foreignaffairs.com/articles/1998-09-01 /power-and-interdependence-information-age (accessed April 8, 2018).

Keynes, John Maynard. 1948. *Treatise on Probability*. New York: Macmillan & Co.

Khosravi, Shahram. 2011. *'Illegal' Traveller: An Auto-Ethnography of Borders*. Basingstoke: Palgrave Macmillan.

Knight, Frank H. 1921. *Risk, Uncertainty and Profit*. Memphis: General Books.

Koslowski, Rey. 2002. "Human Migration and the Conceptualization of Pre-Modern World Politics." *International Studies Quarterly* 46 (3): 375–399.

Kovic, C. and Arguelles, F. 2010. "The violence of security: Central American migrants crossing Mexico's southern border." *Anthropology Now* 2 (1):87–97.

Kristof, Nicholas. 2016. "We're Helping Deport Kids to Die." *New York Times*, July 17, https://www.nytimes.com/2016/07/17/opinion/sunday/were-helping-deport-kids-to -die.html (accessed April 2, 2017).

Kyle, David. 2000. *Transnational Peasants: Migrations, Networks, and Ethnicity in Andean Ecuador*. Baltimore: Johns Hopkins University Press.

Kyle, David, and Christina A. Siracusa. 2005. "Seeing the State Like a Migrant: Why So Many Non-criminals Break Immigration Laws." In *Illicit Flows and Criminal Things: States, Borders, and the Other Side of Globalization*, edited by Willem van Schendel and Itty Abraham, 153–176. Bloomington: Indiana University Press.

Kyle, David, and Marc Scarcelli. 2009. "Migrant smuggling and the violence question: evolving illicit migration markets for Cuban and Haitian refugees." *Crime, Law and Social Change* 52 (3): 297–311.

Lakhani, Nina. 2016. "Mexico Tortures Migrants and Citizens in Effort to Slow Central American Migration Surge." *The Guardian*, April 4, https://www.theguardian .com/world/2016/apr/04/mexico-torture-migrants-citizens-central-america (accessed April 8, 2018).

LeBron, Marisol. 2009. "Migracorridos: Another Failed Anti-Immigration Campaign." *North American Congress on Latin America*, March 17, https://nacla.org/node/5625 (accessed August 4, 2011).

Levi, Primo. 1988. *The Drowned and the Saved*. New York: Vintage.

Lie, Jon Harald Sande. 2013. "Challenging Anthropology: Anthropological Reflections on the Ethnographic Turn in International Relations." *Millennium Journal of International Studies* 41 (2): 201–220.

Logan, Samuel. 2009. "Los Zetas: Evolution of a Criminal Organization." *ISN Security Watch*, March 11, http://www.isn.ethz.ch/isn/Current-Affairs/Security-Watch/Detail /?lng=en&id=97554 (accessed February 20, 2011).

Luibhéid, E. 2005. "Introduction: Queering Migration and Citizenship." In *Queer Migrations: Sexuality, U.S. Citizenship, and Border Crossings*, edited by E. Luibhéid and L. Cantú Jr., ix–xlvi. Minnesota: University of Minnesota Press.

Lynch, Kevin. 1960. *The Image of the City*. Cambridge: MIT Press.

Magañas, Rocio. 2011. "Dead Bodies: The Deadly Display of Mexican Border Politics." In *A Companion to the Anthropology of the Body and Embodiment*, edited by F.E. Mascia-Lees, 157–171. Chichester: Wiley Blackwell.

Mahler, Sarah J. 1995. *American Dreaming*. Princeton: Princeton University Press.

———. 1999. "Engendering Transnational Migration: A Case Study of Salvadorans." *American Behavioral Scientist* 42 (4): 690–719.

Maillet, Pauline, Alison Mountz, and Keegan Williams. 2017. "Researching migration and enforcement in obscured places: methodological challenges to fieldwork." *Social & Cultural Geography* 18 (7): 927–950.

Mainwaring, Ċetta. 2014. "Small States and Nonmaterial Power: Creating Crises and Shaping Migration Policies in Malta, Cyprus, and the European Union." *Journal of Immigrant & Refugee Studies* 12 (2): 103–122.

———. 2016. "Migrant agency: Negotiating borders and migration controls." *Migration Studies* 4 (3): 289–308.

Mainwaring, Ċetta, and Noelle Brigden. 2016. "Beyond the Border: Clandestine Migration Journey." *Geopolitics* 21 (2): 243–262, doi: 10.1080/14650045.2016.1165575.

Mainwaring, Ċetta, and Stephanie J. Silverman. 2017. "Detention as Spectacle." *International Political Sociology* 11 (1): 21–38.

Marcus, George E. 1995. "Ethnography in/of the World System: The Emergence of Multi-Sited Ethnography." *Annual Review of Anthropology* 24: 95–117.

Marosi, Richard. 2005. "Border Patrol Tries New Tune to Deter Crossers." *Los Angeles Times*. July 4, http://articles.latimes.com/2005/jul/04/local/me-bordersongs4 (accessed August 4, 2011).

Marroquín Parducci, Amparo. 2008. "Crónica de la prensa salvadoreña: imaginarios que migran." *Encuentro* 80: 23–45.

———. 2012. "All Roads Lead North: A Reading of News of Migration through the Figure of the Coyote." *Hemispheric Institute*, http://hemisphericinstitute.org/hemi/en /e-misferica-82/marroquin (accessed July 27, 2013).

Martel, Roxana, and Amparo Marroquín. 2007. "Crónica de fronteras: la música popular y la construcción de la identidad salvadoreña migrante." *Istmo*, http://istmo.denison .edu/n14/articulos/cronica.html (accessed July 28, 2013).

Martínez, Óscar. 2010. *Los Migrantes Que No Importan: En el camino con los centroamericanos indocumentados en Mexico*. San Salvador: Icaria.

———. 2011. "The border: funneling migrants to their doom." *North American Congress on Latin America* 44 (5): 5.

Martinez, Marcy. 2013. "Cartels recruiting women to become trained assassins." *Action 4 News*, March 18, http://www.valleycentral.com/news/story.aspx?id=873804# .UVYAms3BD4i (accessed March 29, 2013).

Martinez, Ruben. 2001. *Crossing Over: A Mexican Family on the Migrant Trail*. New York: Metropolitan Books.

McEvoy, J. et al. 2012. "Gendered Mobility and Morality in a South-Eastern Mexican Community: Impacts of Male Labour Migration on the Women Left Behind." *Mobilities* 7 (3): 369–388.

McIlwaine, Cathy. 2010. "Migrant machismos: exploring gender ideologies and practices among Latin American migrants in London from a multi-scalar perspective." *Gender, Place and Culture* 17 (3): 281–300.

Médecins Sans Frontières (MSF). 2005. "Violence from Authorities and Gangs Are Major Threat to Immigrants in Morocco." Press Release, September 30, https://www.doctorswithoutborders.org/news-stories/press-release/violence-authorities-and-gangs-are-major-threat-immigrants-morocco (accessed January 5, 2012).

——. 2010a. *Sexual Violence and Migration: The hidden reality of Sub-Saharan women trapped in Morocco en route to Europe*. Special Report, http://www.msf.org/en/article/msf-denounces-sexual-violence-against-migrants-travelling-europe (accessed January 5, 2012).

——. 2010b. "Morocco: Expelled Migrants Left in Precarious State." Press Release, September 30, https://www.doctorswithoutborders.org/news-stories/press-release/morocco-expelled-migrants-left-precarious-state (accessed January 5, 2012).

Medellin, Jorge Alejandro. 2004. "Reconocen a 13 ex militares como Zetas." *El Universal*, May 11.

Menjívar, Cecilia. 2000. *Fragmented Ties: Salvadoran Immigrant Networks in America*. Berkeley: University of California Press.

——. 2002. "The Ties that Heal: Guatemalan Immigrant Women's Networks and Access to Medical Treatment." *International Migration Review* 36 (2): 437–466.

——. 2008. "Violence and Women's Lives in Eastern Guatemala: A Conceptual Framework." *Latin American Research Review* 43 (3): 109–136.

Meyer, Maureen. 2007. "At a Crossroads: Drug Trafficking, Violence and the Mexican State." Briefing Paper Thirteen, November. Washington, DC: Washington Office on Latin America.

Migdal, Joel S. 2004. "Mental Maps and Virtual Checkpoints: Struggles to Construct and Maintain State and Social Boundaries." In *Boundaries and Belonging: States and Societies in the Struggle to Shape Identities and Local Practices*, edited by Joel S. Migdal, 3–23. Cambridge: Cambridge University Press.

Miles, M., and J. Crush. 1993. "Personal Narratives as Interactive Texts: Collecting and Interpreting Migrant Life-Histories." *Professional Geographer* 45 (10): 95–129.

Miroff, Nick. 2012. "For Mexico's Middle Class, Drug War Deepens Trust Deficit." *Washington Post*, June 1.

Mollett, Sharlene. 2013. "Mapping Deception: The Politics of Mapping Miskito and Garifuna Space in Honduras." *Annals of the Association of American Geographers* 103 (5): 1227–1241.

Moodie, Ellen. 2010. *El Salvador in the Aftermath of Peace: Crime, Uncertainty and the Transition to Democracy*. Philadelphia: University of Pennsylvania Press.

Moorehead, Caroline. 2005. *Human Cargo: A Journey among Refugees*. London: Vintage Books.

Mountz, Alison. 2007. "Smoke and Mirrors: An Ethnography of the State." In *Politics and Practice in Economic Geography*, edited by E. Sheppard et al., 38–48. Thousand Oaks: Sage.

———. 2010. *Seeking Asylum: Human Smuggling and Bureaucracy at the Border.* Minneapolis: University of Minnesota Press.

———. 2013. "Shrinking Spaces of Asylum: Vanishing Points Where Geography Is Used to Inhibit and Undermine Access to Asylum." *Australian Journal of Human Rights* 19 (3): 29–50.

Mountz, Alison, and J. Lloyd. 2014. "Transnational Productions of Remoteness: Building Onshore and Offshore Carceral Regimes across Borders." *Geographica Helvetica* 69 (5): 389–398.

Müller, Martin. 2008. "Situating Identities: Enacting and Studying Europe at a Russian Elite University." *Millennium: Journal of International Studies* 37 (1): 3–25.

Najar, Alberto. 2012. "Mexico: quienes son los muertos de Cadereyta?" BBC Mundo, May 22, http://www.bbc.co.uk/mundo/noticias/2012/05/120521_cadereyta_mexico_ao .shtml (accessed May 23, 2012).

Nazario, S. 2006. *Enrique's Journey: The Story of a Boy's Dangerous Odyssey to Reunite with His Mother.* New York: Random House.

Nordstrom, Carolyn. 2007. *Global Outlaws: Crime, Money and Power in the Contemporary World.* Berkeley: University of California Press.

Nyers, Peter, and Kim Rygiel. 2012. *Citizenship, Migrant Activism and the Politics of Movement.* Routledge.

O'Dogherty, Laura. 1989. *Central Americans in Mexico City, Uprooted and Silenced.* Washington, DC: Hemispheric Migration Project.

O'Donnell, Guillermo. 2004. "Why the Rule of Law Matters." *Journal of Democracy* 15 (4): 32–46.

Otero, Silvia and Carlos Aviles. 2003. "Recompensa por 31 exmilitares." *El Universal,* June 19.

Pachico, Elyssa. 2012. "Lazcano Death May Hasten Zetas' Decline." *InSight Crime*, October 9, http://www.insightcrime.org/news-analysis/lazcano-death-may-hasten-zetas -decline (accessed July 27, 2013).

Pachico, Elyssa, and Steven Dudley. 2012. "Why a Zetas Split Is Inevitable." *InSight Crime*, August 24, http://www.insightcrime.org/news-analysis/why-a-zetas-split-is -inevitable (accessed July 27, 2013).

Pachirat, Tim. 2013. *Every Twelve Seconds: Industrialized Slaughter and the Politics of Sight.* New Haven: Yale University Press.

Papachristos, Andrew V. 2005. "Gang World." *Foreign Policy* 147 (March/April): 48–55.

Pedersen, David. 2012. *American Value: Migrants, Money, and Meaning in El Salvador and the United States.* Chicago: University of Chicago Press.

Pessar, Patricia R., and Sarah J. Mahler. 2006. "Transnational Migration: Bringing Gender." *International Migration Review* 37 (3): 812–846.

Pieke, Frank N. 1995. "Witnessing the 1989 Chinese People's Movement." In *Fieldwork Under Fire: Contemporary Studies of Violence and Culture*, edited by Carolyn Nordstrom and Antonius C.G.M. Robben, 62–79. Berkeley: University of California Press.

Powell, Kimberly. 2010. "Making Sense of Place: Mapping as a Multisensory Research Method." *Qualitative Inquiry* 20 (10): 1–17.

Pratt, G. 2000. "Research Performances." *Environment and Planning D: Society and Space* 18: 639–651.

Ramos, Jorge. 2005. *Dying to Cross: The Worst Immigrant Tragedy in American History.* New York: Harper Collins.

Ramsey, Geoffrey. 2011. "Migrants Accuse Mexico Immigration Officials in Kidnap Case" *InSight Crime*, May 12, http://www.insightcrime.org/news-analysis/migrants -accuse-mexico-immigration-officials-in-kidnap-case (accessed July 27, 2013).Reineke, Robin. 2013. "Arizona: Naming the dead from the desert." BBC, January 16, http:// www.bbc.co.uk/news/magazine-21029783 (accessed July 19, 2013).

Richardson, Laurel. 2000. "Evaluating Ethnography." *Qualitative Inquiry* 6 (2): 253–255.

Roberts, Bryan et al. 2010. "An Analysis of Migrant Smuggling Costs along the Southwest Border." Working Paper, November. Washington, DC: Office of Immigration Statistics, U.S. Department of Homeland Security.

Rosas, Gilberto. 2010. "Cholos, Chuntaros, and the Criminal Abandonments of the New Frontier." *Identities* 17 (6): 695–713.

——. 2012. *Barrio Libre: Criminalization States and Delinquent Refusals of the New Frontier.* Durham: Duke University Press.

——. 2016. "The Border Thickens: In-Securing Communities after IRCA." *International Migration* 54 (2): 119–130.

Rose, G. 1997. "Situating Knowledges: positionality, reflexivities and other tactics." *Progress in Human Geography* 21 (3): 305–320.

Roth, Robin. 2009. "The challenges of mapping complex indigenous spatiality: from abstract space to dwelling space." *Cultural Geographies* 16 (2): 207–227.

Ruggie, John G. 1993. "Territoriality and Beyond: Problematizing Modernity in International Relations." *International Organization* 47 (1): 139–174.

Ruiz Parra, Emiliano. 2011. "Solalinde." *Gatopardo* (September), http://www.gatopardo .com/ReportajesGP.php?R=104 (accessed July 19, 2013).

Ruiz, Olivia. 2001. "Los Riesgos de Cruzar. La Migracion Centroamericana en La Frontera Mexico-Guatemala." *Revista Frontera Norte* 13 (25).

Sadiq, Kamal. 2009. *Paper Citizens: How Illegal Immigrants Acquire Citizenship in Developing Countries.* Oxford: Oxford University Press.

Salter, Mark B. 2004. "Passports, Mobility, and Security: How Smart Can the Border Be?" *International Studies Perspectives* 5 (1): 71–91.

——. 2008. "When the Exception Becomes the Rule: Borders, Sovereignty and Citizenship." *Citizenship Studies* 12 (4): 365–380.

Sanchez, G. 2016. "Women's Participation in the Facilitation of Human Smuggling: The Case of the US Southwest." *Geopolitics* 21 (2): 387–406.

Sassen, Saskia. 1996. *Losing Control? Sovereignty in an Age of Globalization.* New York: Columbia University Press.

——. 2006. *Territory, Authority, Rights: From Medieval to Global Assemblages.* Princeton: Princeton University Press.

Schatz, Edward, ed. 2009. *Political Ethnography: What Immersion Contributes to the Study of Power.* Chicago: University of Chicago Press.

Scheel, Stephen. 2017. "Re-signifying the Self, and the Walking Dead of Traditional IR." In *Walking with Migrants: Ethnography as Method in IR*, Meera Sabaratnam et al. An International Studies Quarterly Online Symposium.

Schlossberg, Linda. 2001. "Introduction: Rites of Passage." In *Passing: Identity and Interpretation in Sexuality, Race, and Religion*, edited by Maria Carla Sanchez and Linda Scholssberg, 1–12. New York: New York University Press.

Schneider, Jane, and Peter Schneider. 2008. "The Anthropology of Crime and Criminalization." *Annual Review of Anthropology* 37: 351–73.

Scott, James C. 1985. *Weapons of the Weak*. New Haven: Yale University Press.

———. 1998. *Seeing Like a State: How Certain Schemes to Improve the Human Condition Have Failed*. New Haven: Yale University Press.

———. 2009. *The Art of Not Being Governed: An Anarchist History of Upland Southeast Asia*. New Haven: Yale University Press.

Seyer-Ochi, Ingrid. 2006. "Lived Landscapes of the Fillmore." In *Innovations in Educational Ethnography: Theory, Methods and Results*, edited by George Dearborn Spindler and Lorie Hammond. Mahwah: Lawrence Erlbaum Associates.

Shelley, Louise. 2010. *Human Trafficking*. Cambridge: Cambridge University Press.

Sheridan, Lynnaire M. 2009. *"I Know It's Dangerous": Why Mexicans Risk Their Lives to Cross the Border*. Tuscan: University of Arizona Press.

Siegel, Dina, and Sylvia de Blank. 2010. "Women who traffic women: the role of women in human trafficking networks—Dutch cases." *Global Crime* 11 (4): 436–447.

Singer, Audrey, and Douglas S. Massey. 1998. "The Social Process of Undocumented Border Crossing Among Mexican Migrants." *International Migration Review* 32: 561–592.

Sladková, J. 2007. "Expectations and Motivations of Hondurans Migrating to the United States." *Journal of Community & Applied Social Psychology* 17: 187–202.

Solomon, A. 2005. "Trans/Migrant: Christina Madrazo's All-American Story." In *Queer Migrations: Sexuality, U.S. Citizenship, and Border Crossings*, edited by E. Luibhéid and L. Cantú Jr., 3–29. Minneapolis: University of Minnesota Press.

Soysal, Yasemin Nuhoglu. 1995. *Limits of Citizenship: Migrants and Postnational Membership in Europe*. Chicago: University of Chicago Press.

Spener, David. 2001. "Smuggling Migrants through South Texas: Challenges Posed by Operation Rio Grande." In *Global Human Smuggling: Comparative Perspectives*, edited by David Kyle and Rey Koslowski. Baltimore: Johns Hopkins University Press.

———. 2004. "Mexican Migrant-Smuggling: A Cross-Border Cottage Industry." *Journal of International Migration and Integration* 5 (3): 295–320.

———. 2009. *Clandestine Crossings: Migrants and Coyotes on the Texas-Mexico Border*. Ithaca: Cornell University Press.

———. 2010. "Movidas Rascuaches: Strategies of Migrant Resistance at the U.S.-Mexico Border." *Aztlan: A Journal of Chicano Studies* 35 (2): 9–36.

Spijkerboer, Thomas. 2007. "The Human Costs of Border Control." *European Journal of Migration and Law* 9: 127–139.

Squire, Vicki. 2011. *The Contested Politics of Mobility: Borderzones and Irregularity*. Abingdon: Routledge Press.

———. 2014. "Desert 'trash': Posthumanism, border struggles and humanitarian politics." *Political Geography* 39: 11–21.

Stacey, J. 1988. "Can There Be a Feminist Ethnography?" *Women's Studies International Forum* 11 (1): 21–27.

Stephen, Lynn. 2002. "Sexualities and Genders in Zapotec Oaxaca." *Latin American Perspectives* 29 (2): 41–59.

Sundberg, Juanita. 2008. "'Trash talk' and the production of quotidian geopolitical boundaries in the USA-Mexico borderlands." *Social & Cultural Geography* 9 (8): 871–890.

Surdin, Ashley. 2009. "Crossover Appeal: Border Patrol Uses Music to Cross a Cultural Line." *Washington Post*, March 15, http://www.washingtonpost.com/wp-dyn/content/article/2009/03/13/AR2009031304234.html (accessed August 4, 2011).

Surowieki, James. 2004. *The Wisdom of Crowds*. New York: Doubleday.

Tagliacozzo, Eric. 2005. *Secret Trades, Porous Borders: Smuggling and States Along a Southeast Asian Frontier, 1865–1915*. New Haven: Yale University Press.

Taylor, Charles. 2004. *Modern Social Imaginaries*. Durham: Duke University Press.

Thompson, Ginger. 2005. "Mexico Fears Its Drug Traffickers Get Help from Guatemalans." *New York Times*, September 29, http://query.nytimes.com/gst/fullpage.html?res=9C02E4DD1330F933A0575AC0A9639C8B63.

Tilly, Charles. 2006. "Afterword: Political Ethnography as Art and Science." *Qualitative Sociology* 29: 409–412.

Tuckman, Jo. 2013. "Central American Migrants flee turf wars and corrupt states for refuge in Mexico." *The Guardian*, December 31, http://www.theguardian.com/world/2013/dec/ 31/central-america-migrants-flee-mexico (accessed January 5, 2014).

U.S. Department of Homeland Security (DHS). 2003. *Yearbook of Immigration Statistics 2003*. Washington, DC, https://www.dhs.gov/immigration-statistics/yearbook/2003 (accessed July 27, 2013).

———. 2011. *Yearbook of Immigration Statistics 2011*. Washington, DC, https://www.dhs.gov/immigration-statistics/yearbook/2011 (accessed July 27, 2013).

Ustubici, Aysen. 2016. "Political Activism Between Journey and Settlement: Irregular Migrant Mobilisation in Morocco" *Geopolitics* 21 (2): 303–324.

Valdez, Al. 2011. "The Origins of Southern California Latino Gangs." In *Maras: Gang Violence and Security in Central America*, edited by Thomas Bruneau, Lucia Dammert, and Elizabeth Skinner, 23–42. Austin: University of Texas Press.

Van Schendel, Willem. 2005. "Spaces of Engagement: How Borderlands, Illicit Flows, and Territorial States Interlock." In *Illicit Flows and Criminal Things: States, Borders, and the Other Side of Globalization*, edited by Willem van Schendel and Itty Abraham, 38–68. Bloomington: Indiana University Press.

Vogt, Wendy. 2012. "Ruptured Journeys, Ruptured Lives: Central American Migration, Transnational Violence, and Hope in Southern Mexico." PhD Dissertation, School of Anthropology, University of Arizona, Tucson.

———. 2013. "Crossing Mexico: Structural violence and the commodification of undocumented Central American migrants." *American Ethnologist* 40: 764–780.

———. 2016. "Stuck in the Middle with You: The Intimate Labours of Mobility and Smuggling along Mexico's Migrant Route." *Geopolitics* 21 (2): 366–386.

Waever, Ole. 1993. "Societal Security: The Concept." In *Identity, Migration, and the New Security Agenda*, edited by Ole Waever et al. New York: St Martin's Press.

Wainwright, Joel, and Joe Bryan. 2009. "Cartography, territory, property: postcolonial reflections on indigenous counter-mapping in Nicaragua and Belize." *Cultural Geographies* 16: 153–178.

Walters, William. 2015. "Migration, vehicles, and politics: Three theses on viapolitics." *European Journal of Social Theory* 18 (4): 469–488.

Watts, Laura. 2008."The Art and Craft of Train Travel." *Social & Cultural Geography* 9 (6): 711–726.

Wilkinson, Tracy. 2010. "A Top Salvadoran Ex-Guerrilla Commander Advises Mexico's Conservative President." *Los Angeles Times*, October 22, http://articles.latimes.com /2010/oct/22/world/la-fg-mexico-guru-20101023 (accessed July 18, 2013).

——. 2012. "Mexico Government Sought to Withhold Drug War Death Statistics." *Los Angeles Times*, January 11, http://articles.latimes.com/2012/jan/11/world/la-fg-mexico -dead-numbers-20120112.

Wolf, Sonja. 2011. "Street Gangs of El Salvador." In *Maras: Gang Violence and Security in Central America*, edited by Thomas Bruneau, Lucia Dammert, and Elizabeth Skinner, 43–70. Austin: University of Texas Press.

Wolf, Sonja. 2017. *Mano Dura: The Politics of Gang Control in El Salvador*. Austin: University of Texas Press.

Wood, Elisabeth Jean. 2003. *Insurgent Collective Action and Civil War in El Salvador*. Cambridge: Cambridge University Press.

Yanow, Dvora. 2001. "Learning in and from Improvising: Lessons from Theater for Organizational Learning" *Reflections* 2 (4): 58–62.

Yanow, Dvora. 2005. "Dear Author, Dear Reader: The Third Hermeneutic in Writing and Reviewing Ethnography." In *Political Ethnography: What Immersion Contributes to the Study of Power*, edited by Edward Schatz, 275–302. Chicago: University of Chicago Press.

——. 2009. "Dear Author, Dear Reader: The Third Hermeneutic in Writing and Reviewing Ethnography" In *Political Ethnography: What Immersion Contributes to the Study of Power*, edited by Edward Schatz, 275–302. Chicago: University of Chicago Press.

Zilberg, Elana. 2004. "Fools Banished from the Kingdom: Remapping Geographies of Gang Violence in the Americas (Los Angeles and San Salvador)." *American Quarterly* 56 (3): 759–779.

——. 2011. *Space of Detention: The Making of a Transnational Gang Crisis Between Los Angeles and San Salvador*. Durham: Duke University Press.

INDEX